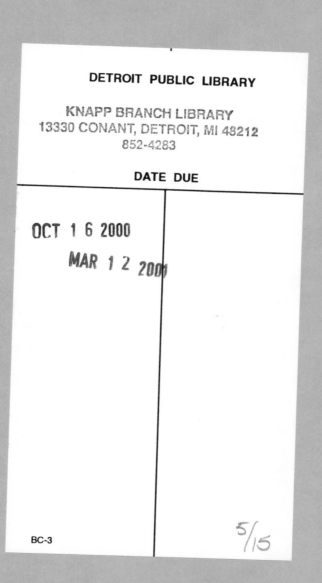

FACTASTIC MILLENNIUM FACTS

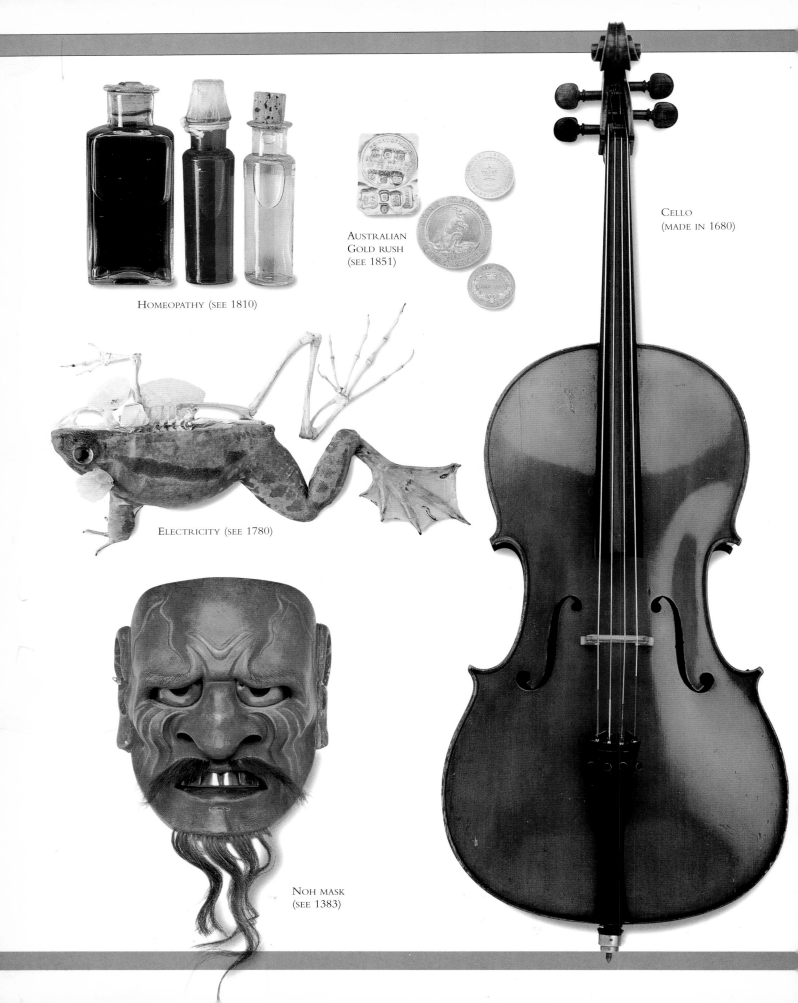

HOMEOPATHY (SEE 1810)

AUSTRALIAN
GOLD RUSH
(SEE 1851)

CELLO
(MADE IN 1680)

ELECTRICITY (SEE 1780)

NOH MASK
(SEE 1383)

FACTASTIC MILLENNIUM FACTS

RUSSELL ASH

KNIGHT
(SEE 1264)

HOMEOPATHY
PLANT
(SEE 1810)

SPIDER
(SEE 1314)

DK Publishing, Inc.
www.dk.com

A DK PUBLISHING BOOK

DK www.dk.com

Produced for DK Publishing by PAGE*One*
Cairn House, Elgiva Lane, Chesham
Buckinghamshire HP5 2JD

EDITORIAL DIRECTOR Helen Parker
ART DIRECTOR Bob Gordon
EDITORS Charlotte Stock, Marion Dent
DESIGNER Melanie McDowell

FOR DK PUBLISHING
MANAGING EDITOR Jayne Parsons
MANAGING ART EDITOR Gillian Shaw
ART EDITOR Nomazwe Madonko
JACKET DESIGN Joe Hoyle
PICTURE RESEARCH Mollie Gillard
DK PICTURE LIBRARY Richard Dabb,
Neale Chamberlain
US EDITORS Lilan Patri, Tom Reilly,
Constance Robinson

First American Edition, 1999
2 4 6 8 10 9 7 5 3

Published in the United States by
DK Publishing Inc.
95 Madison Avenue
New York, New York 10016

Library of Congress Cataloging-in-Publication Data

Ash, Russell.
  Factastic millennium facts / by Russell Ash. – 1st American ed.
    p.   cm.
  Includes index.
  Summary: Presents facts, milestones, and key political and
cultural events from the year 1000 to the present, highlighting
important periods and inventions.
  ISBN 0–7894–4710–X (hc.). – ISBN 0–7894–4948–X (pb.)
  1. Civilization–History Miscellanea Juvenile literature.
  2. World history Miscellanea Juvenile literature. 3. Millennium
Miscellanea Juvenile literature. [1. Civilization–History Miscellanea.
2. World history Miscellanea.] I. Title.
CB69.2.A84   1999
909–dc21   99–27624
                                    CIP

Color reproduction by Colourscan, Singapore
Printed and bound in Spain by Artes Gráficas Toledo, S.A.
D.L. TO: 329-2000

CONTENTS

THE AGE OF RELIGION   10
1000–1199

THE AGE OF CONQUEST   16
1200–1399

Here's to the next 1,000 years

INTRODUCTION

The word "**millennium**" was first used around 300 years ago and means a period of **1,000** years, or a **thousandth anniversary**. The end of a millennium is an obvious moment to take stock of major **events**, advances, and developments as the years unfold.

At the **beginning** of the millennium, people believed that Earth was the center of the universe and knew of only six planets and 12 elements. Printing had yet to be **invented**, and **communications** were primitive. Since travel was laborious, few people journeyed far from their homes, and the **Americas**, much of Asia, and all of **Australasia** were unknown to Europeans. Contrast this with an age that has witnessed the rise of automobile, air, and space **travel**, and of the instant communications of TV, radio, telephone, and the **Internet**.

In the pages that follow, I have charted some of the important and also the unfamiliar and unusual **milestones** along this 1,000-year journey: **inventions** and **discoveries**, some of which were destined to become part of our everyday lives, and others that have been long forgotten; remarkable **achievements** and **triumphs**; and some of the more **bizarre** behavior of our fellow humans.

"Millennium" can also mean the completion of a 1,000-year period when the **world will end**. Thousands of such predictions have been made in the past, but since we are all here, every one of them has been wrong. These, as well as failed attempts to fly and other activities that now seem **ludicrous**, are chronicled in **Extra Extra!** facts. **Century Statistics** tells us the world population, tallest building, and most influential book of each century, and **Then and Now** boxes compare past with present. Four-page special **features** focus on some of the most important developments of the past millennium.

From the comparative **simplicity** of the **medieval** era to the **complexity** of our "Information Age" the story of the past millennium is one of immense change, of calamitous **wars** and religious and racial **intolerance**, of wicked crimes and human **greed**, and of errors that have wrought disastrous effects on the **environment**. Yet it is also a tale of human achievement – of fine architecture and works of **art**, books and music, and of incredible **breakthroughs** in **science** and technology – many of which go to make today's world a better place. Some of the most radical developments of the last millennium, such as transportation, communications, and **medicine**, have occurred in the past century, giving us hope that the next 100 and even 1,000 years will be even more **factastic**.

THE STORY SO FAR

IN THE FIRST MILLENNIUM after the birth of Christ, the flame of civilization burned bright in China, where the emperors ruled. It flared later in the millennium in the Islamic world, too, where Arab astronomers and mathematicians laid the foundations of science. But in Europe, the collapse of the classical civilizations of Greece and Rome plunged the world into the so called Dark Ages. Only the growing network of Christian monks and scholars kept the torch of knowledge alight.

EUROPE: EBB AND FLOW

At the dawn of the first millennium, the Roman Empire was at its zenith, but as it gradually declined over the next 400 years, a power vacuum was left in Europe. Over the centuries, different peoples swept across Europe and held center stage briefly – the Goths, the Franks, the Danes, the Anglo-Saxons, the Vikings – yet none achieved lasting dominance. Gradually, though, Christianity began to emerge as a cohesive force. Yet even Christianity was riven between two great centers of power: Rome in the west and Byzantium (now Istanbul) in the east.

CHARLEMAGNE
(SEE 800)

64 The Roman emperor Nero begins the persecution of Christians – and witnesses the **BURNING OF ROME**.

140 **PTOLEMY** writes the *Almagest*. This last great work of classical scholarship is lost to the west and preserved only in the Islamic east.

EMPRESS THEODORA
(SEE 527)

330 **CONSTANTINE**, the first Christian emperor of the Roman Empire, founds Constantinople (the modern city of Istanbul, Turkey).

410 The **VISIGOTHS** sack Rome, followed by the Vandals in 455.

433 **ATTILA THE HUN** from Asia attacks western Europe.

450 **SAXONS** from Germany begin to invade Britain.

496 Clovis, king of the **FRANKS**, a German people who settled in France, is baptized.

527 Justinian I begins his reign of the **BYZANTINE EMPIRE** with his empress Theodora.

590 Pope Gregory the Great sends out missionaries from Rome to spread **CHRISTIANITY**.

602 **SLAVIC** tribes begin settlement of the Balkans.

711 The **MOORS** invade Spain, but the Muslim advance into Europe is halted in 732 by Frankish king Charles Martel. The Christian west begins to hold.

789 Scandinavian **VIKINGS** start to raid the coasts of Britain.

800 Charlemagne, king of the Franks, is crowned emperor of the **HOLY ROMAN EMPIRE** in Rome.

862 Descendants of the Swedish **VIKINGS**, the Varangians, establish themselves in Russia.

989 Vladimir of Kiev chooses **ORTHODOX CHRISTIANITY** from Byzantium for his people.

THE FLOWERING OF ISLAM

After 632, followers of the Arab Muhammad began to spread his teachings about Allah, the "one true God." So emerged the Islamic religion which, in just a few centuries, built an empire stretching from Spain to India. Islam spread by systematically conquering neighboring countries. But it became a great civilizing force, and Islamic culture flourished under its rulers the caliphs, notably Harun al-Rashid. Muslim artists created beautiful buildings and decorated books, while Arab scholars such as Avicenna and Alhazen laid the foundations of modern medicine, astronomy, and mathematics.

570 MUHAMMAD is born in the Arab town of Mecca.

622 Muhammad flees to MEDINA and the Islamic calendar begins.

632 Muhammad dies. He is succeeded by ABU BAKR – the first caliph. Islam starts to spread rapidly through invasion.

HINDU TEMPLE, INDIA (SEE 711)

638 The Muslims capture JERUSALEM from the Christians and soon begin their conquest of Egypt.

674 The ISLAMIC EMPIRE now reaches as far as Pakistan, and spreads through North Africa.

711 The MOORS (Muslims from Morocco) invade Spain and by 718 hold most of the Spanish peninsula.
• Muslims start to invade India, but the Hindu religion remains strong.

750 The ABBASID DYNASTY overthrows the Umayyads and founds Baghdad, in what is now Iraq.

786 HARUN AL-RASHID becomes caliph of Byzantium.

813 Caliph MAMUN THE GREAT presides over a golden period in the arts.

825 The Indian DECIMAL SYSTEM, eventually used worldwide, is adopted by an Arab mathematician.

900 The TALES of *One Thousand and One Nights* are started.

916 Arab scholar AL-MASUDI travels through Africa to Mozambique.

930 CÓRDOBA in Spain becomes the center of Arab learning.

971 The world's FIRST UNIVERSITIES are established in Muslim cities, such as Cairo.

CHINESE CIVILIZATION

Of the four great empires that held much of the world in thrall in the year one – the Roman, the Gupta in India, the Sassanian in the Middle East, and the Chinese – the Chinese alone survived the first millennium. Linked to the west only by the ancient Silk Road, Chinese civilization flowered almost in isolation.

25 The HAN DYNASTY of emperors, which presides over the first great flowering of Chinese culture, is restored. Its inventions include wheelbarrows, suspension bridges, and calligraphy.

45 Chinese poet, historian, and astronomer PAN CHAO is born.

58 Emperor Ming Ti introduces the BUDDHIST religion into China.

220 The Han dynasty falls, and China splits into THREE KINGDOMS.

589 SUI DYNASTY reunites China and builds the Grand Canal.

618 The TANG oust the Sui and preside over a second flowering of Chinese culture.

970 The Chinese government introduces PAPER MONEY.

Córdoba mosque, Spain, was built by Muslim invaders from Africa

THE AGE OF RELIGION

As the Muslims expand their territory, increasing their hold on Asia and gaining control over northern Africa, Christianity dominates European feudal life. In time, tension between Islam and Christendom results in a series of bloody holy wars called the Crusades. The movement of Crusaders across Asia and Europe leads to the establishment of new trade routes, and trade begins to prosper. Thousands of miles away are the Maoris, who settled in New Zealand a century earlier, while in the Americas, the Chimu and cliff-dwelling Anasazi people flourish.

EAR ORNAMENTS PRODUCED DURING
THE CHIMU DYNASTY (SEE 1000)

1000 Start of the pre-Inca **CHIMU** civilization in Peru.

1001 Emperor Basil II resumes the conquest of **BULGARIA**.

1002 English soldiers kill Danish settlers on **ST. BRICE'S DAY**.

1003 Vikings retaliate for the St. Brice's Day **MASSACRE**.

1004 Riots break out as Henry II is **CROWNED** king of Italy.

1005 Arab scholar Al-Sufi produces an illustrated manuscript on **GEOGRAPHY**.

1006 Brightest-ever **SUPERNOVA** visible in daylight appears.

1007 *The Tale of Genji*, the earliest known **NOVEL**, is written by a noblewoman at the Japanese imperial court.

1008 Abbot Berno writes a book on the theory of **MUSIC**.

1009 The Holy Sepulcher Church in Jerusalem is **RUINED**.

1010 The **LEECH BOOK** of common cures is written.

1011 An **ALTAR** in Rome is dedicated to the handkerchief of St. Veronica, which was said to carry the imprint of Christ's face.

1012 **RICE** reaches China and becomes the staple diet.

1013 A timber **CHURCH** is built in Greensted, England.

1014 Defeated Bulgarian soldiers are **BLINDED** on the orders of Byzantine Emperor Basil II.

1015 Monks at Pomposa monastery in Italy learn to sing by **SIGHT-READING**.

1016 Ethelred the Unready, the **TWICE-MARRIED** Saxon king of England, dies.

1017 Cnut, king of England, abandons Ethelred's **FIRST WIFE**, to marry his widow.

1018 **IVAN OF BULGARIA** is killed in battle.

1019 The founder of the Islamic **DRUZE** sect dies.

1020 The use of a floating magnet for **NAVIGATION** is first recorded in China.

1021 **OUTBREAKS** of St. Vitus' dance in Europe.

1022 The bones of **VENERABLE BEDE**, a learned scholar, are laid to rest in Durham Cathedral.

1023 *Seven Tablets in a Cloudy Satchel* is the mysterious title of a Chinese book on **ALCHEMY**.

1024 China uses paper receipts as official **CURRENCY**.

1025 Sieradz, one of **POLAND**'s oldest cities, is founded.

1026 Guido d'Arezzo, an Italian monk and music teacher, develops **DO, RE, MI, FA, SO**.

1027 William (the Conqueror) is born to Robert the **DEVIL**.

1028 Zoe, the daughter of Constantine VII, **INHERITS** the Byzantine Empire.

1029 Work starts on England's **GLOUCESTER CATHEDRAL**.

1030 Chinese use wooden blocks for **PRINTING**.

1031 Moorish **KINGDOMS** form in Andalusia, Spain.

1032 Benedict IX becomes **POPE** – the first of his three appointments to this post.

1033 An impending sense of doom surrounds the **MILLENNIUM** of Christ's death.

1034 Poland becomes **PAGAN** again with the king's death.

1035 Japan **RECYCLES** used paper to make new paper.

1036 Al-Munstansir heads the **FATIMID** Dynasty in Egypt.

1037 Kiev Cathedral, admired for its **MOSAICS**, is built.

1038 **EARTHQUAKE** in Shansi, China, kills 23,000 people.

1039 A team of Chinese scholars compiles a **PHONETIC** dictionary (one that spells words according to how they sound).

1040 Lady Godiva rides naked through the streets of Coventry in England to persuade her husband to ease the burden of **TAXES**.

1041 Pi Sheng invents clay blocks for **PRINTING**.

1042 All hostilities are suspended in Normandy, France, under the Church's first **TRUCE OF GOD**.

1043 Domenico Contarini is the first of the eight family members to become **DOGE OF VENICE**.

1044 Northern Korea **WALLS** itself in from Manchurians.

1045 Gregory VI is elected pope after paying his rival Benedict IX to **RESIGN** from the post.

1046 **POLYPHONIC** music is popular in Europe.

1047 France's earliest known set of **LAWS** and customs.

1048 The learned Arabic **WRITER** Al-Biruni dies.

1049 Bruno, the son of **COUNT HUGH OF EGISHEIM**, Alsace, is appointed Pope Leo IX.

1050 Earliest known German **CHRISTMAS CAROL** *Sys willekommen heirre kerst* is sung.

1051 Japanese **WARRIOR** Yoshiie Minamoto takes part in the battles of the Earlier Nine Years' War.

1052 Pisa finally gains control of Sardinia after 300 years of **OCCUPATION** by the Arabs.

1053 Pope Leo IX is captured by the **NORMANS**.

1054 **CRAB NEBULA** is created by a supernova.

1055 **BATTERING RAMS** are used by Spanish soldiers to take the city of Coimbra from the Muslims.

1056 MACEDONIAN DYNASTY in Greece ends after 500 years.

1057 Macbeth, king of Scotland, is KILLED by Malcolm, whose father was murdered by Macbeth.

1058 Macbeth's stepson is killed by his father's MURDERER, Malcolm, who then seizes the crown.

1059 A treatise on CRABS, *Hsieh-p'u*, is written in China.

1060 Berbers and Arabs fight alongside each other to gain control of the Ankar SALT MINES.

1061 Total ECLIPSE of the Sun is witnessed in Baghdad.

1062 Marrakech is founded as capital of BERBER empire.

1063 *Vocabularium*, a Latin DICTIONARY, is compiled.

1064 The book *Decisive Word on Sects, Heterodoxies, and Denominations* compares RELIGIONS.

1065 A church window installed in Augsburg, Germany, is the first to feature STAINED GLASS.

1066 SAXONS believe that a comet foretells their defeat by the Normans at the Battle of Hastings.

1067 World's first center for LEPERS is set up by El Cid.

1068 Norman troops embark on the SIEGE of Bari, Italy.

1069 As FAMINE takes its toll in England (claiming 50,000 lives), reports of cannibalism emerge.

1070 Roquefort CHEESE is first reported, in France.

1071 A LATIN translation of *Liber Regius* brings Greek medicine to the Western world.

1072 China develops the first CENSORSHIP laws.

1073 Sa-skya MONASTERY is established in Tibet.

1074 In his attempt to REFORM the Church, Pope Gregory VII bans priests who are married.

1075 Henry IV of Germany defeats the Saxon army at the BATTLE OF UNSTRUT RIVER.

1076 Berbers DESTROY Kumbi, capital of ancient Ghana.

1077 King Henry IV of Germany stands BAREFOOT in snow for three days to receive a Papal pardon.

1078 Pope Gregory VII founds cathedral SCHOOLS.

1079 Persia adopts the ASTRONOMICAL calendar.

1080 Work begins in ITALY on a list of medicinal drugs.

1081 BANISHED from Castile, El Cid becomes a mercenary.

1082 CUZCO, Aztec and Spanish capital of Peru, is founded.

1083 Marianus Scotus, an IRISH monk, writes *Chronicon*, a history of the world since Creation.

1084 Norman forces DESTROY Rome, which they were asked by the Pope to protect.

1085 CNUT II, king of Denmark, plans to invade England.

1086 All landowners in England are required to list their possessions in the DOMESDAY BOOK so that taxation can be assessed.

1087 William the Conqueror dies after falling from his horse; at the BURIAL, his body bursts open, releasing its noxious contents.

1088 In Cluny, France, work starts on the world's largest ABBEY.

1089 Crazed victims of ergotism run amok in France; they ate grain infected with the ERGOT fungus.

1090 A mechanical CLOCK driven by water is invented in China by Su Sung.

1091 The longitudes of England and Italy are assessed by timed sightings of LUNAR ECLIPSES.

1092 MAPS OF STARS are included in a treatise by Chinese astronomer Su Sung.

1093 Last INDEPENDENT prince of South Wales dies.

1094 St. Mark's BASILICA in Venice is completed.

1095 Pope calls for a crusade to FREE Jerusalem.

1096 Norman-French barons lead the FIRST CRUSADE.

1097 Odo, who commissioned the BAYEUX TAPESTRY, dies on his way to the Holy Land.

1098 The Turkish city of Antioch falls to the crusaders when a treacherous captain lets them enter through the WINDOWS of the fort.

1099 Crusaders take Jerusalem, KILLING 40,000 people.

CRUSADERS CAPTURE JERUSALEM (SEE 1099)

30,000 men killed in first crusade

1100 Henry I assumes **ENGLISH THRONE** when his brother William dies in a hunting accident.

1101 Emperor Hui Tsong, a noted **CALLIGRAPHER**, founds China's Imperial Academy of Painting.

1102 Public **MEDICAL SERVICE** is established in China.

1103 **NORWAY**'s King Olavsson III dies in battle in Ireland.

1104 **MOUNT HEKLA** erupts, devastating Icelandic farms.

1105 Hindu maritime power Srivijaya, based on island of **SUMATRA**, controls Southeast Asia.

1106 Floods and fires destroy large parts of **VENICE**.

1107 The **NAHUA** of Mexico dominate Mayan city-states.

1108 Rival Japanese **CLANS**, the Taira and Minamoto, join forces against influential Enryakuyi sect.

1109 **HENRY I** rejects personal combat with Louis the Fat.

1110 **MIRACLE PLAYS**, derived from legends about the saints, become popular in England.

1111 Guibert of Nogent **WRITES** about the First Crusade.

1112 The Church **BANS** Holy Roman Emperor Henry V.

1113 The Church of St. Nicholas, Novgorod, Russia, is given a Greek-Orthodox-style "onion" **DOME**.

1114 International **TRADE FAIRS** are first held in France.

1115 A Cistercian **MONASTERY** is founded by St. Bernard at a bleak location in Clairvaux, France.

1116 The first **CANAL LOCK** goes into operation in Belgium.

1117 **PARMA** Cathedral is rebuilt after earthquake damage.

1118 Hugues de Payens founds the **ORDER OF THE KNIGHTS TEMPLAR** to protect pilgrims during their journey to Jerusalem.

1119 Guido the Geographer details **MAPS** of Italy and the world in his book *Geographica*.

1120 **TIME** is used to measure latitude and longitude.

CALLIGRAPHY OF EMPEROR HUI TSONG (SEE 1101)

1121 The king of **CONNAUGHT** builds Ireland's first castle.

1122 The German city of Worms settles a **DISPUTE** between Holy Roman Emperor and the Church.

1123 The Church forbids the practice of **SIMONY**, such as the sale of pardons to forgive sins.

1124 English **COIN-MAKERS** have their right hands cut off as punishment for poor-quality work.

1125 Aristotle's works are translated into **LATIN**.

1126 The Jurchen (**CHIN DYNASTY**) defeat the Liao and establish rule of Northern China.

1127 Death of Duke William IX of Aquitaine, France, who championed the use of French rather than Latin for writing **LOVE POETRY**.

1128 Afonso Henriques gains controls of Portugal after defeating forces of his **MOTHER**, Teresa.

1129 Henry I's shield of golden lions launches **HERALDRY**.

1130 Work begins on the Cistercian **ABBEY** of Fontenay in France.

1131 **FULK** of Anjou, France, is declared king of Jerusalem.

1132 The rebuilt Abbey of St. Denis in Paris, France, is the first example of **GOTHIC** art.

1133 **RIBBED VAULTING**, a way of strengthening a roof, is first used in Durham Cathedral, England.

1134 Work starts on the first **GOTHIC-STYLE TOWER** at Chartres Cathedral in France.

1135 Henry I of England dies from **FOOD POISONING**.

1136 Freiburg, Saxony, becomes the center for silver-mining, when **SILVER**-bearing ore is discovered.

1137 Louis VII, married to **ELEANOR OF AQUITAINE**, assumes throne in France.

1138 Vladislav II becomes first **GRAND PRINCE** of Poland.

1139 The Russian Federation collapses when Vsevolod II seizes the Ukrainian city of **KIEV**.

1140 Conrad III allows women at the **BESIEGED** fortress of Weinberg, Germany, to go free, taking any property with them; each woman leaves with a male relative on her back.

1141 Hildegard von Bingen of Germany is the first woman to compose a **MASS**.

1142 Dressed in white, **MATILDA** escapes from her husband King Stephen across the snow-covered winter landscape of England.

1143 Afonso I grants **PORTUGAL** its independence.

1144 Edessa, in **MESOPOTAMIA**, falls to the Muslims.

1145 Byzantine Emperor Manuel I launches an unsuccessful invasion of Norman **ITALY**.

1146 Pope Eugenius III organizes the **SECOND CRUSADE**.

1147 Louis VII of France puts his wife, Eleanor, in **PRISON**.

1148 Crusaders return from the Middle East with **SUGAR**.

1149 **OXFORD UNIVERSITY** is founded in England.

1150 Southeast Asian Hindu king completes **ANGKOR WAT**, the largest religious complex in history.

1151 Geoffrey of Anjou dies; he was called **PLANTAGENET** for the sprig of genet, a yellow-flowered plant, worn in his cap.

1120! The church orders that men keep their hair cut to above their eyes and ears.

1152 Ireland recognizes the **SUPREMACY** of the Pope.

1153 English King Stephen recognizes his stepson, Henry Plantagenet, as **HEIR TO THRONE**.

1154 Nicholas Breakspear is elected as **HADRIAN IV**, the first and only English Pope.

1155 The monastery of the Hermits of Mount Carmel is founded in Israel by monks seeking the way of life of the prophet **ELIJAH**.

1156 Henchun Seiken writes on **PERFUME** in *Ko yo sho*.

1157 Henry the Lion founds the city of **MUNICH**, Germany.

1158 The military order of the **KNIGHTS OF CALATRAVA** is founded in Spain.

1159 The English Pope chokes to death, apparently on a **FLY**.

1160 French miracle **PLAY**, *Le Jeu de St. Nicholas*, is written.

1161 The first **TURKISH BATHS** are built by Kilij Arslan II.

1162 Future Mongol leader **GENGHIS KHAN** is born; he is said to descend from the union of a gray wolf and a white deer.

1163 Waldemar the Great leads **DENMARK** to the status of a major power in northern Europe.

1164 Constitution of Clarenden makes English **SECULAR** courts supreme over ecclesiastical ones.

1165 German settlers move east into Prussia and **BOHEMIA**.

1166 The building of **PRISONS** is ordered in England.

1167 A Danish soldier, Absalon, founds **COPENHAGEN**.

1168 **AZTEC TRIBES** attack the Toltec Empire in Mexico.

1169 More than 15,000 are killed when **MOUNT ETNA** erupts, causing tidal waves and earthquakes.

1170 **THOMAS A BECKET**, archbishop of Canterbury, is murdered.

1171 Muslim leader Saladin becomes **SULTAN** of Egypt.

1172 New Christian converts, the **POOR MEN OF LYON**, sell all their possessions to feed the poor.

1173 A French poem, *Le Conte du Graal*, contains the first reference to the **HOLY GRAIL**.

1174 A thirteen-year-old **LEPER**, Baldwin IV, becomes king of Jerusalem.

1175 **TOLTEC EMPIRE** crumbles in Central America.

1176 Work starts on the first stone **LONDON BRIDGE**.

1177 **BELFAST CASTLE** is built to guard the Irish Lagan River.

1178 Han Ch'an-chih writes about 27 different types of **ORANGE** in *Ch, lu*.

1179 The Pope disapproves of knights in **TOURNAMENTS**.

1180 **RUDDERS** replace oars for steering European ships.

KING RICHARD I OF ENGLAND, KNOWN AS RICHARD THE LIONHEART (SEE 1192)

1181 Nicholas of Verdun creates a gothic **ALTARPIECE** of metal and enamel for an abbey in Austria.

1182 Ibn-Munqidh, an **ARAB** soldier, writes his memoirs.

1183 Byzantine Emperor Alexius is **STRANGLED** by his uncle.

1184 Canterbury Cathedral is rebuilt in **GOTHIC** style.

1185 Minamoto clan takes power in Japan; Yorimoto is declared **SHOGUN**.

1186 Italy revives Roman title of **CAESAR** for its rulers.

1187 Saladin defeats crusaders and retakes **JERUSALEM**.

1188 Sultan Ali bin Hasan of Kilwa, who controlled much of Islamic **EAST AFRICA**, dies.

1189 Frederick Barbarossa (**RED-BEARD**) leads the Third Crusade.

1190 Frederick **DROWNS**; Third Crusade is halted.

1191 Aeisai, a priest, brings **ZEN BUDDHISM** to Japan.

1192 English king and crusader Richard the Lionheart wins free **ACCESS** to Jerusalem for pilgrims.

1193 Saladin's **DEATH** sparks war among successors.

1194 **FIRE** completely destroys Chartres Cathedral, France.

1195 Emperor Isaac II is **BLINDED** and jailed by his brother.

1196 **TEMUJIN**, or Blacksmith, begins his rise to power in Mongolia.

1197 Arabs destroy Buddhist **MONASTIC** center at Nalanda, India.

1198 The newly elected Pope Innocent III declares the start of the **FOURTH CRUSADE**.

1199 **RICHARD THE LIONHEART** is killed in dispute over French treasure.

EXTRA EXTRA! Saracen of Constantinople dies as he tries to fly from a tower, in 1162.

15

In 1309, the Pope moved from Rome to the Palais des Papes in Avignon, France

THE AGE OF CONQUEST

In the 1200s, the fierce Mongol hordes led by Genghis Khan and his family push through Asia and establish a vast empire. A century later in Turkey, the Islamic Ottomans begin to threaten the Christian Byzantine empire. New trade routes that are opening up between Asia and Europe act as a channel for ideas – but also disease. In just 50 years, the Black Death – a highly infectious bubonic plague – spreads from India to China and Europe, where it kills a third of the population. In the meantime, in South America, the Inca empire is constantly expanding.

DETAIL FROM A STAINED GLASS WINDOW OF ST. FRANCIS OF ASSISI (SEE 1207)

1200 Start of the **INCA** Empire in the Cuzco Valley, Peru.
•**LETTERS** are used to communicate between European monasteries.

1201 Opening of **ST. GOTTHARD PASS** through the Alps, linking Switzerland and Italy.

1202 The first **JESTERS** appear in European courts.
•The use of **ZERO** is introduced to Europe from India by Italian mathematician Leonardo Fibonacci.

1203 **PHILIP AUGUSTUS** expels English from France.
•Muslims take **MAJORCA**.

1204 **CONSTANTINOPLE** falls to crusaders, who sack the city for three days.

1205 Venetian crusaders return with the famous four bronze horses of **SAN MARCO**, captured during the Conquest of Constantinople.

1206 Temujin is declared *Chinghiz Khan* (or Genghis Khan); it translates as **WORLD RULER**.

1207 Francis of Assisi is **DISOWNED** by his father after selling goods from the family business to pay for church repairs.

1208 Kamo Chomei, a Japanese poet and hermit, begins work on his **NAMELESS NOTES**, a book of anecdotes, poetic lore, and criticism.

1209 Students at Oxford University, England, **DEFECT** to start Cambridge University.

1210 Rather than renounce their faith to the strict Christians known as Albigensians, 140 men and women in Minerve, France, plunge into fire and are **BURNED ALIVE**.

1211 Led by **GENGHIS KHAN**, Mongols invade China.

1212 A French shepherd boy leads the **CHILDREN'S CRUSADE** to the Holy Land. About 50,000 of the children are kidnapped and sold as slaves in Egypt.

THE QUADRIGA, OR FOUR HORSES OF SAN MARCO (SEE 1205)

Stolen from a race course in Constantinople

1213 Christian armies inflict massive defeat upon **MUSLIMS** in Spain.

1214 English scholar Roger Bacon predicts the invention of **CARS** and **AIRCRAFT**.

1215 John I of England contests the **MAGNA CARTA**, a charter that places restrictions on royal power and which he has just signed.

The rose is a symbol of a knight's love for a lady

1216 St. Dominic sets up an order of **PREACHERS** in Italy to defend the Catholic faith.

1217 The Fifth Crusade fails to retake **JERUSALEM** from the Egyptians.

1218 Mongols take **BEIJING**, capital of northern China.

1219 Denmark adopts the **DANNENBORG** as its flag.

1220 Work on the Cathedral of **NOTRE DAME**, built on the site of a Roman temple in Paris, France, is completed.

1221 Chinese warriors use highly destructive **IRON FIRE BOMBS** that produce shrapnel.

1222 Mongol warrior Genghis Khan conquers Herat and massacres its inhabitants to secure his control of **AFGHANISTAN**.

1223 The Mongols make their first invasion of **RUSSIA**.

1224 **NAPLES UNIVERSITY** is founded in Italy.

1225 **COTTON** manufacturing starts in Spain, becoming as important as wool and linen production.

1226 Louis IX becomes king of France at the **AGE OF 12**.

1227 The death of Genghis Khan is kept **SECRET** until his son is established as his successor.

1228 Francis of Assisi is made a **SAINT** by Pope Gregory IX.

1229 In Toulouse, France, the Albigensians **FORBID** Bible-reading by anyone who is not a member of the Church's clergy.

1230 Guillaume de Lorris starts the first part of *Le Roman de la Rose* (*The Romance of the Rose*), a poem about **LOVE** and good manners.

1231 Poverty-stricken families in Japan continue the forbidden practice of selling their children into the **SLAVE TRADE**.

1232 Messages for help are sent by **KITE** when the Mongol army besieges China.

1233 Pope Gregory IX establishes the **INQUISITION** under the direction of the Dominican Order.

1234 French women use weapons to protect themselves from arrest for **HERESY** by the Albigensians.

1235 Frederick II **SUPPORTS** the dissection of human bodies at the Salerno school of medicine.

1236 **PAPER MONEY** is issued in the Mongol Empire.

1237 Mongol warriors use **GUNPOWDER** to battle their way through Europe.

LE ROMAN DE LA ROSE CONJURES UP ROMANCE (SEE 1230)

1238 Six **GOLDSMITHS** are appointed in England to protect their trade from fraud.

1239 Pope Gregory IX bans Frederick II from the church, declaring him to be a heretic and the **ANTICHRIST**.

1240 The Mongols conquer Russia; **KIEV** is destroyed.

1241 Mongols destroy German-Polish-Hungarian **ARMY**.

1242 German invaders are defeated by Russia in a battle on the frozen **LAKE PEIPUS**.

1243 Black rats travel into Europe with the Mongol **INVADERS**.

1244 Jerusalem is lost to the **MUSLIM** forces of Egypt.

1245 Unwell and against his mother's advice, Louis IV of France leads the **SEVENTH CRUSADE**.

1246 A Franciscan monk blames leprosy on eating hot food, pepper, garlic, and diseased **DOG MEAT**.

1247 An **ANTI-JEWISH** inquisition in France is stopped by Pope Innocent IV.

1248 The Lombards storm Italy's **WOODEN** town of Vittoria.

1249 The use of convex lens eyeglasses to correct **FARSIGHTEDNESS** is described.

CENTURY STATISTICS

World population, 1200: 450 million
Bookmark: Printed in Korea in 1234, *Sangjong yemun,* or *Compendium of Rites and Rituals*, is one of the first books to be printed using movable type.
Landmark: Amiens Cathedral, France, built in the Gothic style in 1260, stands at 440 ft (134 m) high.

EXTRA EXTRA! Horse riding is the fastest mode of transport with a top speed of 35 mph (55 km/h).

STONE FIGURE OF A KNIGHT IN CHAIN-MAIL ARMOR (SEE 1264)

Heavy chain mail and thick mud prove fatal for a knight

1250 King Louis IX of France is taken prisoner whilst on a crusade in Egypt. A ransom is paid to the **SULTAN** of Egypt to secure his release.

1251 French shepherds and farm workers lead an unruly **PEASANTS' CRUSADE** in a revolt that spreads as far as Syria.

1252 Pope Innocent IV orders the use of **TORTURE** in the inquisition, which hunts out followers of nonapproved religions.
• Italy's **FLORENCE** mints its own coin, the gold florin.

1253 A Franciscan friar comes across a silver **FOUNTAIN** built for a Mongol prince in Karakorum. The four spouts offer wine, mead, rice wine, and kumyss, made from mare's milk.
• In England, the mathematician John Halifax introduces the **DECIMAL SYSTEM** of counting.

1254 The **HOLY ROMAN EMPIRE** is left without a ruler.
• The Pope turns over the rule of **SICILY** to the House of Anjou.

1255 **CITY-STATE** of Africa's Great Zimbabwe is at its height.

BAKERS USE TRADEMARKS TO IDENTIFY THEIR LOAVES (SEE 1266)

1256 **KUBLAI KHAN** becomes the recognized leader of the Mongols.

1257 The jealous Shajar orders the murder of her husband, Aybak, **SULTAN** of Egypt, but is then killed by members of her harem.

1258 Victorious Mongols kill **ISLAMIC LEADER** Caliph al-Musta'sim; his body is rolled in a carpet, and he is kicked and stomped to death by soldiers and horses.

1259 Fearing that the widespread outbreaks of famine and disease in Italy are punishment from God, many believers cleanse their bodies of sin by **WHIPPING** themselves.

1260 Egypt is saved from conquest by the Mongols, thanks to a Muslim army composed largely of **EX-SLAVES**, the Mamelukes.

1261 **BYZANTINES** regain their capital, Constantinople, from Western crusaders.

1262 Crusaders recover the Spanish city of **CADIZ** from the 500-year rule of the Moors.

1263 Scotland gains the islands of the **HEBRIDES** from Norway.

1264 Baron Fulke Fitzwarine, an English knight returning from victory, **SUFFOCATES** inside his chain-mail armor when his horse becomes trapped in mud.

1265 Italian poet **DANTE ALIGHIERI**, is born in Florence; he is later banned for life from his home town for opposing the Pope.

1266 English bakers are required to **STAMP** their bread with a trademark so that the makers of poor-quality loaves can be identified.
•In Florence, two opponents play chess while wearing **BLINDFOLDS**.

1267 English scholar Roger Bacon writes *Opus Majus*, describing many of his **INNOVATIONS**, such as eyeglasses, magnifying glasses, and the camera obscura for projecting images onto a screen.

1268 A violent **EARTHQUAKE** in Cilicia, Asia Minor, kills 60,000 people.

1269 **TOLLS** are charged for the use of roads in England.
• **COMPASS** with 360 degrees is described by Petrus Peregrinus of Maricourt in his *Epistola de Magnete*.

1270 Knights use the little-known practice of **MAP-READING** to guide the St. Louis Crusade.
•Yekuno Amlak founds Solomonic Dynasty in **ETHIOPIA**, the Christian stronghold of Africa.

1271 **MARCO POLO** sets sail from Venice, Italy, for China.
•A **WATERMARK** of the letter "F" is used to represent Fabriano, a papermaking center in Italy.

1272 Thomas Aquinas moves from France to Italy, where his masterpiece of Christian intellectual thought, *Summa Theologica*, earns him the title of **UNIVERSAL TEACHER**.

1273 Londoners complain about the **POLLUTION** caused by the burning of coal.

1274 **DEER HUNTING** on skis is prohibited in Norway.

1275 **MARCO POLO** enters the service of Mongol emperor Kublai Khan as a traveling diplomat.

1276 Old Bushmills, the oldest known **WHISKEY** distillery, is founded in Northern Ireland.
•Gregory X, Innocent V, and Hadrian V are each appointed **POPE**, in turn.

1277 Thousands are killed by **FLOODS** in Holland.

1278 London Jews found guilty of shaving off the edges of gold and silver coins are hanged for **COIN-CLIPPING**, while Christians are given only a fine for the offense.

1279 A Franciscan monk makes the first **GLASS MIRRORS**.

1280 Egyptians are summoned to China to reveal their secret of how to make **WHITE SUGAR**.
•China produces the earliest known **CANNON** from bronze and iron.

1281 A second attempt by Kublai Khan to conquer Japan is foiled when his invasion fleet is again wiped out by a typhoon known as **KAMIKAZE**, or "divine wind."

1282 The wealthy merchants of Florence **REBEL** against the nobility and receive the Pope's approval for their self-styled government.

1283 David III, **PRINCE OF WALES**, is hanged, drawn, and quartered by the king of England, and his head is displayed in London.
•The great city of Mayapan is founded by the Itza in **YUCATAN**.

1284 Kublai Khan's army of 500,000 Mongol warriors is **DECIMATED** by Vietnamese guerillas.

1285 Roads between English towns are widened to prevent travelers from being **ROADBLOCKED** and robbed by bandits.

1286 Alexander III of Scotland **BREAKS HIS NECK** while out riding his horse in the dark.

1287 Rufinus compiles *Herbal*, a book detailing **MEDICINAL** herbs and general botany.

1288 Valencia, Spain, is one of the first towns to come under attack from **ROCKETS**.
•The **GRAND CANAL**, built in AD 618, is extended to link the Chinese capital of Peking with the Yellow Sea.

1289 **BLOCK** printing is first used in Europe in Ravenna, Italy.

1290 An **EARTHQUAKE** in China kills 100,000 inhabitants.

THEN AND NOW

1288 Women in Scotland are allowed by law to propose to men – but only on Leap Year Day.
1999 More than 4,000 English people marry each year in the Scottish village of Gretna Green – the first village over England's border with Scotland, where runaway couples can marry without their parents' consent.

1291 A protection league is established in Austria, forming the origins of **SWITZERLAND**.
•The last Crusaders are expelled from Middle East, marking end of **CRUSADES**.

1292 The Venetian masters of glass-making move their **HIGH-TEMPERATURE** ovens to the island of Murano, to remove the risk of fire breaking out in Venice.

1293 Missionaries bring **CHRISTIANITY** to China.

1294 **KUBLAI KHAN** dies at the Imperial Court in Beijing.

1295 **MARCO POLO** returns to Venice with fantastic accounts of his travels in China.

1296 At the Battle of Curzola, Marco Polo is captured and held **PRISONER** by the Genoese.
•Sultanate of **DELHI** in India is founded by Ala-nd-din.

1297 Scottish patriot William Wallace, known as **BRAVEHEART**, defeats the English army.

1298 At the Battle of Falkirk, Scotland, the efficiency of English **ARROWS** over solid square spears is proven, when the Scots are defeated by Edward I of England.

1299 The use of Arabic numerals is **BANNED** in Florence.
•**EYEGLASSES** appear in northern Italy.

A SPIDER PROVIDES INSPIRATION FOR ROBERT THE BRUCE (SEE 1314)

As determined as a spider, Scotland fights on

1300 On January 1, two million Christians gather in Rome to **CELEBRATE** the **turn of the century**.
•**ANASAZI** towns are mysteriously destroyed in southwestern America.

1301 The death of Andrew III ends the 400-year rule of the Arpàd dynasty in **HUNGARY**.

1302 Exiled **DANTE ALIGHIERI** starts to write his epic poem, *The Divine Comedy*.

1303 Edward I allows foreign merchants to buy and sell any goods in England, except **WINE**.

1304 Italian painter Giotto di Bondone of Florence produces his first **FRESCO**.

1305 William **BRAVEHEART** Wallace of Scotland is found guilty of treason and hanged.

GIOTTO'S *LAMENTATION OF THE DEAD CHRIST*, ARENA CHAPEL IN PADUA, ITALY (SEE 1304)

1306 In China, as part of the entertainment to celebrate the coronation of Fo-Kin, revelers perform **PARACHUTE** jumps.

1307 A primitive **GUILLOTIN E** is used in Ireland to cut off the head of Murcod Ballagh.

1308 France's Philip the Fair continues a campaign against the Knights Templar, to whom he owes money. Members of the order are **TORTURED** to extract confessions.

1309 **PAPACY** moves from Rome to Avignon in France.

1310 Accused of being a **WITCH**, Marguerite Porrett, a mystic, is burned to death in Paris, France.

1311 **PAPER CURRENCY** is abandoned in China when the amount of paper money printed exceeds the reserves of precious metals held by the treasury.

1312 The order of the Knights Templar is **ABOLISHED**.

1313 The Holy Roman Emperor **HENRY VII** dies while on a campaign to attack Robert of Naples.

1314 Inspired by a spider's perseverance, **ROBERT THE BRUCE** wins independence for Scotland when his army of 30,000 men defeats the 100,000 soldiers of the English army.

1315 Spanish philosopher Raymond Lully is **STONED** to death by his Algerian audience for trying to convert them to Christianity.
•Swiss defeat **HAPSBURGS** at Lake Zug.

1316 **RUMORS** of a Christian king, Prester John, in Ethiopia, are investigated by eight Dominican monks sent by the Pope.

1317 The study of **ALCHEMY**, an early form of chemistry, is banned by Pope John XXII.

1318 As the worst famine in Europe enters its fourth year, rumors spread of **DEAD BODIES** being dug up and eaten in Ireland.

1319 Horses are used for **PLOWING** in England when oxen are struck by disease.

1320 The first surgery manual to propose **STITCHES** and the cleaning of wounds is written.
•Scottish **INDEPENDENCE** from England is spelled out in the Declaration of Arbroath, a letter written by the Scottish Parliament to Pope John XXII.

1321 The Soji Temple in Japan, becomes the headquarters of the Soto sect of **ZEN BUDDHISM**.

1322 **PHILIP V** of France, who imposed heavy taxes on all Jewish residents in the country, dies.

1323 A school for musical poets, known as **TROUBADOURS**, is founded in Toulouse, France.

1324 Mansa Musa, ruler of the Mali Empire, makes his great **HAJJ** (pilgrimage) to Mecca.

1325 **TENOCHTITLAN**, Mexico, is founded by the Aztecs; it later becomes Mexico City.
•Jean Froissart embarks on his travels around Europe; he records events in his *Chronicle*, which is written by hand in a script called **SECRETARY** that is fast to write and easy to read.

1349! In the mass graves for plague victims, lead crosses are placed alongside the bodies.

SECRETARY SCRIPT USED BY JEAN FROISSART IN HIS *CHRONICLE* (SEE 1325)

1326 In Italy, a written order for iron bullets contains the first European reference to a **HANDGUN**.

1327 Edward II, king of England, is forced by followers of his wife to abdicate the throne; he is later found murdered by **RED-HOT POKER**, in the dungeons of Berkeley Castle.

1328 England tries to claim the **FRENCH CROWN** when the last heir of the Capetian dynasty dies.

1329 Ivan I becomes Grand Prince of **MOSCOW**.

1330 William of Ockham establishes the principle known as **OCKHAM'S RAZOR**, which states that scientists should look for the simplest explanations.

1331 The practice of **SEPPUKU**, ritual suicide, ends when the military rule of the Kamakura shogunate collapses in Japan; seppuku was often performed by plunging a sword into one's stomach.

1332 The British Parliament **DIVIDES** into two "houses"– the Commons and the Lords.

1333 The **BLACK DEATH** sweeps quickly across China when the population becomes weakened by famine and malnutrition.

1334 Turkish **PIRATES** in the Gulf of Edremit, Turkey, are defeated by the crusader navy.
•The Feast of the Holy Trinity (held 50 days after Easter) is formally **APPROVED** by Pope John XXII.

1335 A clock installed in the San Gottardo Chapel in Milan, Italy, is the first public **TIMEPIECE** to strike the hour.

1336 The Japanese Imperial Court is established at **KYOTO**, leading to a flowering of classic Japanese culture.

1337 England's attempt to claim the French throne starts the **HUNDRED YEARS' WAR**, which actually lasts for 116 years.

1338 Despite having married three times, John III the Good, Duke of Brittany, France, has no **HEIR**; he therefore arranges the marriage of his niece to Charles of Blois.
•**FLEMISH REVOLT** against France is backed by the English.

1339 *The Christopher*, which was built in England, is the first ship to feature **IRON CANNONS** and a handgun.
•The first **ZEN** garden is created by Muso-Suseki of Kyoto, Japan.
•Construction begins of the **KREMLIN** (Russian for "fortress") in Moscow.

1340 Blast furnaces and water-driven hammers are first used in **IRON-MAKING**.
•Moved by his visit to the shrine of our Lady of Guadalupe in Spain, Alfonso XI of Castile builds a monastery on the site; the building later becomes a famous center of **PILGRIMAGE**.

1341 Francesco Petrarca, the Italian poet known as Petrarch, is honored by Rome as a classical poet and receives a laurel crown. He is the first to write **SONNETS**.

CENTURY STATISTICS

World population,1300: 432 million
Bookmark: The first history of the world *Jami'u't-Tawarikh,* or *Great Universal History* by Rashid-eddin is published in Persia in 1311.
Landmark: At 334 ft (102 m), Siena Town Hall in Italy, built 1348, makes its mark as the world's tallest brick building in the 14th century.

1342 The people of Thessalonica, Greece, rise up against the Byzantine Emperor John V and, under the leadership of John Cantacuzene, create a virtually **INDEPENDENT** state.

1343 Marauding Tatars who attack merchants from Genoa, Italy, are struck down by the Black Death, probably because the merchants' baggage is **INFESTED** with black rats.

1344 Amda Tseyon, ruler of Ethiopia, Africa, dies a **HERO**, having constantly repelled Muslim forces and thereby increased his empire.

1345 The **PONTE VECCHIO**, a unique bridge with a two-story gallery, is built in Florence, Italy, by Taddeo Gaddi, the son of a famous family of Florentine religious painters and architects.
•The great banking houses, Peruzzi and Bardi, go **BANKRUPT** in Florence, Italy.

1346 At the Battle of Neville's Cross, David II of Scotland tries to invade England. Scotland is defeated and David is held for **RANSOM**; it takes his country ten years to complete the ransom payment.
•Edward III of England invades France and wins the Battle of Crécy. Blinded by the evening sun, the army of Philip VI runs out of missiles and is outshot by the English **LONGBOW**; it can pierce armor at a range of 300 ft (91 m).
•The **BLIND** king of Bohemia, eager to help fight for France at Crécy, is tied to two knights who guide him into battle.

1347 Calais finally **SURRENDERS** to England, having resisted capture for almost a year.
•The Black Death arrives in **GREECE** and southern Italy.

1348 The Most Noble Order of the Garter, a form of knighthood, is founded by Edward III of England. Embroidered on the **GARTER** is "Evil to him who thinks evil," the words used by the king when he returned a lost garter to his dancing partner.

1349 Imported by rat-infested ships, the **BLACK DEATH** kills half the population of England; one London grave holds 50,000 bodies.

A TYPICAL MASK WORN IN JAPANESE NOH THEATER (SEE 1383)

1350 The kingdom of **SIAM** is established.

1351 The Red Turban Rebellion breaks out in **CHINA**.

1352 **JOHN THE GOOD** founds France's Order of the Star.

1353 Italian author Giovanni Boccaccio's *Decameron* gives a first-hand account of the **PLAGUE** in his country.

1354 The **SHROUD OF TURIN**, believed to be Christ's burial cloth, comes into the possession of a knight named Geoffroi de Charnay. •The **OTTOMANS** cross into Europe at Gallipoli.

1355 A portrait in the Doge's palace, Venice, is covered by a curtain when its subject, Marino Falieri, is **BEHEADED** for treason.

1356 Two thousand French knights are **KILLED** and another two thousand **CAPTURED** by England's Black Prince Edward at the Battle of Poitiers in France.

1357 Rebellious French peasants kill and cook a **KNIGHT**, forcing his wife to eat him.

1358 Up to 300 French protesters are burned to death for not paying **RANSOM** money for King John II.

1359 Belgian workers **PROTEST** in Bruges, wearing red hats.

1360 English workers are jailed for asking for a **WAGE** raise.

1361 Sir John Hawkwood leads an army of **MERCENARIES** involved in fighting in northern Italy.

1362 England's law courts start to use **ENGLISH**, although official documents remain in French.

1363 John II of France volunteers to go to **JAIL** in place of his son, who has escaped from the English.

1364 Poor **HARVEST** yields lead to famine in France.

1365 Crusaders sack the city of **ALEXANDRIA** in Egypt.

1366 Irish Parliament **OUTLAWS** the marriage of Irish citizens to anyone of English descent.

1367 After being repeatedly burned down, Moscow's wooden **KREMLIN** is rebuilt in stone.

1368 Chu Yuan-chang, a former **PEASANT** and monk, takes the title of Emperor Hung-Wu of China.

1369 Pedro the Cruel of **CASTILE** is killed by his half-brother.

1370 Henri de Vick installs a mechanical **CLOCK** at the royal palace in Paris, France.

1371 **STUART DYNASTY**, which eventually rules the British Isles, takes the throne of Scotland.

1372 Coming to the aid of the French, **CASTILIAN** fleet destroys English fleet off La Rochelle.

1373 Arab author Al-Damiri writes *The Lives of Animals*, detailing real and mythical **ANIMALS**.

1374 A frenzy of unexplained **DANCING MANIA** breaks out in Aix-la-Chapelle, France.

1375 Heartbroken by the death of Petrarch, **BOCCACCIO** dies.

1376 The **AZTEC** dynastic rule of Mexico begins under King Acamapichtli.

1377 An Italian mystic persuades the **POPE** to leave Avignon, France, and return to Rome, Italy.

1378 The **PAPACY** becomes divided, with one pope in France and the other in Italy.

1379 **PERSIA** is part of the second Mongol Empire, ruled by Genghis Khan's grandson Tamerlane.

1380 **POISONOUS MUSHROOMS** kill Charles V of France.

1381 The Peasants' Revolt in England protests against the **POLL TAX**, charged on a per-head basis.

1382 Ireland is hit by an outbreak of the **BLACK DEATH**.

1383 Zeami Motokiyo pioneers **NOH** theater in Japan.

1384 **GRAPEPICKING** before September 29 is banned in Tuscany, Italy, to ensure quality wine.

1385 **RICHARD II** permits the building of Bodiam Castle.

1386 **LITHUANIA** is converted to Catholicism and unites with Poland, creating Europe's largest state.

1387 Tamerlane, conquering **THE CAUCASUS**, enters Europe.

1388 The **SIDESADDLE** is adopted by horsewomen in England.

1389 Serbia falls to the Ottomans at the Field of Blackbirds in the **BATTLE OF KOSOVO**.

1390 English author Geoffrey **CHAUCER** begins the *Canterbury Tales*.

1391 **JEWS** living in Spain are forced to become Christian or die.

1392 French painter Jacques Gringonneur designs a standard for **PLAYING CARDS**.

1393 Mesopotamia is taken over by **TAMERLANE**.

1394 The Holy Roman Emperor is captured and imprisoned by the **LEAGUE OF THE LORDS**.
• King Charles VI issues a decree to **EXPEL** Jews from France.

1395 **LOCKS** are installed on the Po River in Italy to enable the transportation of marble by barge for use in the building of Milan Cathedral.

THEN AND NOW

1351 The Black Death, the worst plague in the history of the Western world finally ends, claiming 25 million lives in Europe alone.
1999 Each year, heart disease claims 7.2 million lives worldwide.

1396 Ottoman Turks conquer much of **HUNGARY**.

1397 Denmark's Queen Margaret rules all of **SCANDINAVIA**.

1398 Tamerlane conquers northern **INDIA**, bringing the powerful Delhi Sultanate to an end.

1399 French writer Christine de Pisan produces *L'Epistre au dieu d'amours* in defense of **WOMEN**.

THE MOATED CASTLE OF BODIAM IN ENGLAND (SEE 1385)

EXTRA EXTRA! Two French housewives are found guilty of witchcraft and burned alive at the Paris Pig Market, in 1391.

25

In 1420, Beijing became the northern capital of China and armed itself against Mongol invaders.

THE AGE OF EXPANSION

During the 15th century, territories and ideas expand, as international commerce increases. Africa prospers through trade with Europe and Asia, Chinese merchants voyage west in search of precious raw materials, the Portuguese reach India, and at the end of the century Columbus sails across the Atlantic. In Europe, there is a rebirth, or renaissance, of Greek and Roman styles of art and literature, and interest in science and technology is rekindled. In Central America the Aztec empire grows and a third of South America is under Inca rule.

1400 England's King **RICHARD II** is believed murdered while imprisoned in Pontefract Castle.

1401 The Tatar conqueror **TAMERLANE** (Timur the Lame) sacks Damascus in Syria.

1402 Tamerlane captures Ottoman Turk **SULTAN BEYAZID I** in a terrible battle at Angora, Turkey.

1403 In Italy, Venice implements the world's first **QUARANTINE** against the Black Death, while Florence legalizes interest being charged on loans.
•A Chinese encyclopedia, *Yung-lo Ta-tien*, is completed by 2,000 scholars, but later all its 22,937 volumes will be lost.

1404 In Holland, the first known use of the **ARCHIMEDEAN SCREW**, powered by a windmill, is employed to aid drainage.

1405 Tamerlane dies en route to invade China, and his body is brought back for burial at **SAMARKAND**, his capital city.

1406 James I of **SCOTLAND** is sent to France for safety, but he is captured at sea by the English, who keep him a prisoner until 1423.

1407 The **BLACK DEATH** hits London, England.

1408 **DONATELLO** creates his marble statue of David at Florence Cathedral; he is the Italian founder of modern sculpture and leader of the early Renaissance, with a realist style that breaks with classical tradition.

1409 The antipope **ALEXANDER V** agrees to end the division of the papacy, but the two rivals already in power refuse to give way, and now three popes vie for control.

1410 The first **COIL SPRINGS** are used in clocks designed by Filippo Brunelleschi, Italian pioneer of Renaissance architecture.

1411 France's Duke of Orléans arms his men with 4,000 **HANDGUNS**, the first instance of their use in warfare.

AN ODD FISH TO CATCH (SEE 1433)

1412 Benedictine monk, John Lydgate, begins *The Troy Book*, which contains flattering references to his friend, the English poet, Geoffrey Chaucer.

1413 **A CANAL LOCK** is built in Holland.
•**DOLLS** with movable arms are made in Nuremberg; from the 1500s onwards, this city will be the centre of Germany's toy industry.

1414 The Fonte Gaia (**PUBLIC FOUNTAIN**) is begun in Siena, Italy, by Jacopo della Quercia, a leading early Renaissance sculptor.

1415 The Flemish artist Hubert van Eyck paints in **OILS**.
•At the **BATTLE OF AGINCOURT**, the French are defeated by English archers under Henry V; there are 7,000 French dead and only 500 English.
•The *Très Riches Heures du Duc du Berry*, one of the finest **ILLUMINATED MANUSCRIPTS** of all time, is created.

1416 Dutch fishermen are the first to use **DRIFT NETS**.

1417 The **HANSEATIC LEAGUE** of merchants sets low prices for meat and grain in North German towns; this move which does nothing to improve the lot of poor rural peasants.

1418 Sent by Portugal's Henry the Navigator, Portuguese seamen discover the **MADEIRA ISLANDS**.

1419 **PHILIP THE GOOD**, Philip the Bold's grandson, is France's Duke of Burgundy when his father, John the Fearless, is murdered.

1420 Construction of the **GREAT TEMPLE OF THE DRAGON** is completed in Peking, China.
•*Feuerwerkbuch* (*The Book of Fireworks*), containing instructions for the developing science of guns and explosives, is compiled in Germany.

1421 Italian architect Filippo Brunelleschi receives the world's first **PATENT**, to make a canal boat with cranes to transport marble.
•The first **ARTILLERY SHELLS** are used at the Siege of St Boniface, Corsica, France.

1422 On the death of Henry V, nine-month-old **HENRY VI** becomes the youngest-ever English king.

1423 Chinese **BLOCK PRINTING** comes to Europe; block-printed playing cards begin to appear.

1424 Thomas à Kempis writes *On the Following (or Imitation) of Christ*; apart from the Bible, it becomes the most widely read book in the world for more than 100 years.

1425 Henry the Navigator takes the islands off the African coast and names them *Islas Canarias* after the wild dogs there; in turn canary birds are named after the islands.
•France's **JOAN OF ARC**, just 13 years old, claims to have been visited by the spirit of St Michael, who calls her to rescue the Paris region from the English.

1426 The Mediterranean island of **CYPRUS**, to be ruled by both Britain and Turkey in later centuries, now falls to the Egyptians.

1427 Britain's first **LIGHTHOUSE** is begun by a hermit, Richard Reedbarrow, in Yorkshire.

1428 **JOHANN GUTENBERG**, Germany's inventor of printing from movable type, begins his printing experiments.

1429 Joan of Arc becomes a heroine at the **SIEGE OF ORLÉANS**, liberating central France.

1430 Mad Megî, a giant **CAST IRON GUN**, is made.

CENTURY STATISTICS

World population, 1400: 374 million
Bookmark: *On the Following (or Imitation) of Christ* is published by German religious writer Thomas à Kempis. A treatise on the principles of religion, it becomes an important book for all Christians.
Landmark: St. Peter's in Louvain, Belgium, soars to 152 m (500 ft). Built in 1497, it collapses to the ground in 1606.

1447! The rules for the ceremony of drinking tea are established by Japanese Shogun Ashikaga Yoshimasa.

1431 Joan of Arc, accused of being a witch and a heretic, is **BURNED AT THE STAKE** in France.

1432 Portuguese noble Gonzalo Cabral discovers the **AZORES**; Prince Henry the Navigator later makes him a gift of the islands.

1433 A **BISHOP FISH** is presented to King of Poland, Ladislas II; the legendary mermaidlike creature appears in natural history books in subsequent centuries as authentic.

1434 **PHNOM PENH** becomes the capital of Cambodia.

1435 **JOANNA II** of Naples dies, having ruled in Italy during constantly troubled times; her kingdom now passes to René of Anjou.

1436 In Florence, Italy the **DUOMO** Cathedral, begun in 1420, is completed.

1437 **JAMES I** of Scotland is murdered at Perth and is succeeded by James II.

1438 Pachacuti founds the **INCA DYNASTY** in Peru.

1439 The **SPIRE** of Strasbourg Cathedral, Europe's tallest at 466 ft (142 m), is completed in the Holy Roman Empire.

1440 Johannes Gutenberg invents the **PRINTING PRESS**.

1441 The African **SLAVE TRADE** begins in the Lisbon markets of Portugal, started by an explorer with 12 captured Africans.

1442 The first known **GYPSIES** in Europe arrive in Spain.

1443 **ALBANIA** defeats the Turks.

1444 Italian explorer **NICCOLÚ DE CONTI** returns to Venice and will be ordered by Pope Eugene IV to relate his travels to the papal secretary.

1445 Founded in the 12th century, **COPENHAGEN** is recognized as Denmark's capital.

1446 Ireland's Blarney Castle is completed; anyone who kisses its **BLARNEY STONE** is blessed with the gift of the gab.

1447 India, Persia, and Afghanistan gain **INDEPENDENCE** when Scanderbeg, Albanian leader and hero, defeats Murad II, sultan of Turkey.

1448 **BAR LINES** are introduced in musical manuscripts.

1449 Turkestan prince **ULUGH BEG** is murdered after his son orders his execution; a noted astronomer, he had accurately calculated the movements of Mars and Venus and produced precise tables of the stars.

The towering Duomo dwarfs every building in Florence

BRUNELLESCHI DARES TO BUILD IL DUOMO (SEE 1436)

EXTRA EXTRA! Mountain sledding is the fastest mode of transportation with a top speed of 45 mph (70 km/h), in 1400.

29

A DAINTY DISH IS SET BEFORE THE KING (SEE 1454)

1450 Italian architect Leon Alberti devises a primitive **ANEMOMETER** to measure wind speed.

1451 Jean Lieburc invents a **TRAVELING CLOCK**.

1452 The first **MIDWIVES'** professional association is established in Germany.

1453 The Byzantine civilization ends when **OTTOMAN** Muhammad II conquers Constantinople.

1454 **ITALY** is divided into several regions: Venice, Milan, Florence, the Papal States, and Naples are the largest, and there are numerous smaller regions as well.
•The *Four and 20 blackbirds baked in a pie* **NURSERY RHYME** derives from the Duke of Burgundy's banquet in France, at which 24 musicians appeared in a pie.

1455 **CAST-IRON** pipes are installed at Germany's Castle of Dillenburgh to transport water.
•**PAPER MONEY** is no longer issued in China, after 500 years of its use.
•Johannes **GUTENBERG** prints the first Bible, in Latin; it is named after him.

1456 An **EARTHQUAKE** in Naples, Italy, kills 35,000 people.

1457 Ladislas V, King of Hungary, flees after the beheading (at his instruction) of the Hungarian **HERO**, Laszlò Hunyadi.

1458 The 12-mile (19-km) Bereguardo **CANAL** is built in Italy complete with locks.

1459 Massacres are begun by Prince **DRACULA** of Wallachia, known as "Vlad the Impaler."

1460 Written in Latin and German, Friar Johannes Balbus Januensis of Mainz, Germany, writes the first printed **DICTIONARY**.

1461 Famine and plague in **JAPAN** lead to an uprising against the country's ruler, Yoshimasa.

1462 **VLAD THE IMPALER** is defeated by Ottoman Sultan Muhammad II, after killing 20,000 Turks along the Danube River.

THEN AND NOW

1451 Nicholas of Cusa invents concave lens spectacles to correct nearsightedness.
1987 Holographic lenses are introduced by the UK glassmaking company, Pilkington, for people who suffer from both near- and farsightedness.

1463 François Villon, a French poet who stabbed a priest to death, is **BANISHED** from Paris.

1464 A **POSTAL** system (*la poste*) is established in France by King Louis XI, with a horse relay system set up to make deliveries for the King.

1465 A cap knitter in Yorkshire provides the first known records of **KNITTING** in England.

1466 Henry VI is recaptured and imprisoned in the Tower of London by Yorkists as the **WAR OF THE ROSES** continues in England.

1467 The Lyons **SILK** industry is established by France's Louis XI, using Italian workers.
•A ballad praises **WILLIAM TELL**, the Swiss national hero who was ordered to shoot an apple off his own son's head.

1468 To strengthen its defenses, England extends its **BAN** on soccer to dice and quoits, in order to encourage people to practice archery.

1469 **RICE**, planted near Pisa, Italy, becomes a major crop.

1470 **PAGE NUMBERS** first appear in a printed book, published in Cologne, Germany.

1471 The foundations of modern **GARDENING** are laid when the *Opus Ruralium Commodorum* is published, based on a manuscript written in the 1300s by Pietro Crescenzi.

1472 The first scientific study of a **COMET** is made by Johann Müller in his observatory in Germany.

1473 Adam von Rottweil produces the first printed **GUIDE BOOK** to Rome, Italy.

1474 Venice introduces a patent **LAW** to protect inventors.
•English printer William **CAXTON** prints the first-ever book in English.

1475 The first **ILLUSTRATED BIBLE** is printed by Jodocus Pflanzmann in Augsburg, Germany.
•**HOURGLASSES**, in different sizes to cover different time spans, are invented in Nuremberg, Germany.

CANNONBALLS MAKE A HIT
(SEE 1495)

1476 Three young Italian nobles **ASSASSINATE** a cruel tyrant, the Duke of Milan, outside the cathedral.

1477 The tradition of **DIAMOND** engagement rings is started when a gold ring set with diamonds forming the letter "M" is given to Mary of Burgundy by Archduke Maximilian.

1478 To root out and punish heretics, the **SPANISH INQUISITION** is ordered by King Ferdinand and Queen Isabella; the dreaded Grand Inquisitor is Tomás de Torquemada.

1479 **VENICE** loses most of her islands in the Aegean, when she loses a naval war to Turkey.

1480 Ivan III stops paying tribute to the Tartars and proclaims himself **TSAR OF RUSSIA**.

1481 Five Italian artists, including Botticelli, paint frescoes in the **SISTINE CHAPEL** in Rome.

1482 Johannes Campanus's translation of *Euclid's Elements* is the first major book to be printed on **MATHEMATICS**.

1483 In England, Edward IV's sons (the **PRINCES IN THE TOWER**) are believed murdered.

BOTTICELLI'S
THE BIRTH OF VENUS
(SEE 1486)

1484 New pope Innocent VIII denounces witchcraft, with severe punishments for "**WITCHES**," who are often innocent midwives.

1485 *Le Morte d'Arthur* by English writer Sir Thomas **MALORY** is published; it is a shortened version of a French Arthurian romance.

1486 Italian Sandro **BOTTICELLI** paints *The Birth of Venus*.

1487 The Genoese use **LAND MINES** for the first time, against the Florentines, in Italy.

1488 Italian artist Leonardo da Vinci designs the **MULTIPLE CROSSBOW GUN**

1489 **CYPRUS** comes under the rule of the state of Venice, and becomes its main source of sugar.

1490 Corpse **DISSECTIONS** are carried out at Padua, Italy.

1491 England's **HENRY VIII** is born at Greenwich, London.

1492 **CHRISTOPHER COLUMBUS**, the Genoese explorer, sails west from Spain and discovers America.

1493 The *Nuremberg Chronicle*, printed in German and Latin, is the first **BOOK** on world history.

1494 Columbus discovers the island of **JAMAICA**.

1495 Cast-iron **CANNONBALLS** are used for the first time by France in her conquest of Naples.

1496 *The Crucifixion* is painted by the early **RENAISSANCE** master, Il Perugino, in Florence, Italy.

1497 Portuguese explorer, Vasco **DA GAMA**, rounds the Cape of Good Hope and arrives in India.

1498 A Chinese encyclopedia is first to detail a modern-style **TOOTHBRUSH**.

1499 Vasco de Gama loses 100 of his 160 men to **SCURVY** (a disease caused by a lack of Vitamin C).

EXTRA EXTRA! A Scottish monk distills the first whisky in 1494.

St. Peter's Basilica in Rome was lavishly rebuilt in the 16th century

THE AGE OF REVELATION

In the 16th century, the growing science of navigation enables European sailors to travel farther afield to hitherto uncharted coasts. But the desire for trade turns to greed in Central and South America and the Aztec and Inca empires are destroyed. The Renaissance that began in the last century is now widespread in Europe, and as printing develops, books are cheaper and more plentiful, and more people read about new ideas. Powerful monarchs rule over Europe, while the Ottoman empire continues to expand in southeastern Europe and the Middle East.

1500 Italian explorer Amerigo Vespucci and his men return from South America, where they had found the mouth of the **AMAZON RIVER**.

1501 **GRANADA** in Spain declares itself a Christian kingdom.

1507 The first stone arch **BRIDGE** in Paris, France (the Pont Notre Dame) is completed.

1508 Italian playwright Lodovico Ariosto's *Cassaria* is the first play to use painted **STAGE SCENERY**.

1517 Cassowaries (flightless birds) from the East Indies are stuffed in Amsterdam, Holland; it is the earliest record of **TAXIDERMY**.

1518 A German inventor, Anthony Blatner, builds a **FIRE ENGINE**.

Leonardo believed that people could learn from birds how to fly

1502 Amerigo **VESPUCCI** returns to Spain from America, which is named after him.

1503 Christopher Columbus and his men arrive in **PANAMA**; they are the first to see Native Americans playing with a rubber ball.

1504 Henry VII, the English ruler, is depicted on a **COIN**.

1505 Italian painter, sculptor, mathematican, and scientist **LEONARDO DA VINCI** studies the flight of bats and birds, and produces designs for ornithopters (flapping-wing aircraft).

1506 Work starts on rebuilding **ST PETER'S** in Rome, Italy.

CENTURY STATISTICS

World population, 1500: 460 million
Bookmark: Every church in England is ordered to have a copy of the *New Testament Bible*, first translated into English by William Tyndale in 1526; most copies are chained to desks to prevent them from being stolen.
Landmark: Rouen Cathedral in France is built in 1530; it pays the price for being 156 m (512 ft) high, when the spire is toppled by lightning in 1822.

1509 The first Portuguese settlement is founded near Porto Seguro in **BRAZIL**.

1510 Portuguese explorer Alfonso de Albuquerque seizes **GOA**, gaining Europe's first territory in the Far East.

1511 Spain seizes control of the Caribbean island of **CUBA**.

1512 The Battle of Brest, between France and England, is the first **SEA BATTLE** in which cannons sink ships.

1513 Explorer Vasco Núñez de Balboa is the first European to see the **PACIFIC OCEAN**; he calls it the South Sea and claims it for Spain.

1514 Ottoman sultan Selim the Grim invades **PERSIA**; his troops massacre the people of Tabriz.

1515 Spanish Juan de Bermudez reaches an archipelago in the Atlantic, naming it the **BERMUDAS**.

1516 Carlos I, the first Hapsburg ruler of Spain, receives a gift of the first **SUGAR** grown in America.

1519 Austrian author Johan Haselberger prints the first ever picture of a **RAILWAY**.

1520 The wheel-lock **MUSKET** is first made, replacing its unreliable predecessor, the matchlock; gun barrels are rifled (cut with spirals to improve velocity).

SLAVES ARE CHAINED TOGETHER BY ANKLE FETTERS WHILE TRAVELLING (SEE 1526)

1521 Aztec emperor **MONTEZUMA II** is killed by invading Spanish soldiers.

1522 The world's first circumnavigation is completed: 15 out of 265 sailors survive the perilous voyage, but their Portuguese leader Ferdinand **MAGELLAN** is killed.

STOP PRESS! Giovanni Danti attempts to fly by leaping from a tower in Perugia, Italy, in 1503

1523 TURKEYS are taken to Europe from the Americas for the first time ever.

1524 German astrologer Johann Stöffler predicts a terrible FLOOD; believers construct arks, and a nobleman is trampled to death by a mob trying to board his vessel.

MODEL OF A FLYING MACHINE BY LEONARDO DA VINCI (SEE 1505)

1525 The harquebus, the first PORTABLE FIREARM, is made by Spanish soldier Fernando de Avalos, Marquis of Pescara.

1526 Spanish explorer Lucas Vasquez de Ayllon takes the first African slaves to MAINLAND America, for a colony in Florida.

1527 Spanish and German MERCENARY soldiers sack Rome, taking Pope Clement VII prisoner.

1528 The ODOMETER (a device for measuring distance) is invented by French scientist Jean Fernel.

1529 German historian Georg Bauer, known as Agricola, employs MUSICAL BAR LINES.

1530 At the wedding feast of Eleanor of Hapsburg and Francis I of France, PLATES, not bowls or wooden trenchers, are first used.

Over seven million slaves were shipped to America

1531 An EARTHQUAKE strikes Lisbon in Portugal and 30,000 people are killed.

1532 Spanish explorer Francisco Pizarro starts the conquest of Peru; the first HORSES are taken from Europe to South America.

1533 England's King Henry VIII is excommunicated by the Pope for declaring his first marriage void; the king proceeds to have SIX MARRIAGES during his reign.

1534 The first printed description of a TOMATO appears in an Italian chronicle that refers to it as a *pomo d'oro*, or golden apple.

1535 DIVING BELLS are first used in Italy for investigating shipwrecks in Lake Nemi.

1536 CATHERINE OF ARAGON, the first wife of England's Henry VIII, dies under house arrest; she was banished for failing to bear a son.

1537 Tyrannical Duke of Florence Alessandro DE MEDICI is stabbed to death by a relative in Italy.

1538 The MENNONITES, a group of nonmilitant Anabaptists, are founded by Menno Simons, a former Dutch Catholic priest influenced by the work of Germany's Martin Luther.

1539 The first PRINTING PRESS in the New World is set up by Antonio de Mendoza, Spain's viceroy in Mexico.

1540 Spanish explorer Francisco Vazquez CORONADO discovers California; his deputy Lopez de Cardenas finds the Grand Canyon.

1541 Francisco PIZARRO completes his conquest of Peru, but he is assassinated.

1542 YOGURT is brought to Europe from Asia Minor.
•AKBAR THE GREAT, the future Mogul Emperor in India, is born.

1543 The Polish astronomer, Nikolaus COPERNICUS, shows that the Sun is the center of the solar system, but he dies immediately after publishing his theory; the word "revolution" (as in revolutionary idea) comes from the title of his work.

COPERNICUS'S THEORY: CHART OF THE SOLAR SYSTEM (SEE 1543)

1544 The dissolution of the monasteries in England causes a HONEY SHORTAGE (since the monks kept bees), thus creating a demand for sugar from the New World.

1545 The *Mary Rose*, flagship of England's HENRY VIII, sinks in Portsmouth harbor, drowning 73 sailors; the ship is recovered in 1982.

1546 Italian doctor Girolamo Fracastoro suggests that EPIDEMICS are caused by tiny seeds transmitted from one person to another.
•Flemish geographer and mapmaker Gerhardus Mercator states that Earth has a MAGNETIC POLE.

1547 England's King Henry VIII dies and is buried at WINDSOR CASTLE.

1548 Italian engineer Giacomo da Vignola constructs CANAL LOCKS, using da Vinci's designs.

1549 Roman Catholic MISSIONARIES begin work in South America and Japan.

THE RENAISSANCE

THE 16TH CENTURY in Europe was an age of astonishing and revolutionary change. From beginnings in Italy, Europeans started to throw off the shackles of medieval superstition, entering a modern "humanist" age in which people tried to look and think about the world for themselves. A new thirst for knowledge grew hand in hand with the spread of ideas through new universities and the remarkable innovation of printed books. This period is called the Renaissance, or rebirth, because it found its inspiration in the rediscovery of ancient Greek and Roman ways of thinking. But it fostered ideas and discoveries in the arts and in sciences, such as medicine, that were entirely new. Above all, it led to the cataclysmic shift in religious beliefs called the Reformation that split the western church from top to bottom.

MEDICINE AND ANATOMY

The ideas of Greek physician Galen (c. 130–201) about the human body were unquestioned for a thousand years. But the Renaissance spurred some thinkers into studying the body for themselves. Physicians such as Belgian Andreas Vesalius (1514–1564) began to obtain dead bodies from graveyards and dissected them to make the first detailed pictures of anatomy – the way the human body is put together. They followed up with growing insights into physiology and disease, which form the basis of modern medicine.

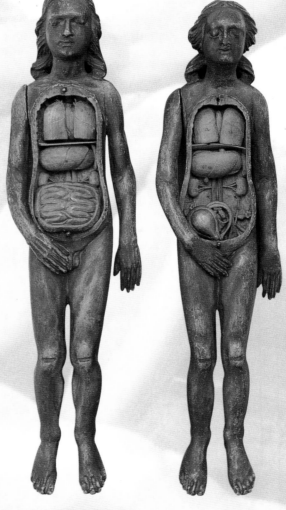

THE ART OF ANATOMY
Renaissance artist Ghiberti (1378-1455) designed these bronze figures as models for medical study.

BREAKTHROUGHS IN MEDICINE

ANATOMICAL DRAWINGS are first seen in detailed sketches of parts of the human body by artists such as Leonardo da Vinci (1452–1519).

A CAESAREAN BIRTH takes place in 1500, when Swiss Jakob Nufer operates on his wife.

MODERN ANATOMY is founded when in 1543 Andreas Vesalius, one of the most famous anatomists working in Padua, Italy, writes *De Humani Corporis Fabrica* ("What the Human Body is Made of").

DISEASE Paracelsus (1493–1541) argues that disease is not an upset in the body's "humors" but is caused by an outside agent.

REPRODUCTIVE ORGANS and bones are studied by physicians such as Italian Gabriel Fallopius (1523–1562).

PHYSIOLOGY, the study of body functions, begins in the 1590s, when Italian physician Sanctorius (1561–1636) shows how to measure pulse and temperature.

CREATION OF ADAM
In 1510, Michelangelo Buonarroti painted the fresco on the ceiling of the Sistine Chapel in Rome.

ART AND ARCHITECTURE

The effect of Renaissance ideas on art and architecture was startling. Painting and sculpture were revolutionized by a series of remarkable artists in Italy – especially Leonardo da Vinci, Michelangelo, Raphael, and Titian – and many more who were inspired not only by the great classical works of Greece and Rome, but also by the world in which they lived. Almost overnight, the flat, iconic images of the medieval era were superseded by images of three-dimensional realism as they discovered the rules of perspective and began to explore space, form, and light. In architecture, similarly, the genius of men like Brunelleschi and Bramante reinvented classical approaches to buildings to create masterpieces such as the cathedrals in Florence and Rome.

Artists are inspired by ancient Greece and Rome

TROMPE L'OEIL
Painted by Andrea Mantegna (1431–1506) on the ceiling of the Gonzaga Palace in Italy, this fresco makes good use of perspective by creating the illusion that it opens out to the sky.

MASTERPIECES

1436 Brunelleschi (1377–1446) completes the dome of **FLORENCE CATHEDRAL** with a design inspired by the Pantheon of ancient Rome, and develops the first rules of perspective.

1503 In his masterpiece *Mona Lisa*, Leonardo da Vinci (1452–1519) uses the technique of fading colors to create a sense of aerial **PERSPECTIVE**.

1508 Michelangelo (1475–1564) begins to create a painting of almost sculptural presence on the ceiling of the **SISTINE CHAPEL** in Rome.

1510 The paintings of Raphael (1483–1520) for the **VATICAN**, such as *The School of Athens*, set the standard artists aspired to for centuries.

1515 Prolific Italian painter **TITIAN** (d. 1576) combines romantic realism and classical idealism in his painting *Sacred and Profane Love*.

1586 Greek-born Spanish artist **EL GRECO** (1541–1614) finishes his painting – the *Burial of Count Orgaz* – in Toledo, Spain.

NEW FAITH AND IDEAS

The Renaissance saw a profound shift in ideas and a new interest in learning as thinkers began to question religious dogma and gradually shift the focus away from God's role in the world to that of humankind. Print played a crucial role in disseminating first the humanist ideas of Erasmus and then the protests of Luther.

NEW IDEAS

HUMANISM Dutch scholar Erasmus (1466–1536) pokes fun at the church in his best-seller *In Praise of Folly*.

THE REFORMATION sees the breakaway from the Catholic Church of Protestant reformers, inspired by the protests of Martin Luther (1483–1547) against Church abuses and his insistence that faith could be found in the Bible by anyone – not just priests.

THE SPREAD OF IDEAS

1432 **UNIVERSITIES** are founded at Caen and Poitiers in France.

1450 German printer Johannes Gutenberg (1398–1468) finds a way of casting movable type from metal, making **PRINTING** multiple books easy.

1475 William Caxton (c. 1422–1491) prints the **FIRST BOOKS** in England, including *The Canterbury Tales*.

1508 Italian humanist Girolamo Aleandro begins to teach **GREEK CLASSES** at Paris University, France.

RENAISSANCE PEOPLE

THE NEW IDEAS of the Renaissance began, for the first time, to place a high value on individual ideas and achievements – and on the individual search for truth. The "Universal Man," the cultured man versed in everything from science to music, was held up as the ideal. Yet though few lived up to this ideal – men like Leonardo da Vinci are the exceptions – there was no shortage of remarkable individuals who made their mark in their own field, in literature, in sciences such as astronomy, and in the political world.

STATESMAN AND POET
Lorenzo de Medici (1449-1492) was a true Renaissance prince.

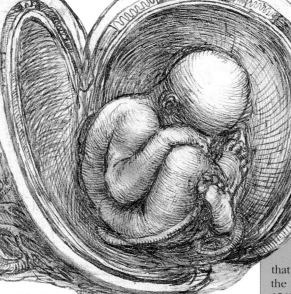

HUMAN WOMB
A sketch from Leonardo da Vinci's detailed notebooks

MEN OF SCIENCE

Renaissance ideals gave people new confidence to observe and analyze the world for themselves for the first time. There gradually emerged a series of men who laid the foundations of modern science. They did not call themselves scientists but natural philosophers. Their prolific studies and discoveries soon revolutionized the world.

LEONARDO DA VINCI

LEONARDO DA VINCI (1452–1519) is a genius from Tuscany, Italy, who exemplifies Renaissance ideals. He is perhaps best known for his few master paintings, such as the *Mona Lisa* and the *Last Supper,* but is also a remarkable illustrator, producing sketches that reveal detailed scientific studies – from human anatomy to astronomy. His inventive mind leads him to create designs for tanks, crossbows – even an early flying machine.

NATURAL PHILOSOPHERS

NICOLAUS COPERNICUS (1473–1543) Until the 16th century, people thought that Earth was at the center of the universe. However, in his 1543 book *De Revolutionibus Orbius Coelestium,* Polish astronomer Copernicus shows that Earth is just one of the planets circling the Sun – an idea so disturbing it is banned by the Church for the next 300 years.

GEORGIUS AGRICOLA (1494–1555) of Germany is the first great geologist. He devotes his life to classifying minerals and studying mining techniques.

TYCHO BRAHE (1546–1601), a Danish astronomer, builds an observatory and becomes the greatest observer of the heavens with the naked eye, measuring the positions of 777 stars with unprecedented accuracy.

JOHANNES KEPLER (1571–1630) a German astronomer, discovers three fundamental laws that show how all the planets move.

FRANCIS BACON (1561–1626), an English philosopher, lays down the basis of modern science by insisting that ideas must come from observation and experiment – not reasoning.

WILLIAM GILBERT (1544–1603), an English physician at the court of Queen Elizabeth I, writes *De Magnete,* a study of magnetism and Earth's magnetic field. He is first to use the term "electricity."

GREAT WRITERS

The Renaissance was the age when European writers began to create literature. Instead of the largely anonymous ballads and religious mystery plays of the medieval period, individual poets and playwrights, including William Shakespeare, began to write fictional works about real life in their own literary style.

POETS AND PLAYWRIGHTS

MIGUEL DE CERVANTES (1547–1616), a storyteller from Spain, writes *Don Quixote* – the first great work of prose fiction.

CHRISTOPHER MARLOWE (1564–1593) is the first of the great dramatists of the vibrant theater of Elizabethan and Jacobean England, which spawns writers such as Shakespeare and Ben Jonson (1572–1637).

LOPE DE VEGA (1562–1635) is the first great playwright of the Golden Age of Spanish drama. He pens such masterpieces as *El Castigo sin Venganza* and *La Dama Boba*.

PIERRE CORNEILLE (1606–1684), whose greatest play is *Le Cid* (1637), is the first great French dramatist. He is later eclipsed by Jean Racine (1639–1699).

LITERARY HERO El Cid (c. 1030-1099) was a Spanish hero who inspired many poems as well as Corneille's masterpiece Le Cid.

WILLIAM SHAKESPEARE

WILLIAM SHAKESPEARE (1564–1616), born in Stratford, England, is the greatest poet and playwright of the age. His plays such as *Romeo and Juliet* and *Hamlet* are still performed around the world today.

Science and literature enter a golden age

SCHOLARS AND STATESMEN

With the coming of the Renaissance, the old certainties of the feudal way of life and the Catholic church crumbled, and people began to look for new ways of ordering society. Some writers, such as Thomas More in *Utopia*, tried to imagine ideal worlds. Others, like Niccolò Macchiavelli in *The Prince*, explored how a society could be secured by skillful statecraft. Soon princes and men of power, such as the Italian Medicis and England's William Cecil, began to try out for themselves the arts of politics and statecraft.

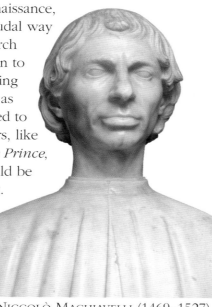

NICCOLÒ MACHIAVELLI (1469–1527)
Machiavelli's famous book The Prince *inspired many politicians and statesmen.*

THE NEW STATESMEN

NICCOLÒ MACHIAVELLI (1469–1527) argues that to govern well a prince must be cunning and, sometimes, unethical. His philosophy inspires generations of "Machiavellian" politicians.

THOMAS MORE (1478–1535), an Englishman, imagines the ideal social system on his mythical island of Utopia, in which everyone shares equally in government, education, and wars.

WILLIAM CECIL (1520–1598), Lord Burghley, masterminds the reign of England's Elizabeth I.

THE BORGIAS are one of the great political families of Renaissance Italy. Rodrigo Borgia (1431–1503) becomes Pope Alexander VI, one of the most powerful of all popes.

LORENZO DE MEDICI (1449–1492) is the best known of the Medici family who ruled Florence. Known as Lorenzo the Magnificent, he is the embodiment of the Renaissance prince – hugely powerful and a great patron of the arts.

1550 The earliest known records of **REFRIGERATION** are published in Rome, Italy; they detail the method of dissolving saltpeter in water, for cooling the wine and water of the Roman nobles.

St. Basil's Cathedral (SEE 1555)

1551 Taverns and alehouses in England and Wales receive their first **LICENSES**.

1552 English butchers face **IMPRISONMENT** for selling meats other than those decreed by Parliament, under a newly issued law.

1553 Spanish physician Miguel Servetus describes the circulation of **BLOOD** through the lungs; the Church orders him burned at the stake for heresy, in Geneva, Switzerland.

1554 The first of the Italian city's huge sculptures, *Mars and Neptune* by Jacopo Tatti Sansovino, is erected at the Doge's Palace in **VENICE**.

1555 **ST. BASIL'S CATHEDRAL** in Moscow, Russia, is begun; it follows the design of architect Posnik Yakovlev and was commissioned by Ivan the Terrible in honor of his conquest of Kazan three years earlier.

1556 A terrible **EARTHQUAKE** in China is said to have buried alive 830,000 Chinese peasants.

1557 The **EQUALS SIGN** (=) is invented by Englishman Robert Record, who records it in his algebraic work, *The Whetstone of Witte*.

1558 The earliest **DOLLHOUSE** is made in Munich, Germany, for Bavaria's Duke Albrecht V.

1559 **HENRY II** of France dies in agony after being wounded in the head at a jousting tournament.

1560 Diplomat Jean Nicot brings the **TOBACCO** plant to France; it is named *Nicotiana* after him, hence the word in English, nicotine.

1561 Pieter Brueghel, Flemish painter, is commissioned to design a **DREDGER**, which will be used to clean Holland's Rupel-Scheldt canal.

Ivan the Terrible celebrates victory in style

1562 The **TULIP** arrives in Europe when bulbs are brought to Antwerp in Holland from Contantinople (now Istanbul) in Turkey.

1563 Pieter Brueghel "The **Elder**" paints his *Tower of Babel*.

1564 Graphite deposits are discovered at Borrowdale in England by Germans digging for copper; next year Switzerland's Konrad Gesner will invent **PENCILS WITH LEAD** made from Borrowdale graphite.

1565 England's Royal College of Physicians are allowed by law to carry out **HUMAN DISSECTIONS**.

1566 The French astrologer **NOSTRADAMUS**, who achieved world fame through his prophecies, dies at age 63.

SAILORS GET A NAP
(SEE 1597)

Life on the ocean waves becomes more comfortable

1567 Lord Darnley, the husband of **MARY, QUEEN OF SCOTS**, is blown up with gunpowder, probably on her orders; later she marries the Earl of Bothwell, his likely murderer.

1568 Flemish mathematician and mapmaker Gerhard Kremer produces his Mercator projection, a **MAP** of all the known world, with the globe displayed as a rolled flat cylinder.

1569 Queen Elizabeth I of England establishes the first **NATIONAL LOTTERY**, with 400,000 tickets issued at ten shillings each and a winning prize of £5,000.

1570 Dutch geographer Abraham Ortelius publishes the first modern **WORLD ATLAS** in Antwerp.

1571 English mathematician Leonard Digges invents the **THEODOLITE**, which facilitates greater accuracy in mapmaking.

1572 The **ST. BARTHOLOMEW'S DAY** massacre occurs in Paris, France, when Royalist (Catholic) supporters of Charles I go on a rampage against the Huguenots (Protestants).

1573 The Germans establish their first **CANE SUGAR** refinery.

1574 The drunken Ottoman Sultan **SELIM II** slips in the Turkish baths, cracks his skull, and dies.

1575 **STEPHEN BÁTHORY** becomes King of Poland.

1576 Italian astrologer Jerome Cardan **PREDICTS** when he will die, starving to make it come true.

1577 English explorer **FRANCIS DRAKE** sets out on a round-the-world trip, using five vessels.

1578 The **CATACOMBS**, underground tunnels with tombs, are rediscovered in Rome, Italy.

1579 Seven Dutch provinces, now the modern Netherlands, are united by the **UNION OF UTRECHT**.

1580 Francis Drake is knighted by **QUEEN ELIZABETH I** on his successful return to England.

1581 Balthazar de Beaujoyeux's *Ballet comique de la Reyne*, the first **BALLET**, is performed in France.

1582 October 4 follows October 15 by order of Pope Gregory XIII, to allow for **LEAP YEAR** days.

1583 Galileo Galilei discovers the **PENDULUM**'s properties.

1584 Reginald Scot writes a book against **WITCHHUNTS**.

1585 **FIRE SHIPS** are used at the Siege of Antwerp, Belgium.

1586 **MOTHER GOOSE**'s death is registered in England.

1587 Antonio da Ponte's design wins the competition for a new **RIALTO BRIDGE** in Venice, Italy.

1588 The English, led by Admiral Charles Howard, defeat the "invincible" **SPANISH ARMADA**.

1589 The **FLUSHING TOILET** is invented in England.

1590 Dutch eyeglasses maker Zacharias Janssen invents the **COMPOUND MICROSCOPE**.

1591 When German property owners in Hamburg each agree to pay a certain amount to help any other member who has a fire, **FIRE INSURANCE** begins.

1592 **POMPEII**, the Roman city in Italy ruined by Mount Vesuvius in AD 79, is rediscovered.

1593 English dramatist **CHRISTOPHER MARLOWE** is stabbed to death in a tavern brawl.

1594 The first **DESK DIARY** is published in Poland.

1595 The English army stops the use of **BOWS AND ARROWS**.

1596 English poet **EDMUND SPENSER**'s greatest work, *The Faerie Queen*, is completed.

1597 **HAMMOCKS** are used in England's Royal Navy.

1598 The **FLAGEOLET** is invented by Juvigny in Paris, France.

1599 The **RIKSDAG** (Swedish Parliament) deposes its king, Sigismund III, because he supports the Catholics.

THEN AND NOW

1559 London's Globe Theatre, a round, wooden structure named after its sign depicting Hercules with the world upon his shoulders, is built. Shakespeare's *Julius Caesar* opens here. **1997** The New Globe Theatre is built in London, 656 ft (200 m) from the original site, and designed mainly for the performance of Shakespeare's plays.

Moghul emperor Shah Jahan built the Taj Mahal in memory of his wife

THE AGE OF COMMERCE

During the 17th century, Europeans set up trading posts on every continent, guaranteeing people at home a constant supply of exotic goods and spices. Fleeing religious persecution or poverty, increasing numbers of pilgrims cross the Atlantic to settle in North America. Central Europe comes close to being overrun by the powerful Ottomans. Art and architecture, such as the Taj Mahal, flourish under the Moghul dynasty in India, while China's Manchu rulers lead her into a period of prosperity helped by trade of ceramics and silk.

1600 The **BRITISH EAST INDIA COMPANY** is founded.
•William **SHAKESPEARE**'s play *Hamlet* opens in London, England.

1601 France and Germany establish **POSTAL SYSTEMS**.

1602 The United (Dutch) East India Company is the first to issue **SHARE CERTIFICATES**.

1603 The first English horse-drawn **RAILROAD WAGONS** are built to carry coal from the pits of Newcastle-upon-Tyne to the harbor.
•A new fuel, **COKE** (made from heating up coal), is discovered by Hugh Platt.
•Italian Girolamo Fabrici studies leg veins and discovers valves that allow **BLOOD** to flow only towards the heart.
•A shortage of **BREAD** in Russia leads to widespread famine; 50,000 die.
•England's **QUEEN ELIZABETH I** dies.

1604 Italian **GALILEO** Galilei observes by dropping objects from the Leaning Tower of Pisa that the distance they fall is equal to the square of the time it takes to fall.
•England's King James I attacks the new fashion of **SMOKING** in his book, *A Counterblaste to Tobacco*.

DON QUIXOTE, THE WOULD–BE KNIGHT, TACKLES AN IMAGINARY ENEMY (SEE 1605)

Don Quixote tilts at windmills

1605 Amritsar's **GOLDEN TEMPLE**, the holiest of the Sikh religion, is built in the middle of the sacred pool of Amrita Saras in India.
•**SANTA FE**, capital of New Mexico, is founded by Don Pedro de Paralta.
•People travel between English cities on horse-drawn wagons; the horses are changed regularly, at stages, from which the term **STAGECOACH** is derived.
•Spanish novelist Miguel de Cervantes writes the first part of *Don Quixote*, the tale of a man who longs to become the perfect knight. The word **QUIXOTIC** comes to mean foolishly idealistic.
•Catholic conspirator Guy Fawkes is found in the vaults of the Houses of Parliament with 36 barrels of **GUNPOWDER**. He is hanged, drawn, and quartered for plotting to destroy the king of England and his Parliament.

1606 The British **UNION JACK** flag links the crosses of the patron saints of Scotland and England, which are now united under James I.
•**AUSTRALIA** is discovered by a Portuguese expedition led by Luis Vaz Torres.

1607 John Smith founds **JAMESTOWN**, the British colony of Virginia in America. Captured by a Native American tribe and condemned to death, he is saved by Pocahontas, the chief's daughter.

1608 The Dutch state rewards eyeglass-maker Hans Lippershey with money for inventing the **LOOKER**, an early telescope.
•The Canadian city of **QUEBEC** is founded by the French explorer Samuel de Champlain.

1609 The **NETHERLANDS** gain independence from Spain.
•The colony of Virginia is granted a royal charter.
•The first newspapers, or **CORANTOS**, are published in Strasbourg, Germany; they are translated throughout Europe.
•**TEA DRINKING** becomes popular in Europe when the Dutch East India Company returns from China with a small trial consignment of green tea.

•Johannes Kepler, German astronomer, discovers three laws of planetary motion that become known as **KEPLER'S LAWS**.

1610 The **FLINTLOCK GUN** is invented in France by Marin Le Bourgeois; its efficient ignition mechanism makes it popular on the battlefields and in private duels.

1611 The **DANISH ARMY** introduces service rifles.
•Marco de Dominis presents his **THEORY OF RAINBOWS** in Italy.
•The **KING JAMES VERSION** of the Bible is published.

1612 In an operation to reclaim 17,000 acres (6,880 hectares) of fertile land, 43 **WINDMILLS** are used to drain Lake Beemster in Holland.
•A flag is flown at **HALF-MAST** for the first time, by the crew of the *Heartsease* in honor of their Captain James Hall, killed by Greenland's Inuits (Eskimos).
•Of the 20 accused **WITCHES ON TRIAL** in Lancashire, England, ten are hanged, including an 11-year-old girl.
•The **DECIMAL POINT** is first used by Bartholemew Pitiscus.
•Russia defeats invading **POLISH** army.

1613 Early **DIVING** apparatus is described in Diego Ufano's *Trado dela artilleria*, which shows a hooded diver with a tube that reaches the water's surface.
•**MIKHAIL ROMANOV** is chosen to be tsar of Russia.
•Protestant Englishmen and Scots colonize **IRELAND**.
•During a performance of William Shakespeare's *Henry VIII* at the Globe Theatre in London, England, a **CANNON BLAST** sets the thatch roof on fire, and the building burns down.
•The first daily **TEMPERATURE** readings are recorded on Galileo's thermometer by Francesco Sagredo in Venice, Italy.

1614 Basil Besler describes more than 660 types of **FLOWERS** in his two-volume work, *Hortus Eystettensis*, published in Germany; the two volumes are so hefty that they have to be transported by wheelbarrow.
•Scottish mathematician and inventor John Napier publishes a table of figures, or **LOGARITHMS**, which speed up the multiplication and division process in mathematical calculations.
•Dutch map the island of **MANHATTAN**.

•Erzebet Bathory, known as Countess Dracula, the **MASS MURDERESS** accused of killing 650 girls, is walled up in her castle in Csejthe, Hungary.

1615 "Honesty" tobacco boxes, the first-known **VENDING MACHINES**, are installed in English taverns; a penny is inserted in the machine to open a box of pipe tobacco supplies.
•Salomon de Caux makes the first **SOLAR-POWERED** motor, in France, to run a fountain for the royal family.

1616 William Shakespeare dies on April 23, his **BIRTHDAY**, the same day as the death of Miguel de Cervantes, author of *Don Quixote*.

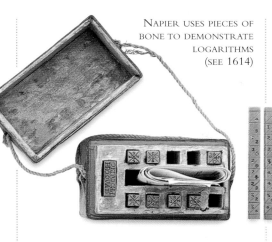

NAPIER USES PIECES OF BONE TO DEMONSTRATE LOGARITHMS (SEE 1614)

•Italian professor Santorio Santorio makes the first medical **THERMOMETER**.

1617 The works of French theologian **JOHN CALVIN** are published posthumously.
•Princess **POCAHONTAS** dies while waiting for a ship to return to America and is buried in Gravesend, England.

1618 The **EXPLORER** and poet Sir Walter Raleigh falls out of favor with the English court and is beheaded; his wife proceeds to carry his head around until she dies; then Raleigh's son continues the tradition.
•Two Catholic supporters of the Hapsburg Emperor Ferdinand II are thrown out of a palace window by Bohemian Protestants in Prague; it sparks Europe's **THIRTY YEARS' WAR**.
•The earliest **PAWNBROKER** shop sets up business in Belgium, lending money in exchange for personal goods that owners can "buy" back later.

1619 The first **AFRICAN SLAVES** are brought to the colony of Virginia and sold by Dutch merchants.

1620 English philosopher Francis Bacon inspires a fresh approach to scientific research when he champions the value of **OBSERVATION** in his *Novum Organum*.
•In a demonstration of the first **SUBMARINE**, a wooden boat coated in tallow, with 12 oarsmen breathing through a hollow mast, is presented to England's King James I by Dutch physicist Cornelis J. Drebbel.

THE SOLEMN DRESS CODE OBSERVED BY PURITANS (SEE 1620)

•**SIGN LANGUAGE** is first detailed by Juan Pablo Bonet in Spain.
•Edmund Gunter invents a **WOODEN RULE** to replace printed log tables.
•English Puritans set sail in *The Mayflower* and arrive in Massachusetts to set up "godly" colonies.
•America's Virginia Company is given the English tobacco **MONOPOLY**.

1621 Pilgrims celebrate the first **THANKSGIVING** in Plymouth colony.
•Pope Gregory XV declares January 1 the beginning of the **NEW YEAR**.

1622 Fearful that religious influence may threaten their imperial power, Japanese **SHOGUNS** crucify 55 Christians in Nagasaki.
•One-third of the European settlers in Virginia are **MASSACRED** by Native Americans for moving in on Indian cornfields.
•Thousands of Spanish emigrants are drowned at sea when a **HURRICANE** hits their convoy outside Havana, Cuba.

1623 The first mechanical **CALCULATING MACHINE** is invented by German Wilhelm Schickard.
•John Mason founds **NEW HAMPSHIRE**.
•Persia takes **MESOPOTAMIA** from the Ottoman Empire.
•England establishes a **PATENTS LAW** to protect inventors.

1624 Anti-Spanish **RIOTS** occur in Mexico.
•Louis XII appoints **CARDINAL RICHELIEU** the chief minister of France.
•Flemish alchemist Jan Baptista van Helmont gives the name **GAS** to compressible liquids.

CENTURY STATISTICS

World population, 1600: 579 million
Best-seller: The world's largest book, a world atlas measuring 5 ft 10 in by 3 ft 6 in (1.78 m by 1.07 m) is presented to King Charles II of England by Dutch merchants in 1660.
Landmark: St. Peter's, the central church of the Roman Catholic faith, is built in Rome. The dome designed by Michelangelo takes the church to a height of 433 ft (132 m).

1625 *La Liberazione di Ruggiero* is the first opera to be written by a female composer, Francesca Caccini of Florence, Italy.
•**CATHOLIC** Charles I becomes England's king.
•A patent for steel **SPRING-SPRUNG** coaches is granted to English inventor Edward Knapp, making travel by road a more comfortable experience.

1626 A devastating earthquake hits **NAPLES**, killing 70,000 and destroying 30 neighboring villages.
•English philosopher Francis Bacon dies after trying to invent **DEEP-FREEZING** by stuffing a chicken with snow.

1627 Hunters kill the last **AUROCH**, a cow-like wild animal that roamed Europe's forests.
•**CIVIL UNREST** spreads in Ming China.

THEN AND NOW

1646 The magic lantern is described by Athanasius Kircher, a German priest; it projects hand-painted images from slides onto a white screen and is lit by candle or oil lamp.
1952 Panoramic movie-viewing is introduced to the US at Fred Waller's Cinema, where a curved screen and three projectors are used to try to produce an effect that is more akin to real-life vision.

1628 English physician William Harvey establishes how blood is circulated around the body, via the heart. **BLOOD CIRCULATION** and the structure of the heart is described in his new book *Exercitatio Anatomica de Motu Cordis et Sanguinis*, which is the first to apply measurement and mathematics to biology.
•The *Vasa*, the Swedish navy's brand-new 60-gun flagship, sinks in Stockholm harbor when the crew forgets to close the gunports before setting sail.

1629 **KING CHARLES I** dissolves parliament and attempts to rule England on his own.

•France issues a **DECREE OF TOLERATION** for Protestants, but excludes them from politics and the military.
•Mutineers kill over 100 people in the *Batavia* shipwreck off Australia.
•Women are banned from the **KABUKI THEATER** in Japan.

1630 English mathematician Richard Delamain invents the circular **SLIDE RULE**, an instrument for multiplying and dividing numbers.
•Bubonic **PLAGUE** kills 1,000,000 in northern Italy.
•**BOSTON** becomes the capital of Massachusetts.

1631 American colonist John Winthrop uses the Bible to justify the **PURITANS'** seizure of Native-American lands.
•The first **FERRY TRIPS** begin in America on the Charles River in Massachusetts.
•**REMBRANDT** begins painting in Amsterdam, Holland.
•Sweden defeats Russia in the **BALTIC**.
•Mt. Vesuvius, a **VOLCANO**, erupts in Italy, killing 4,000 people.
•Frenchman Pierre Vernier's **AUXILIARY SCALE** allows precision measurements.

•Englishman William Oughtred introduces new mathematical **SYMBOLS** for algebra and arithmetic, including multiplication and proportion signs.

1632 Italian astronomer **GALILEO GALILEI**'s new theory that the Earth orbits the Sun is met with great disbelief.
•The "Water-bow" **FIRE ENGINE** is invented by Thomas Grent.
•Lord Baltimore founds **MARYLAND** as a haven for Catholics in America.
•Drought followed by excessive rains causes severe **FAMINE** in Dekhan, India.

1633 British establish a trading post in **BENGAL**, India.

1634 Russia **DEFEATS** and forces out the Polish army.
•Samuel Cole opens the first **TAVERN** in Boston, Massachusetts.
•Johannes Kepler publishes his story about a trip to the **MOON**.
•After the previous year's Black Death plague, Germany's Bavarian village of Oberammergau pledges to perform a **PASSION PLAY** every ten years, forever.

1635 **RELIGIOUS WARS** (Catholic versus Protestant) engulf Europe from Portugal to Poland.

1636 Englishman William Gascoigne invents an astronomical device, the **MICROMETER**.
•The will of English-born John Harvard awards his library and a grant to found a new college; built in Cambridge, Massachusetts, it is named **HARVARD** after its founder and becomes one of America's most prestigious universities.

1637 To save costs, the body of Ben Jonson, Shakespeare's fellow dramatist and multitalented friend, is buried standing up in Westminster Abbey in London, England.
•The earliest **OPERA HOUSE**, Teatro San Cassiano, opens in Venice, Italy.
•French philosopher and mathematician René **DESCARTES** publishes the first account of analytic geometry.

1638 In the **SHIMABARA REBELLION**, 20,000 Japanese peasants are massacred by an army organized by the nobility.
•Swedes and Finns settle Delaware Valley, founding Christiana, the capital of **NEW SWEDEN**.

1626! The island of Manhattan in America is sold to Dutch colonists for $24-worth of trinkets.

•Disenchanted with Puritan Massachusetts, Thomas Hooker and others found **CONNECTICUT**.

1639 America's first **PRINTING PRESS** begins operations in Cambridge, Massachusetts.
•English astronomer Jeremiah Horrocks observes the transit of **VENUS**.
•Russian explorers cross **SIBERIA** and reach the Pacific Ocean.

1640 Robert Burton, author of *The Anatomy of Melancholy*, dies in Oxford, England, on January 25 – the day he had predicted astrologically as the date of his death.
•The Taxis family sets up Germany's first regular **STAGECOACH SERVICE**.
•Cardinal Richelieu establishes the **ROYAL PRINTING WORKS** in France.

1641 **COTTON** is imported from Cyprus and used in Britain's first cotton-manufacturing establishment at Manchester, England.

1642 Led by Li Tzu-ch'eng, a former member of the Emperor's postal service, rebels against China's **MING DYNASTY** capture the town of Kaifeng, by breaking the river dikes. The city and surrounding area is completely flooded; 300,000 people die.
•At age 19, French physicist Blaise Pascal invents his calculator, known as the **PASCALINE**, an adding and subtracting machine to help his father with the accounts.
•Dutch navigator Abel Tasman discovers **TASMANIA** and New Zealand.
•The Tavernier Blue, later known as the **HOPE DIAMOND**, is found in India by French traveler Jean Tavernier; it is said to bring bad luck to all who own it.
•Dutch painter **REMBRANDT** creates his materpiece *The Night Watch* in the year that his wife Saskia van Ulenburgh dies; because the work, largely set in shadow, goes against convention, the popularity of this great artist wanes.
*Italian astronomer and physicist **GALILEO GALILEI** dies.

1643 The first Native-American **DICTIONARY**, *A Key into the Language of America*, is compiled by Roger Williams.
•The **MERCURY BAROMETER** invented by Italian physicist Evangelista Torricelli, demonstrates that air has its own weight.

THE MOON'S FEATURES ARE MAPPED OUT (SEE 1647)

•Santiago, **CHILE**, is completely destroyed by a massive earthquake.
•The Dalai Lama's palace, the Potala, is completed in **TIBET**.

1644 English poet **JOHN MILTON** calls for the freedom of expression in his *Areopagitica, A Speech for the Liberty of Unlicensed Printing*.
•China's Ming Dynasty ends with the **SUICIDE** by hanging of Emperor Chongzhen, who pins a note to his lapel.

1645 A large part of Boston, Massachusetts, is destroyed when a store of **GUNPOWDER** explodes.
•The New Netherlands (New York) makes peace with the **MOHAWKS** and other Native-American tribes.

1646 **VIRGINIA** passes the New World's first law providing for the educaiton of poor children.

1647 Massachusetts passes a law barring Catholic priests from the colony. First offense is punished by **BANISHMENT**, second offense by death.
•The first **MAP OF THE MOON** is drawn by astronomer Johannes Hevelius, based on sightings made from Germany's most important observatory, founded by him.

•The **BAYONET** (a dagger attached to the barrel of a rifle) is invented by an armorer in Bayonne, France.

1648 Nitric acid, which will be used in **EXPLOSIVES**, is discovered by German chemist Johann Rudolph Glauber.
•The **HYDRAULIC PRESS** is invented by Blaise Pascal in France.
•Europe's Thirty Years' War ends with the **PEACE OF WESTPHALIA**.
•Margaret Jones of Plymouth becomes the first woman to be executed for **WITCHCRAFT**.

1649 **MARYLAND** passes an act of religious toleration, the first in the colonies.
•A **MECHANICAL TOY** coach and horses is made by Camus for the 11-year-old French king, Louis XIV.
•King **CHARLES I** is beheaded; he was found guilty of waging war against his kingdom and the English Parliament.
•Turkish ruler **SULTAN IBRAHIM** is ousted by his family, when his mother helps to have him deposed and murdered. He is succeeded by his seven-year-old son Mehmet IV.

EXTRA EXTRA! A winged chariot made out of farming machinery is flown across an English barn by a 10-year-old boy, in 1640.

EXPLORATION

WITH THE COLLAPSE of the Mongol empire in the 14th century, roads from Europe to the east were cut off, spurring a remarkable series of bold European mariners to set out westward to find their way to Asia by sea. As they ventured farther and farther into unknown waters, they discovered new lands – including the New World of the Americas – encountered strange peoples, and made conquests that have shaped the modern world.

ASTROLABE
From the 1300s, seafarers used the astrolabe to find their position north or south.

WHERE THEY WENT

After 1400, mariners sailed from Europe, venturing south into the unknown around the west of Africa, often in small ships called caravels. Many mariners were Portuguese, sent out by Prince Henry "the Navigator" (1394–1460) from his base at Sagres. Cape by cape, they pushed south until, in 1488, Bartolomeu Dias rounded Africa's southern tip. Nine years later, Vasco da Gama sailed right around to India. Meanwhile, in 1492, taking a great gamble, Christopher Columbus set out westward across the open Atlantic, hoping to reach China – and instead found the whole New World of the Americas, waiting to be explored. Finally, in 1522, less than 90 years after the voyages began, Ferdinand Magellan's ship *Victoria* sailed all the way around the world.

NAVIGATIONAL AIDS

COMPASS From the 12th century on, European sailors use a magnetic needle to find North.

ASTROLABE The astrolabe is adopted in Europe in the 13th century. By measuring the height of a star or the Sun at noon, sailors can work out their latitude (how far north or south they are).

CROSS-STAFF Navigators in the 16th century adopt the cross-staff to enable them to figure out the angle between the horizon and the North Star to show latitude more accurately than with an astrolabe.

LONGITUDE PROBLEM With an astrolabe or cross-staff, navigators could find their latitude, but not their longitude (how far east or west). The only way was to guess how far they had come by "dead reckoning" – trailing a knotted rope in the water to keep a constant track of their speed.

CHRONOMETER It is not until the 18th century that John Harrison invents the chronometer, finally solving the longitude problem by keeping time accurately enough aboard ship for navigators to know the real time within seconds.

THE GREAT VOYAGES

1434 Portuguese naval officer Gil Eannes sails beyond **CAPE BOJADOR**, Africa's seemingly impassable western cape.

1488 Bartolomeu Dias rounds the Cape of Good Hope at **AFRICA**'s tip.

1492 Genoese adventurer Christopher Columbus sails across the Atlantic to reach land in the **CARIBBEAN** in the New World of the Americas, named after Amerigo Vespucci, who voyages there a few years later.

1497 Vasco da Gama sails south into the Atlantic and then swings east to round Africa and reach **INDIA**.
•John Cabot, trying to find a way north around America to Asia, discovers **CANADA**.

1513 Vasco Balboa leads an expedition across the Isthmus of Panama and sees the **PACIFIC OCEAN**.

1505 Magellan's crew is the first to **CIRCUMNAVIGATE** the world.

1535 Jacques Cartier sails up the St. Lawrence River in **CANADA**.

1648 Seeking a sea route from Europe to the Pacific, Russian explorer Simon Dezhnev reaches the **ARCTIC OCEAN**.

FIRST MAP OF EUROPE
*The great mapmaker Mercator (1512–1594)
was the first to create a map of Europe.*

EXOTIC TREASURES

As they sailed around the world, European mariners brought back with them astonishing wealth, which was to form the foundation of Europe's power. As many goods as were gained by honest trade were obtained by exploitation and conquest.

STRANGE FRUITS

1554 POTATOES are brought to Europe from South America by Spanish explorer Francisco Pizarro. They became a staple in western and northern Europe.

1555 TOBACCO is introduced to Europe from South America. By the early 17th century, tobacco smoking is common throughout Europe, championed by such men as Sir Walter Raleigh.

1596 TOMATOES are brought to Europe from South America. Initially, they are considered poisonous, and are not widely eaten for 200 years.

TOBACCO PLANT

GOLD, SLAVES, AND SPICES

SLAVES In the 16th and 17th centuries, Portuguese trading posts along the African coast form the first slave markets. In 1562, English trader John Hawkins transports slaves from West Africa to the West Indies. By the early 19th century, more than seven million Africans will have been taken into slavery. Today, half Brazil's population is of African origin.

GOLD Rumors of great wealth encourage many adventurers to explore South and Central America. By 1521, Hernando Cortés, a Spanish soldier, has conquered the Aztec empire in Mexico, while another Spaniard, Francisco Pizarro, destroys the Inca empire in Peru in 1532. Both men return to Spain laden with gold. Important gold and silver mines are established, and by 1700, most of the world's silver comes from mines in Peru and Mexico.

SPICES The Portuguese monopolize the Asian trade routes, working from their bases in Indonesia, China, and India. Spices, such as pepper, cloves, cinnamon, and nutmeg, become sought after in Europe. In 1599, the Dutch establish control of the Moluccas, or "Spice Islands," of Eastern Indonesia. In 1602, they found the Dutch East Indies Company.

COLONIZATION

The Europeans were not slow to take advantage of the wealth that their discoveries overseas could bring their nations. During the 17th century, they quickly established themselves, by force and by persuasion, in colonies and settlements in the New World, in Africa and Australia, and even in India and the Far East.

Sailors discover great wealth overseas

COLONIES AND TRADING POSTS

LATIN AMERICA Columbus gives the New World its first European colony in 1492, when he leaves 40 men on Hispaniola (Puerto Rico). In 30 years, Spanish colonies appear all over Central America.

NORTH AMERICA Jamestown, Virginia, the first English settlement, is set up in 1607.

PORTUGUESE TRADING PORTS are established around the world in the 17th century – in Goa, India, in the Moluccas, and in many other places.

CAPE TOWN In 1652, the Dutch East Indies Company sends 80 colonists to found Cape Town, on the tip of South Africa.

AZTEC GOLD
The Aztecs, who ruled in what is now Mexico from 1325 to 1521, fell to European expansion.

PEOPLE OF THE NEW AGE

THE 17TH CENTURY WAS an astonishing age of discovery in Europe. Every decade seafarers brought home news of unknown lands, along with exotic foods, plants, and animals – and much more. Every decade, too, brought new discoveries in science and philosophy. Yet perhaps none of these discoveries had quite so profound an effect as the discoveries people made about themselves – changes that were eventually to bring down kings and overturn society.

SHIP IN A BOTTLE

NEWS BRINGERS

Fired by Columbus's discovery of the New World and the circumnavigation by Magellan's crew, voyagers set off from Europe to probe every corner of the world. Some were looking for fame, some for riches, some for conquest, and some went simply out of curiosity. But each helped to fill in the picture of the world, keeping great mapmakers like Mercator constantly busy.

FERDINAND MAGELLAN (1480–1521)

EXPLORERS

1580 The second voyage around the world is completed by English explorer **SIR FRANCIS DRAKE**.

1606 Dutchman Willem Jansz maps part of the Australian coast.
• Luis Vaez de Torres (d. 1615) explores the coast of New Guinea.

1608 French seafarer **SAMUEL DE CHAMPLAIN** (1567–1635) founds Quebec, in eastern Canada.

1610 Trying to discover a northwest passage linking the Atlantic to the Pacific Ocean, **HENRY HUDSON** (d. 1611) explores Canada's Hudson Bay.

1642 Dutchman **ABEL TASMAN** (1603–1659) sails around Australia – known as the Great South Land.

1673 French-Canadians **LOUIS JOLLIET** and **JACQUES MARQUETTE** press far into the North American interior to explore the Mississippi.

1699 English navigator **WILLIAM DAMPIER** (1652–1715) embarks on a voyage to Australia and New Guinea.

1728 Commissioned by the Russian tsar, Dane **VITUS BERING** (1681–1741) sets off on the first of a series of scientific expeditions across Siberia.

1768 Captain **JAMES COOK** (1728–1779) sets off on his first voyage to explore the Pacific Ocean.

PLACES NAMED AFTER EXPLORERS

AMERICA In 1508, the Italian navigator Amerigo Vespucci is made chief pilot and mapmaker of Spain. All Spanish sea captains must report to him the details of their latest voyages. From this information, Vespucci makes such good maps of the New World that sailors soon start to refer to it as "Amerigo's Land," or "America."

COLOMBIA This South American country is named after Christopher Columbus. It is one of the many places he visits during his voyages of exploration to the New World.

STRAITS OF MAGELLAN Named after Ferdinand Magellan, this sea channel lies between the island of Tierra del Fuego and South America.

DAVIS STRAIT English sailor John Davis (1550–1605) gave his name to the straits between Canada and Greenland, after his (unsuccessful) attempt to discover the Northwest Passage to Asia.

COOK ISLANDS These South Pacific islands are named after the English explorer and navigator, Captain James Cook.

THINKERS

The 17th century was a time of incredible advances in science. Inventions such as the telescope opened up the skies and led to challenges to existing theories about the universe and how it works, the planets and their movements, and the position of Earth within the universe.

ASTRONOMERS
With the invention of the telescope, people were able to see the movement of the stars and planets and form theories on the universe.

INVENTORS AND DISCOVERERS

1610 Observing the night sky with a telescope, Italian **GALILEO GALILEI** (1564–1642) sees moons orbiting Jupiter – proving Copernicus's view that Earth circles the Sun.

1643 Italian **EVANGELISTA TORRICELLI** (1608–1647) invents the mercury barometer to measure air pressure.
• French mathematician **BLAISE PASCAL** (1622–1662) develops the first adding machine.

1660 Developing Galileo's ideas, Dutchman **CHRISTIAAN HUYGENS** (1629–1695) designs an accurate pendulum clock.

• Italian **MARCELLO MALPIGHI** (1628–1694) of Italy discovers blood capillaries.

1661 Irishman **ROBERT BOYLE** (1627–1691) introduces the idea of chemical elements and compounds.

1675 Dutch **ANTON VAN LEEUWENHOEK** (1632–1723) uses convex and concave lenses to make microscopes – and in 1676 discovers microscopic organisms.

1682 **ISAAC NEWTON** (1642–1727) introduces his laws of motion and theory of gravitation.

MEN OF POWER

Most European countries were ruled by monarchs, but thinkers such as John Locke (1632–1704) began to question their right to power. The English monarchy was restored after Cromwell's Commonwealth, but the king's power was no longer absolute.

People begin to question the power of the monarchy

MONARCHS AND LEADERS

LOUIS XIV (1638–1715) is an absolute monarch and claims his power by divine right. He builds the palace at Versailles.

OLIVER CROMWELL (1599–1658) rules England as Lord Protector after Charles I is beheaded at the end of the English Civil War.

WILLIAM OF ORANGE (1650–1702) of Holland is invited to become King of England by assent of Parliament in 1688.

PETER THE GREAT (1689–1725), Russian tsar, introduces policies to "Europeanize" Russia, and builds the city of St. Petersburg.

SUN KING
Louis XIV (1638-1715) is among the world's longest-reigning monarchs.

1650 TEA is drunk for the first time in England.

• French philosopher Descartes dies of a cold in Queen Christina's palace in STOCKHOLM, Sweden.

• The first DAILY NEWSPAPER, *Einkommenden Zeitungen*, is published in Leipzig, Germany.

• A COFFEE HOUSE, England's first, is opened by Christopher Bowman and is funded by a Turkish merchant.

1651 CHARLES II, deposed king of England, flees to France.

Louis XIV dazzles France

1652 In Boston, Massachusetts, John Hull sets up America's first MINT, where silver coins are made bearing the symbol of a pine tree, the word "Massachusetts," and Roman numerals for pence denominations.

• CAPE TOWN, in South Africa, is founded by the Dutch East India Company as a provisions station.

• The MINUET, an elegant dance, sweeps through France.

• RHODE ISLAND bans slavery.

1653 Religious battles kill thousands in RUSSIA.

• OLIVER CROMWELL declares himself Lord Protector of England.

1654 Jacob Barsimson is the first known JEWISH IMMIGRANT to America; he pays 36 guilders to travel along with 22 other Jews from Holland.

THEN AND NOW

1661 Hand stamps are first used in London, England, for marking letters with a small round postmark giving the date of mailing.

1998 The world sends more than 400 billion letters a year, 170 billion of which are handled by the US Postal Service. The Vatican City has the highest average daily postage of 26 letters per person.

LOUIS XIV AS
LE ROI SOLEIL
(THE SUN KING) (SEE 1661)

• Using his AIR PUMP, Otto von Guericke of Germany advances the understanding of vacuums and pressure when he finds that even two teams of eight horses cannot pull apart the two sections of a sphere from which he has pumped out the air.

• Joseph Jencks of Boston builds the first FIRE ENGINE in America.

1655 Robert Hooke builds a model ORNITHOPTER, an aircraft with flapping wings, in England.

• TITAN, the largest of Saturn's many moons, is discovered by Christiaan Huygens, a Dutch scientist.

1656 Accurate to within five minutes a day, the PENDULUM CLOCK invented by Christiaan Huygens is built in Holland.

• Two Spanish galleons collide at night off the BAHAMAS, killing 644 people.

1657 More than 100,000 people die when gale force winds in Tokyo, Japan, send a small fire out of control. For three days flames spread through the city's wooden buildings; many lives are lost by panic-driven STAMPEDES, exposure, and starvation.

1658 The first illustrated book for children, *Orbis Sensualium Pictus*, is published in Germany.

• Protestant Oliver Cromwell dies from MALARIA, because he believes that quinine, supplied by Catholic Jesuits, is the powder of the devil.

1659 RED BLOOD CORPUSCLES are discovered by Jan Swammerdam of Amsterdam, Holland.

1660 When the English monarchy is restored to the throne, the body of former ruler Oliver Cromwell is dug up and beheaded, then placed on public display.

• Naval clerk SAMUEL PEPYS begins writing his *Diary*, which gives a vivid portrayal of daily life in London, England; he keeps his journal until his eyesight fails nine years later.

• Peasants from Holland, known as BOERS, colonize South Africa.

• Friedrich Staedtler founds the first PENCIL factory in Germany.

1661 LOUIS XIV declares "*L'Etat, c'est moi*" (I am the State), when he regains control of France with the death of Cardinal Mazarin, nicknamed "the Second King," who had ruled for Louis since he was crowned at age five.

• The first CHURCH for Indians is founded by John Eliot in Massachusetts.

• Ireland's Robert Boyle devises BOYLE'S LAW. (For a fixed mass of gas at a constant temperature, pressure and volume are inversely proportional.)

1662 Leading scientists and intellectuals found the ROYAL SOCIETY in London, England.

• The first PUNCH AND JUDY puppet show in London's Covent Garden is described by Samuel Pepys in his *Diary*.

1663 The COLONIES of New Jersey, North Carolina, and South Carolina are founded.

1664 Dutch settlement of Fort Orange in the Hudson Valley (New York), surrenders to the British and is renamed ALBANY.

• The Turkish assault on VIENNA, Austria, is stopped.

EXTRA EXTRA! Solomon Eccles marches naked through London with a pan of sulfur on his head, predicting doom, in 1665.

1665 English physicist Isaac Newton conducts **GRAVITY** experiments with apples.
•The British take all of New Netherlands and rename it **NEW YORK**.

1666 The **GREAT FIRE** of London, England, starts in a baker's shop and rages for five days.
•**NEWTON** devises differential calculus.

1667 **HAND GRENADES** are used during the French army's invasion of Holland.
•Englishman **ROBERT HOOKE** transmits sound along tightly drawn strings.
•France's earliest **POLICE FORCE** is set up in Paris by a royal edict.

•The earliest **ART EXHIBITION** is held at the Palais-Royal in Paris, France.
•**BLOOD TRANSFUSION** experiments are performed in France by Jean-Baptiste Denys on a 15-year-old boy.

1668 Newton builds the first **REFLECTING TELESCOPE**.
•Father Jacques Marquette establishes first colony in **THE GREAT PLAINS**.

1669 German alchemist Hennig Brand discovers the element **PHOSPHORUS** (a Latin word meaning "morning star"), while distilling urine.

Ever-active Mount Etna blows its top once more

1670 France's **PALACE OF VERSAILLES** is completed.
•French astronomer Jean Picard finds the exact **RADIUS** of Earth.

1671 The moon **IAPETUS**, a satellite of Saturn, is discovered by Giovanni Domenico Cassini, first director of the Paris Observatory in France.
•Herds of bulls are sent to trample Welsh pirate Sir **HENRY MORGAN** and his band of men as they plunder Panama.

1672 Germany's Otto von Guericke invents the first weather **BAROMETER**: a 34-ft (10-m) water-filled tube, containing a model that floats in good weather and sinks in bad weather.

1673 The first American woman writer, **PURITAN POET** Anne Bradstreet, dies in Massachusetts.
•Jean-Baptiste **MOLIÈRE**, French actor-playwright, dies on stage in Paris.
•The first-ever American **POSTAL ROUTE** operates monthly between New York City and Boston, Massachusetts.

1674 Morel, a French surgeon, devises the **TOURNIQUET**, which restricts blood flow to a limb and controls the bleeding.
•Marquette and Joliet return to Montreal, Canada, after completing their 2,500-mile exploration of the **MISSISSIPPI RIVER**.

1669! Mount Etna erupts in Sicily, Italy, killing 20,000 people.

AN ILLUSTRATION OF THE NOW-EXTINCT DODO (SEE 1680)

1678 The French fleet is sunk in the **CARIBBEAN**.
•French explorer Robert Cavalier de la Salle is the first European to see **NIAGARA FALLS**.
•During his imprisonment for preaching, English author John Bunyan writes *The Pilgrim's Progress*, which follows a Christian's journey from Earth to heaven. It immediately becomes a success, and sells 100,000 copies in Bunyan's lifetime.

1679 The German mathematical writer Gottfried Wilhelm Leibnitz invents the **BINARY SYSTEM** of counting, using only two digits.
•The Muslim Moghul Emperor Aurangzeb orders **HINDU TEMPLES** to be destroyed throughout India.

1680 The **DODO**, a tame flightless bird (its name derives from *doudo*, the

A hungry sailor polishes off the last dodo on Earth

Portuguese for simpleton), becomes extinct after the last of its number is killed and eaten by hungry sailors in Mauritius.
•John Calpepper of South Carolina is acquitted of treason after leading the first **POPULAR UPRISING** against the British.

1675 The Royal **GREENWICH OBSERVATORY** is founded by England's King Charles II to provide reliable information for sea navigation.
•Italian anatomist Marcello Malpighi dissects a silkworm and discovers that the **ANATOMY** of small creatures is no less complex than that of larger animals.
•Olaus Roemer, a Danish astronomer, discovers the finite **VELOCITY OF LIGHT** and concludes that light travels through space at 180,000 miles per second.
•George Ravenscroft of England invents flint or **CRYSTAL GLASS**, which closely resembles natural rock-crystal.

1676 America's first **PRISON** is built in Massachusetts.
•Le Grand Vatel, **CHEF** to the Prince de Condé, kills himself when King Louis XIV of France expresses disappointment with his dinner.
•Englishman Robert Hooke invents the **UNIVERSAL JOINT**, which allows astronomical instruments to be turned in any direction.

1677 The Dutch-Jewish philosopher **BARUCH SPINOZA** dies; his great work, *Ethics*, is published a few months later.
•Britain's first female playwright, Aphra Behn, gains popularity with her new comedy, *The Rover*.

1681 Theologian Thomas Burnet publishes *Sacred History of Earth*, his ideas about **EVOLUTION**.
•The Languedoc **CANAL**, a triumph for French civil engineering, connects Toulouse with the Mediterranean.

1682 King Charles II grants William Penn a charter for the American colony of Pennsylvania; Penn founds Philadelphia as a "holy experiment" in tolerance.
•English astronomer Edmund Halley observes the **COMET** that will be named after him, and accurately predicts its return in 1758.

1683 William Penn signs the TREATY of Peace and Brotherhood with the Indians.
•The Poles and Austrians repel a Turkish **INVASION**.
•China seizes **TAIWAN**.

EXTRA EXTRA! A Polish peasant is given a beating for his failed attempt to fly with wings made of mica, in 1680.

•**BACTERIA** are described by Dutch microscopist Antonie van Leeuwenhoek when he discovers "animalcules," or little animals, in the samples of saliva, cow dung, and other material that he has examined under high-powered lenses.

1684 Pope Innocent IX forms the **HOLY LEAGUE** with Venice, Poland, and Austria, against the Turks.
•Iharu Saikuko composes 23,400 **HAIKU** verses in a single day and night.
•Dione and Tethys, two of **SATURN'S** moons, are discovered by Italian astronomer Giovanni Domenico Cassini.

1685 The revocation of the Edict of Nantes, in France, spurs a migration by French Protestant **HUGUENOTS** to the Carolinas in America and to South Africa.
•Judge Jeffreys punishes rebels against King James II at the **BLOODY ASSIZE** in England by condemning 320 men to hang and 840 men to be sold into slavery in the West Indies.

1686 Russia joins the Holy League and Austria annexes Hungary; Turkey falls into **ANARCHY**.
•A **CORDON BLEU** (blue ribbon) for cooking is worn by each girl graduating from France's Institut de Saint-Louis, which teaches cooking to daughters of not-so-wealthy nobles.
•**ICE CREAM** is first served in the English court of King James II.

1687 English physicist Sir Isaac Newton publishes his *Prinicipia*, explaining the **THEORY OF GRAVITY** and the movements of bodies in the universe.
•England's Catholic king, James II, issues the Declaration of Indulgence, granting **RELIGIOUS FREEDOM** to Catholics and nonconformists.
•A basic **STEAM ENGINE** is built by French physicist Denis Papin.
•The science of **STATISTICS** is pioneered by English economist Sir William Petty.
•The **PARTHENON** in Athens is seriously damaged by a gunpowder explosion.

1688 The **GLORIOUS REVOLUTION** occurs in England: Catholic James II is deposed and exiled to France, and Dutch monarchs William of Orange and Mary become England's king and queen.
•As Austria annexes **TRANSYLVANIA**, France invades from the west.

•Lloyd's Coffee House in London, England, becomes the meeting place of underwriters, who form an association known as **LLOYD'S**; it becomes world-famous for offering insurance against most eventualities.

1689 A trained ship carpenter, Peter the Great becomes the absolute ruler of **RUSSIA** at 22.
•England, Spain, Holland, Sweden, Savoy, and Holy Roman Empire form the **GRAND ALLIANCE** and invade France.
•Edmund Halley designs, makes, and successfully demonstrates his new **DIVING** bell and diving helmet.

1690 French colonials and Native Americans **MASSACRE** 60 English settlers in New York state.
•The **ASHANTI** kingdom in Ghana, West Africa, is organized into a confederation of African tribes; Kumasi is the capital.
•William III defeats James II at the Battle of the Boyne, ending **IRISH CATHOLIC** aspirations for independence.
•Boston's *Publick Occurrances* is America's first **NEWSPAPER**.
•The British found **CALCUTTA** in India.

1691 **FREEDOM OF WORSHIP** is granted to all – except the Catholics – in Massachusetts.
•**MAINE** and Plymouth are incorporated into Massachusetts.

1692 Large chunks of Port Royal, Jamaica, tumble into the sea when the city is hit by a **TIDAL WAVE**.
•One man is pressed to death and 19 women are hanged at the **SALEM WITCHCRAFT TRIALS** in America.

1693 Italian **EARTHQUAKES** cause 153,000 to die in Naples and Catania, and 18,000 in the eruption of Mount Etna volcano in Sicily.
•**WILLIAM AND MARY COLLEGE**, America's third college, in Virginia, is granted its charter by the English king and queen after whom it is named.
•France's Louis XIV defeats the Grand Alliance army in the Netherlands and defeats the navy near **GUINEA**, Africa.

1694 **FAMINE** sweeps France; the poor die while speculators stockpile grain.
•German botanist Rudolph Jakob Cammerarius discovers **PLANT POLLEN**.
•The **BANK OF ENGLAND** is founded by Scotsman William Paterson.

1695 **CENSORSHIP** of the press ends in England.
•**PLAGUE** sweeps Mexico.

1696 Etienne Loulié of Paris, France, invents the **METRONOME** to mark time to music.
•Peter the Great seizes Azor from Turks, giving Russia a port on the **BLACK SEA**.

1697 *Cinderella, Sleeping Beauty,* and other **FAIRY TALES** are published in France by Charles Perrault.
•The Pennypack Bridge is built in Pennsylvania and becomes America's oldest **STONE ARCH BRIDGE**.
•A **GOLD RUSH** begins in the Portuguese colony of Brazil.

1698 Nehemiah Grew's Epsom salts are granted the first **MEDICINAL PATENT**; Grew also notes that plants are male and female.
•The Russians must pay a **BEARD TAX**.
•British engineer Thomas Savery patents a **STEAM-DRIVEN WATER PUMP**.
•Peter the Great visits England's shipyards to learn **NAVAL CRAFT**.

1699 **YELLOW FEVER** epidemic sweeps American colonies.
•William Dampier finds an island north-east of **AUSTRALIA**, and names it New Britain.
•**SILHOUETTES** (shadow portraits) are first cut in Holland.
•Peter the Great declares Russia's **NEW YEAR** to be January 1 (not September 1).

THEN AND NOW

1688 Champagne, a bubbly white wine made from black grapes, is invented in France by Dom Pérignon, a Benedictine monk. **1998** In just one year, France consumes 179,004,405 bottles of Champagne and exports 113,453,686 bottles of it.

1680! The earliest known cello is made by Italian Antonio Stradivarius.

Bath was built in the 1700s as an elegant vacation resort for the wealthy

THE AGE OF REVOLUTION

The 18th century is marked by revolution and change. Starting in England, new labor-saving machines enable food and textiles to be mass-produced, leading to peaceful revolutions in farming and industry. In North America, the United States of America is created when the 13 colonies revolt and win independence from Britain. At the end of the 1700s, the French republic is founded, and the king is deposed and later executed. Elsewhere in the world, Europeans continue to map Africa and the Pacific, while China is richer and more powerful than ever.

A GIBBET, OR IRON CAGE, FOR DISPLAYING THE BODY OF AN EXECUTED PIRATE (SEE 1701)

1700 Sweden defeats the Russians at Narva in the **BALTIC**.
•**AMMONIUM CHLORIDE** is discovered in France by J. P. de Tournefort; it is later used to make batteries.
•American Samuel Sewall publishes the first outright appeal against **SLAVERY**.
•The **TAXATION** of unmarried women is introduced in Berlin, Germany.

1701 English agriculturalist **JETHRO TULL** creates the first seed-sewing machine; 270 years later, an English rock band takes his name and becomes world famous.
•Scottish pirate Captain William Kidd is hanged; his body is later displayed in an **IRON CAGE**, called a gibbet, as a warning to other pirates.
•**WILLIAM III** of England dies when his horse stumbles over a molehill.
•Catholics are banned from the **ENGLISH THRONE**.

1702 A monthly **TRANS-ATLANTIC POSTAL SERVICE** between England and the West Indies costs the sum of thirteen cents per item.
•English author Daniel Defoe, sentenced to stand for three days in the **PILLORY**, is showered with flowers by his admirers.
•The *Daily Courant* becomes the **FIRST DAILY NEWSPAPER** to be published in London, England.

1703 Peter the Great founds the city of **ST. PETERSBURG** to manage Russia's trade in the Baltic.
•Forty-six Samurai commit **RITUAL SUICIDE** on the orders of the Japanese shogun.
•In his *A Voyage to the Moon*, David Russen suggests that a man could reach the moon by being **CATAPULTED** off a high mountain.

1704 Tokyo, Japan, is left in ruins by a series of **DISASTERS**: tidal waves (killing 37,000), a fire fanned by hurricane-force winds, and an earthquake.
•**A PETTICOAT REBELLION** breaks out when 25 brides sent from France refuse to marry anyone in Louisiana, because of the terrible conditions they find there.

1705 English astronomer Edmond Halley correctly predicts that a **COMET** he had observed in 1682 will return every 76 years.

1706 The first known use of the Greek letter π (**PI**) to show the ratio of circumference to diameter in a circle appears in *A New Introduction to Mathematics* by William Jones.

1707 **HUNGARY** revolts against Hapsburg rule and declares a short-lived independence; four years later, the Hungarian rebels surrender.
•The **ACT OF UNION** binds Scotland and England together; Scotland loses its parliament, but retains its own legal system and the Presbyterian Church.

1708 While buying tobacco in America, Ebenezer Cook is appalled by the greed of Maryland settlers; on his return to England, he writes a **SATIRE** of his experiences.
•The **AFRICAN KINGDOM** of Dahomey grows rich from the slave trade by selling off the members of other tribes.

1709 A miniature **HOT-AIR BALLOON** is demonstrated by Bartolomeu Lourenco de Gusmão.
•Bartolommeo Cristofori, an Italian keyboard maker, invents the **PIANO**.
•Wind strength and velocity are measured by Wolfius's **ANEMOMETER**.
•Italian perfumier Giovanni Farina creates a mass-produced scent, **EAU DE COLOGNE**, in Cologne, Germany.
•German physicist Daniel Fahrenheit invents the **ALCOHOL THERMOMETER**, and five years later a mercury version.

1710 **TURKEY** joins Sweden in the war against Russia.
•France introduces **INCOME TAX**.

CENTURY STATISTICS

World population, 1700: 679 million.
Bookmark: *Webster's American Spelling Book* published in 1783 sells up to 100 million copies.
Landmark: After 38 years of building work, the new St. Paul's Cathedral in London, England, is completed in 1710. Reaching a height of 365 ft (111 m), its dome is dwarfed only by St. Peter's Church in Rome, Italy.

TODAY'S
STRAWBERRIES
(SEE 1714)

Chilean strawberries are brought to Europe

• The rebuilding of St Paul's Cathedral in London, England, is completed by architect, astronomer and mathematician **CHRISTOPHER WREN**; the original was destroyed during the Great Fire of London in 1666.

1711 The **TUNING FORK** is invented in England, by John Shore, a trumpeter to the court of Queen Anne.
• A **FULL-COLOR PRINTING** process is patented by Jakob Le Bon in Germany.

1712 Johann Boltger of Meissen, Germany, discovers the secret of making Chinese **PORCELAIN** and founds the most influential ceramics factory in Europe.
• The first of Thomas Newcomen's **STEAM ENGINES** is used to drive a pump at a coal mine in England.
• St. Petersburg, now a major cultural center, takes over from Moscow to becomes Russia's **CAPITAL**.
• **HANNAH PENN** takes over the governance of Pennsylvania in America after her husband, William Penn, suffers a stroke; she bans the importation of slaves into the colony.
• To survive the heavy tax imposed by the English government, newspapers resort to **BRIBERY**, promising to withhold their criticism of certain politicians in return for "hush" money.

1713 The **SCHOONER**, a new type of American sailing ship with sails both at the front and the back, is invented by Andrew Robinson.

• The **TREATY OF UTRECHT** ends the War of Spanish Succession; Europe's borders are redrawn.
• France's Louis XIV is given a **COFFEE** bush; ten years later it is stolen and taken to Martinique.

1714 German **GEORGE I**, of Hanover, becomes king of England even though he cannot speak English.
• **WITCH TRIALS** are abolished in Prussia.

• The first known collector of **BIRDS' EGGS** is M. Peters of Belgium.
• François Frézier, a French naval officer, returns from South America with five **STRAWBERRY** plants, from which the modern strawberry evolves.
• The Church of the Transfiguration is built entirely out of **WOOD** on Kizhi, an island on Lake Onega, Russia.

1715 Goaded by Spain, the **YAMASSEE INDIANS** massacre hundreds of English settlers in South Carolina.
• Louis XIV dies, having achieved the **LONGEST REIGN** in European history.

1716 America's first **LIGHTHOUSE**, lit by a whale oil lamp, replaces the warning bonfires at Boston Harbor.

1717 The link between mosquitoes and **MALARIA** is established by Giovanni Lancisi in *On the Noxious Effluvia of Marshes*.
• School attendance is made **COMPULSORY** in Prussia.
• John Lombe returns to England from Italy with the secret of silk throwing (a technique for producing a strong twisted thread). He patents a machine for making **THROWN SILK**, which until now has been a costly import.

1718 The flintlock **MACHINE GUN**, invented by English lawyer James Puckle, is capable of firing 63 bullets in seven minutes, but it is too heavy to be practical.
• Ferocious English pirate Edward Teach, or **BLACKBEARD**, dies in a duel with a lieutenant of the British Navy.
• John Law receives the French king's approval to print paper money. The **BANKNOTES** are payable in silver pieces but soon become worthless when the bank issues too many.

1719 English writer Daniel Defoe publishes *The Life and Strange Surprising Adventures of Robinson Crusoe*, a tale of **SHIPWRECK** on an uninhabited island. It is so realistic that many readers believe it is true; supposed relics of Crusoe's boat and boots are offered for sale.
• US lighthouse keeper John Hayes takes to firing a cannon during fog, starting the first **FOG WARNING SIGNAL**.

FRANCE ISSUES BANKNOTES (SEE 1718)

N.º 1490395 CINQUANTE livres Tournois.

Division Ordonnée par Arrest du 2. Septembre 1720.

LA BANQUE promet payer au Porteur à vûe CINQUANTE livres Tournois en Especes d'Argent, valeur reçue. A Paris le deuxiéme Septembre mil sept cens vingt.

Vû p.ʳ le S.ʳ Fenellon. Giraudeau.

Signé p.ʳ le S.ʳ Bourgeois, Delanauze.

Controllé p.ʳ le S.ʳ Durevest. Granet.

EXTRA EXTRA! Madame de Prie of Paris, France, is the first person known to wash in a bidet, in 1710.

59

1720 Louis Bertrand Castel invents a **HARPSICHORD** that performs a light show. When the instrument is played, beams of light travel through strips of color that are fixed to the keys.

1721 Emperor K'ang Hsi of China celebrates his 60-year rule with a **FESTIVAL OF OLD MEN**, at which men above the age of 90 are presented with gifts of rice and silk.
•In order to provide wives for colonists in New Orleans, **FEMALE PRISONERS** are sent from France.

1722 Dutch navigator Jacob Roggeveen discovers an island in the Pacific on Easter Day and names it **EASTER ISLAND**.
•Peter the Great westernizes the Russian army and **CIVIL SERVICE**.
•Afghanistan conquers **PERSIA**.

1723 After a fight with his brother, 17-year-old **BENJAMIN FRANKLIN** leaves Puritan Boston for the more tolerant city of Philadelphia, where his radical, inventive gifts soon flourish.
•A reduced import **DUTY** on coffee and tea increases their popularity in Britain.

1724 Britain's first **GLASSHOUSE**, built under the supervision of horticulturist Stephen Switzer, houses a grapery at Belvoir Castle.
•In Louisiana, **THE BLACK CODE** legalizes the branding of slaves and bans Jews from the colony.

1725 Adrien de Pauger builds a 62-ft (19-m) **BEACON** near New Orleans to provide a landmark for shipping.
•Italian composer Antonio **VIVALDI**, nicknamed "the Red Priest" because of his red hair, writes *The Four Seasons*.
•Gold diggers in Brazil discover **DIAMONDS** instead of gold; people rush to make their fortunes, and the Tejuco

region is renamed Diamantina; the price of diamonds, inevitably, falls.

1726 **BLOOD PRESSURE** is first measured by Stephen Hales, English botanist and chemist.

1727 After 700 years of seismic inactivity, an **EARTHQUAKE** destroys Tabriz, a city in Persia (modern Iran), and kills 75,000 inhabitants.

1728 In the **TREATY OF SEVILLE**, Spain recognizes British control of Gibraltar.
•Jian Ting-xi completes the **GREAT CHINESE ENCYCLOPEDIA**, which has 10,000 chapters.
•The **NATCHEZ** Indians kill 300 French soldiers in a fierce battle at Fort Rosalie in Louisiana.
•Frenchman Pierre Fauchard, father of modern **DENTISTRY**, publishes his work *The Surgeon Dentist*, which leads the way to making dentistry a profession.

1729 **CAST-IRON** ribbed wheels are introduced to replace the less durable wooden wheels on England's railroad cars.
•German composer Johann Sebastian **BACH** writes the *St. Matthew Passion*.

THE COASTAL STATUES OF EASTER ISLAND (SEE 1722)

Huge carved statues stand guard on Easter Island

1730 Georg Brandt, professor of chemistry at Uppsala University in Sweden, discovers **COBALT**, a silvery blue metal element.
•Benjamin Franklin publishes *A Witch Trial at Mt. Holly*, a **SATIRE** of superstition.
•British mathematician John Hadley's reflecting nautical **QUADRANT** measures the distance between the Sun and the horizon, to determine a ship's location.
•Frenchman René-Antoine Ferchault de Réaumur invents an alcohol **THERMOMETER** with an 80-degree scale between freezing and boiling.

1731 The first **FOREIGN LANGUAGE PAPER** in the colonies is published by Benjamin Franklin.
•Finding himself stranded on Honduras, John Cockburn becomes the first Englishman known to explore the pleasure of smoking a **CIGAR**.

1732 English physician Thomas Dover invents **DOVER'S POWDER** (opium and ipecacuana) to induce sweating, to treat rheumatism, water retention, and cold.
•General James Oglethorpe founds **GEORGIA**, as a colony for debtors; hard liquor and slavery are prohibited.

1733 The first child's **PERAMBULATOR** (stroller) is built for England's Duke of Devonshire by William Kent and is pulled by a dog.
•The **FLYING SHUTTLE** for weaving is patented by John Kay in England, and adopted by the textile industry. Despite the success of the flying shuttle, Kay is hounded by irate workers whose skills have been replaced by his invention. Driven from his home, he dies abroad in poverty, in 1753.
•The poisonous element **ARSENIC** is discovered by Georg Brandt.

1734 A **CHAIN BRIDGE**, built in Prussia by the Palatinate Army of Saxony, is the first-known metal suspension bridge in the West.
•The sultan of Bornu becomes overlord of Kano (modern-day **NIGERIA**) and establishes a vast empire in West Africa.

1735 China's **CH'ING DYNASTY** continues with the coronation of Ch'ien Lung, patron of

A WINTER COURT ROBE DESIGNED BY THE TALENTED EMPEROR CH'IEN LUNG (SEE 1735)

the arts; one of his best-known verses, "In praise of tea," becomes a popular inscription on Chinese teapots.
•Contaminated sausage meat is blamed for an outbreak of **BOTULISM**, a killer food-poisoning bug recorded for the first time in Germany.
•In response to an English bill offering rewards to anyone who could find the longitude at sea, clockmaker John Harrison invents a marine **CHRONOMETER**. Despite the success of his timepiece, Harrison has to fight for many years to win his reward.

1736 While exploring the Amazon in South America, French geographers Charles-Marie de Lacondamine and François Fresneau discover caoutchouc, which is later called **RUBBER**.
•When Britain's Parliament bans the sale of gin to combat the increasing numbers of alcoholics in the country, the illegal production and sale of alcohol, called **BOOTLEGGING**, starts to flourish.
•The first successful operation for **APPENDICITIS** is conducted by English surgeon Claudius Aymand.

1737 Contour lines are first used on a **MAP** of the English Channel produced by French cartographer Philippe Buache.
•A **TIDAL WAVE** from the Bay of Bengal crashes down on Calcutta in India.
•In an attempt to make it as easy as possible to name plants and animals, Swedish botanist Carl von Linné introduces the **LINNAEAN SYSTEM** of classification in his scholarly work *Genera Plantorum*, which identifies 18,000 plant species.
•The master violin maker Antonio **STRADIVARIUS** dies in Cremona, Italy.

1738 Anglican **PRIEST** John Wesley founds the Methodist Movement.
•Work begins in Italy, to excavate **HERCULANEUM**, the city near Naples that was completely obliterated in AD 79 by the eruption of Mount Vesuvius.

1739 Dick Turpin, the legendary **HIGHWAYMAN**, is hanged at York in England for horse stealing; he climbs the ladder, speaks to the hangman briefly, and throws himself off the scaffold to his death.

THEN AND NOW

1727 The first coffee is grown from a bush originally given to Louis XIV of France, and the American coffee industry is founded. Such is the thirst for coffee that Bach even composes a *Coffee Cantata* in its honor.
1998 A world total of 6,946,673 tons of coffee is produced. The top coffee-producing countries are:

Brazil (1,822,140 tons)
Colombia (793,663 tons)
Indonesia (501,682 tons)
Vietnam (416,673 tons)
Côte d'Ivoire (366,358 tons)

EXTRA EXTRA! In 1732, England bans the importation of American hats, to protect local haberdashers.

61

1740 On a trip to Peru and the Amazon River in South America, French geographer Charles Marie de Lacondamine discovers the drug curare, which relaxes muscles; he finds that it is used by Peruvian Indians to **POISON** the tips of their arrows.
• **EMPRESS ANNA** of Russia, known for her cruel jokes, orders an ice palace to be built on the Neva River for the enforced marriage of her court jester.

1741 The **ENSLAVED INCAS** of Peru rebel against Spain.
• English chemist Dr. William Brownrigg makes **BUBBLY** mineral water by using carbonic acid gas.
• The **CELSIUS** scale of temperature is introduced by Swedish astronomer Anders Celsius; it sets the boiling point of water as 0° and its melting point as 100°, but five years later the scale will be inverted by Celsius's colleagues.
• Bering Island and the Bering Sea are named after Danish Arctic explorer Vitus **BERING**, who dies of scurvy on the remote island that will bear his name, off the east coast of Kamchatka Peninsula.
• Sir Robert Walpole resigns as **PRIME MINISTER** of England.

1742 Dublin, Ireland, hosts the first performance of the *Messiah*, which German-English composer George Frederick **HANDEL** wrote in only 24 days; when the work is later performed in London, King George II is so impressed by the *Hallelujah Chorus* that he rises to his feet and remains standing until the end of the performance – a custom that is still observed at *Messiah* performances.

1743 A FLYING CHAIR (*chaise volante*), an early type of elevator, is installed for King Louis XV of France; it transports him between two floors of his private apartment at the Palace of Versailles by a system of weights and pulleys.
• Claude Moët sets up his **CHAMPAGNE** business at Epernay; it later becomes Moët and Chandon, the largest of all France's champagne producers.

1744 The first illustrated reference to **BASEBALL** appears in *A Little Pretty Pocket Book* by the UK's John Newbery.
• **MADAME DE POMPADOUR** comes into favor with King Louis XV of France and becomes his most influential advisor.

1745 The **LEYDEN JAR**, for storing and releasing electrical charges, is invented simultaneously by E. G. von Kleist, the dean of the Cathedral of Kamin in Pomerania, Germany, and Pieter Van Musschenbroek, the professor of physics at Holland's Leyden University.
• The conflict in Europe spreads to America, prompting the French and Indian **WAR** against the English colonies.

1746 ZINC, a metallic element, is discovered by Andreas Marggraf in Germany; it will be used in galvanizing (to protect steel from rusting), batteries, and brass-making.
• On February 13, Frenchman Jean Marie Dubarry is executed for **MURDERING** his father; precisely 100 years later, on February 13, 1846, another Frenchman named Jean Marie Dubarry will be executed for the same crime.

1747 Dr. James Lind discovers that citrus fruits prevent **SCURVY**, a disease that causes bones and teeth to soften because of a shortage of vitamin C in the body; in trials to test this theory, 12 scurvy-ridden sailors report an improvement in their condition after including lemons, limes, and oranges in their diet for six days.
• German chemist Andreas Marggraf extracts **SUGAR** from beetroot, providing the first chemical proof of sugar being present in root vegetables.
• British boxer Jack Broughton, who composed the first set of rules for boxing, invents **BOXING GLOVES**.

1748 A **WINDUP** spring-driven carriage is demonstrated before King Louis XV by French engineer Jacque Vaucanson.

1749 The slave-traders' passage to Newport harbor in America is made safer when the inhabitants of Rhode Island erect the 64-ft (19.5-m) Beavertail **LIGHTHOUSE** on Conanicut Island.

1750 French philosopher **JEAN-JACQUES ROUSSEAU** publishes his highly influential *Discourse on the Science and the Arts*.
• The first of English dramatist **WILLIAM SHAKESPEARE**'s plays known to have been performed in New York City is *Richard III*, at the Nassau Street Theater.

1751 The British Parliament decrees that the **NEW YEAR** of 1752 should be January 1 instead of March 25, bringing Britain into line with the Gregorian calendar. The third of September becomes September 14; as a result, nothing happens in British history during the "lost" 11 days.
• The element **NICKEL** is discovered by Swedish metallurgist Axel Fredrik Cronstedt; it will be used in coins, alloys, and metal-plating.
• English clockmaker Benjamin Huntsman perfects the **CRUCIBLE METHOD** of making steel in a large bowl made of strong earthenware. Efficient but expensive, this method is still used for making steel for special tools.

1752 A steel-tipped **LIGHTNING ROD** measuring 7 ft (2 m) tall, is erected by its inventor, Benjamin Franklin, to safeguard his house on Market Street in Philadelphia; other rods will follow at the State House and the academy building.
• Thomas Boulsover, an English cutler from Sheffield, Yorkshire, discovers while mending a knife handle that by overheating copper and silver the two metals fuse together permanently, a technique known as **SHEFFIELD PLATE**.

1753 The *Scots Magazine* receives a letter from an unknown person who identifies himself as "C. M." and who predicts the coming of the **ELECTRIC TELEGRAPH**.

1754 A model **HELICOPTER** is constructed and flown successfully by Russian scientist Mikhail Vasilyevitch Lomonosov.
• King's College, which will become **COLUMBIA UNIVERSITY**, is founded in New York City.
• In America, Benjamin Franklin calls for a **VOLUNTARY UNION** of the 13 colonies at the Albany Congress.
• **A ROPE-MAKING MACHINE** is invented in England by Richard Marsh; up to then, ropes had been laboriously handmade.

1755 Lisbon, Portugal, is destroyed by an **EARTHQUAKE** so severe, it causes 50 ft (15 m) waves in southwestern England; huge fissures are torn in the land, a massive tidal wave sweeps across the city, and fires spread, killing up to 100,000 of the 275,000 inhabitants and ruining 17,000 of the 20,000 buildings.

• French engineer Garvin constructs an **IRON-GIRDERED** bridge to span the Rhone River; it has one arch made out of forged iron and two out of wood.

• John Outram of England invents the **STREETCAR**, which runs on cast-iron rails and is pulled by two horses.

• Robert Bakewell takes over his father's farm in Leicester, England. He soon develops a strong interest in **STOCK BREEDING** and proves that it is possible to raise animals that have more flesh in the areas preferred by butchers.

1756 A series of severe winters weakens the piers of **LONDON BRIDGE**, and the British Parliament fears for its safety. A decree is issued ordering that all buildings on the bridge be pulled down. The bridge is then widened and provided with a roadway, and traffic using the new road is instructed to keep to the left.

• A **STAGECOACH SERVICE** opens between Philadelphia and New York City. It takes "only" three days to travel from one city to another.

LIMES ARE USED TO PREVENT SCURVY IN SAILORS (SEE 1747)

Citrus fruits help sailors keep scurvy at bay

• Scottish chemist Joseph Black discovers **CARBON DIOXIDE**; his published experiments on magnesia, lime, and other alkaline substances give details of chemical reactions.

• Calcutta, a trading factory set up in India by the British East India Company, is besieged following a surprise attack by the ruler of Bengal. He imprisons some of the residents in the **BLACK HOLE OF CALCUTTA**, an airless cell measuring 18 ft (5.5 m) by 15 ft (4.5 m). After just one night of imprisonment, 43 of the 64 inmates suffocate and die.

1757 The **SEXTANT** is invented as an aid to navigation by Scotland's Captain John Campbell.

• War breaks out again in Europe and continues in **INDIA** and America.

1758 The Wedgwood **POTTERY** factory, one of the first to mass-produce pottery, is founded by Josiah Wedgwood in England; a victim of smallpox when he was young, Wedgwood was left lame by the disease and was never able to work a potter's wheel. His fine cream-colored earthenware allowed ordinary people to buy plates, dishes, and jugs that were just as elegant as porcelain tableware, which only the wealthy could afford.

• On the North American continent, the French are forced out of Fort Duquesne by the British; it is renamed **FORT PITT**.

• Britain's John Dolland constructs the achromatic **TELESCOPE**, which eliminates the blurred imaging caused by chromatic aberration.

• A **REVOLVING STAGE** is installed by Namiki Shozo at the Kado-za doll theater in Osaka, Japan.

• Jedediah Strutt invents the ribbing machine for making **STOCKINGS**.

1759 The government of Portugal expels the **JESUIT ORDER** from the country.

DISTINCTIVE BLUE–AND–WHITE PATTERN OF WEDGWOOD POTTERY (SEE 1758)

• Princess Augusta, mother of King George III, founds the **ROYAL BOTANIC GARDENS** at Kew in London, England.

• English commander James Wolfe and French commander Louis Montcalm are both killed in the **BATTLE OF QUEBEC**; the British take the city in the Battle of the Plains of Abraham.

• Funded by lottery money, the **BRITISH MUSEUM** opens to the public in London, England; among the earliest treasures on display are a rat, a tree trunk gnawed by a beaver, and a mummified thumb.

• A revolutionary **LIGHTHOUSE** at Eddystone in Plymouth, England, is designed by engineer John Smeaton, setting a new standard in tower building.

• **VOLTAIRE**, a French philosopher and writer who often challenged religious and social traditions and was an avid defender of the freedom of speech, publishes his masterpiece, *Candide*.

THEN AND NOW

1746 Dr. Samuel Johnson and his six assistants begin work on *A Dictionary of the English Language* in London; it comprises definitions of more than 40,000 words and includes at least 114,000 quotations.

1928 The first *Oxford English Dictionary* is completed after 70 years' work.

MECHANIZATION

U NTIL THE MID-1800s, most people lived in the country. But two great revolutions that began in Britain soon changed this rural way of life forever. There was a revolution in agriculture that drove the poorest off the land as landowners began to use new farming techniques. And there was a revolution in industry as home-based handicraft industries gave way to the first factories, humming with machinery. Country people flocked to the factories to find work and the first industrial cities grew.

ENGLISH
WHEAT "DOLLY"

NEW FARMING TECHNIQUES

To boost profits from the land, farmers began to abandon small-scale traditional techniques and develop new crops, new breeds of livestock, and new machines that would maximize production.

HEREFORD BULL
First improved in Britain by Benjamin Tomkins during the 1780s, the Hereford is now farmed for its beef in 50 countries worldwide.

NEW LIVESTOCK BREEDS

ABERDEEN ANGUS This cattle breed of small, compact black animals was improved by Hugh Watson of Keillour, Scotland, and is considered to produce the finest-quality beef.

RED POLL This distinctive red cow was bred to provide both meat and milk. Unusually, neither cows nor bulls have horns.

LEICESTER This breed of sheep doubled its body weight as a result of improvements made to the breed by Robert Bakewell, an English pioneer of selective stock breeding.

GOLDEN GUERNSEY An unusually friendly goat first raised in Guernsey and believed to descend from the wild goats of France.

FIELD WORKS

1701 English agriculturalist Jethro Tull (1634–1741) invents a horse-drawn **SEED DRILL** to plant seeds mechanically, provoking a strike by farm workers fearing for their jobs.

1716 Swedish engineer Martin Triewald builds the first-ever hotwater-based central heating system for a **GREENHOUSE** in England.

1730 Viscount "Turnip" Townshend introduces the "Norfolk Four-Course" system of **CROP ROTATION**, using turnips to save soil from being overworked.

1784 A **THRESHING MACHINE** patented by Andrew Meikle of Scotland separates grain from husks automatically.

1793 Eli Whitney (1765–1825) of the US invents the **COTTON GIN**, a machine that strips fibers from cotton seeds; now one person can do the work of 50.

1802 **SUGAR BEETS** are introduced as a field crop in Germany.

1804 The first **FOOD PRESERVATION** factory is built by Nicolas Appert (1750–1841) in France.

1820 The **WHEAT BELT** forms in the US as wheat-growing spreads.

1831 American Cyrus McCormick introduces a new labor-saving **REAPING MACHINE** in Virginia.

GOODS BY WATER

The traditional horse and cart could not cope with all the goods being churned out by the factories, and within a few decades thousands of miles of canals were built across Europe. Canals soon linked towns and cities with the river network and so with the coastal ports. Goods could now be imported and exported.

DUTCH BARGE
Flat-bottomed boats carried cargo in the Low Countries.

IMPORTANT WATERWAYS

BRIDGEWATER CANAL Started in 1761, this English canal is later extended to the sea and becomes the Manchester Ship Canal.

WELLAND CANAL Built in 1829 to link the US and Canada, this canal via Montreal shortens the sea voyage from England to the US by about 450 miles (725 km).

RHINE RIVER An international commission is set up in 1815 to protect this vital route used for carrying heavy raw materials.

Mechanization radically changed people's lives

MASSES OF BUCKLES
Buckles like these were among the first mass-produced items.

MASS-MARKET GOODS

The world opened up by the colonists provided not only cheap materials for the new factories but a huge market for their goods – so big that mass-production techniques were developed to machine-make masses of identical parts for assembly at low cost.

MASS-PRODUCTION

1798 Eli Whitney makes muskets with such **PRECISION** that parts can be interchanged – a vital step to mass-production.

1836 Samuel Colt makes his Colt 45 pistol by mass-producing identical parts.

1851 Robbins and Lawrence mass-produce **RIFLES**, which are displayed at London's Great Exhibition.

THE POWER OF TRADE

SILK Silkworms are imported into Europe from China for the production of raw silk.

IRON Cargoes of iron goods, such as guns, are exchanged for slaves in West Africa.

COTTON Cheap, raw cotton is imported into Britain from the colonies in North America and India and manufactured into textiles. Cotton accounts for half of all British exports.

MONEY As the Netherlands gains wealth from its trading partners, Amsterdam becomes the money capital of Europe.

COAL Deeper and deeper mines are dug to cope with the ever-increasing demand for coal to power machines worldwide.

POTTERY Potteries such as Wedgwood in Britain, Sèvres in France, and Meissen in Germany export fine porcelain worldwide.

MASTERS OF INDUSTRY

THE INDUSTRIAL REVOLUTION unleashed a flood of inventions, as men of all kinds turned their hands to creating machines for the factories. At the same time, it created new breeds of men, like Matthew Boulton and Andrew Carnegie, mill-owners and iron manufacturers to rival the landed gentry in power and wealth, and the masses of factory hands who became the new working class.

MATTHEW
BOULTON
(1728–1809)

INVENTORS

The rise of industry gave endless scope to the inventive mind, and it seemed everyone from humble craftsman to great scientists was filled with enthusiasm for invention.

MEN AND MACHINES

1709 By smelting iron with coke, **ABRAHAM DARBY** (1678–1717) starts to make the huge amounts of iron needed to build machines and factories.

1712 Thomas Newcomen makes the first industrial **STEAM** engine to pump water from mines. Steam power will become the driving force of industry, powering large machines.

1733 John Kay of England patents the **FLYING SHUTTLE** for weaving cloth very quickly.

1764 James Watt improves the Newcomen **STEAM ENGINE**.

1776 Samuel Crompton invents the **MULE**, a spinning machine to spin cloth in vast quantities.

1801 Joseph-Marie Jacquard of France invents a **LOOM** for weaving patterns.

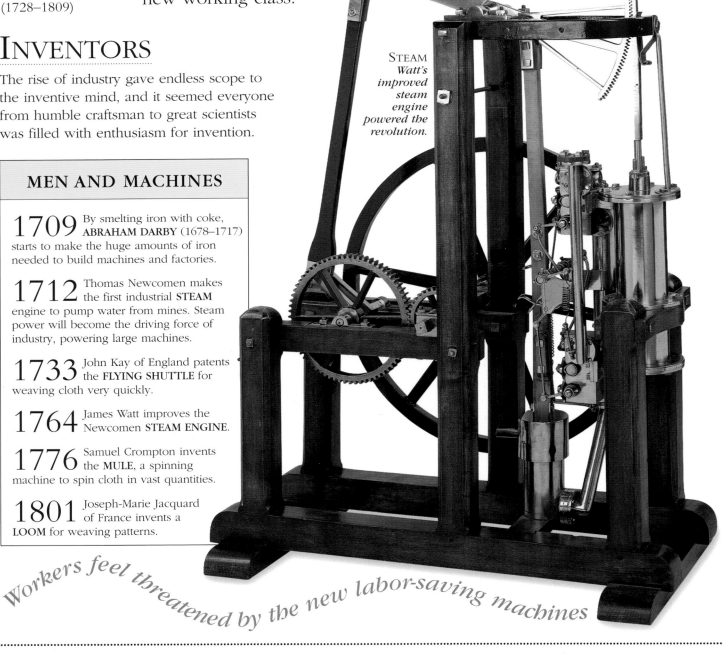

STEAM
Watt's improved steam engine powered the revolution.

Workers feel threatened by the new labor-saving machines

LUDDITE
PROTESTER

THE WORKFORCE

Huge numbers were needed to work in the new factories, and the industrial population soared. But jobs were insecure, and working conditions could be atrocious. Workers and factory owners were soon entrenched in opposition, while reformers demanded changes.

WORKERS IN ARMS

LUDDITES From 1811 to 1816, a group of angry textile workers called Luddites pose as women to smash machines, which they believe will take their jobs.

LES CANUTS From 1831 to 1834, French silk-workers rebel against working conditions.

WORKINGMEN'S ADVOCATE In 1829 American George Evans writes a worker's version of the US Declaration of Independence as a protest call.

FACTORY ACTS

1791 The French government is the first to outlaw **TRADE UNIONS**.

1819 The working day for children in England is set at 12 hours. Most employers ignore the law, because **CHILDREN** are cheap to employ.

1833 Factory **INSPECTORS** are appointed in England to enforce laws introduced to improve conditions in factories.

1847 A maximum ten-hour day becomes mandatory in New Hampshire, and in several other American states shortly after.

ARMED ROBBERY

During the Industrial Revolution, the arms industry boomed. The large-scale wars of the Napoleonic era spurred the production of vast numbers of identical muskets and pistols. The sudden flood of cheap guns was also appreciated by a growing criminal fraternity.

HEADHUNTER
Angry at the damaging effects that pirates were having on seagoing trade, the British sent HMS Harlequin, distinguished by its colorful figurehead, to capture pirate ships.

LETHAL WEAPONS

1718 American James Puckle invents the first repeat-firing **MACHINE GUN**.
• Americans Elisha Collier and Artemis Wheeler both patent **REVOLVERS** – small handguns that fire from rotating cylinders.

1776 The **BREECH-LOADING RIFLE** is designed by Patrick Ferguson of Scotland.

1836 American Samuel Colt (1814–1862) is the first to introduce mass-produced weapons with his **SIX-SHOOTER REVOLVER**. This handgun sells in massive numbers and becomes the symbol of the American West.

1840 The Prussian army adopts a **BATTLEFIELD RIFLE** that has been designed by the German gunsmith, Nikolaus von Dreyse.

FAMOUS BANDITS

CLAUDE DUVAL, originally from France, becomes well known in England for his charming ways. During a holdup, he is said to have danced with a lady before making off with her money and jewels. He is eventually hanged in 1670.

JOHN CLAVEL, a literate highwayman, publishes an insight into the habits of his criminal colleagues, advising people to avoid going out on Sundays, since this is by far the most popular day for holdups.

JACK RANN, a highwayman known as "Sixteen-string Jack" because of the eight silk strings he wore at each knee, wears a pea-green costume at his trial.

EDWARD LOW, an English pirate, leads the slaughter of the crew of a Spanish ship in 1723. He has a fearsome reputation and is said to have cut off a man's lips and fried them in front of him.

1760 The first **ROLLER SKATES** are worn by Belgian instrument maker Joseph Merlin while he plays the violin at a Carlisle House masquerade in London, England.
•A New Jersey **WAMPUM** factory opens to produce strings of the shells used for currency by Native American Indians.
•George Dunhill sells **LICORICE**, a new candy, in Pontefract, Yorkshire, England.

1761 Malignant nose polyps (small stalklike growths) are linked with the fashion for sniffing **SNUFF** (finely powdered tobacco).
•The British ruling that **WHITE PINE TREES** (needed for ship masts) in New England can be cut down only under crown license is met with anger by the American colonists; the first Revolutionary flag will bear a white pine to represent Massachusetts.
•A **VAULTING HORSE** is built at Lund University, Sweden.

1762 The **SANDWICH** is allegedly invented by John Montague, Fourth Earl of Sandwich, England, to snack without breaking from a 24-hour gaming session in London.

1763 Germany's Josef Kohlreauter discovers **POLLINATION**.
•The British Admiralty approves a cork **LIFE JACKET** for use by the Royal Navy.
•**JIGSAW PUZZLES** are first referred to as teaching aids for geography.

1764 Sandy Hook, America's oldest **LIGHTHOUSE**, is completed in New Jersey, standing 103 ft (31 m) high, its lantern 7 ft (2 m) high and with 7-ft (2-m)-thick walls.
•Eight-year-old Wolfgang Amadeus **MOZART** of Austria composes his first piece of music, a symphony.

1765 The first bank in Germany to issue **PAPER MONEY**, the Royal Giro and Loan Bank (later to become the Bank of Prussia, then the Reichsbank), is founded by Frederick II.

1766 A **FIRE ESCAPE**, consisting of a wicker basket worked by a pulley and chains, is invented by David Marie, an English watchmaker.
•British physicist Henry Cavendish discovers a new, extraordinarily light gas ("inflammable air"), named **HYDROGEN** by Antoine Lavoisier 20 years later.

1767 The first **CAST-IRON RAILROAD TRACK** is made on the Coalbrookdale track in Shropshire, England, by fixing cast-iron bars over the wooden rails to strengthen them. These bars are a means of storing pig iron during a price slump so allowing production to continue.
•**MESMERISM**, an early form of hypnotism, is practiced in Vienna, Austria, by Friedrich Anton Mesmer and Professor Hehl, who discover it while investigating "animal magnetism."

1768 A **HYDROMETER** with a graduated scale (the Baumé scale), used for measuring the relative density of liquids, is invented by French chemist Antoine Baumé.

1769 Don Gaspar de Portola leads a Spanish exploration party overland and discovers **SAN FRANCISCO BAY**; in the name of the Spanish king, he takes over San Francisco and San Diego and establishes orange and olive groves.
•**VENETIAN BLINDS** are invented by an Englishman, Edward Bevan.
•Britain's first **CREMATION** takes place when Honoretta Pratt is burned in an open grave in London at her own request; she was concerned that the fumes might be harmful to passersby.

1770 Captain Cook reaches Australia's Botany Bay two years after setting out on a **SCIENTIFIC EXPLORATION** on the *Endeavour*; he reassesses his original naming of their landing spot, Sting Ray Harbor, when a wonderful selection of new plants is collected by his companions, the naturalists Joseph Banks and Daniel Charles Solander.
•In Amsterdam, a whole year's supply of nutmeg and cloves is ruined deliberately to maintain the **HIGH PRICES** that make the Dutch traders rich.
•The first practical **FALSE TEETH** are made from porcelain by France's Alexis Duchateau.
•**MONTEREY** becomes the first capital of California. It was also established by the Spanish.

1771 English manufacturer Sir Richard Arkwright builds the first **SPINNING MILL** in Britain.
•The *Encyclopedia Britannica* appears in Edinburgh, Scotland. It is published in weekly parts and each copy costs sixpence; the **ENCYCLOPEDIA** claims that it contains "all there is to know."

1772 Scottish physician and botanist Daniel Rutherford publishes his discovery of the difference between "noxious air" (later called **NITROGEN**) and carbon dioxide.
•England's Flight and Kelly, a London firm of organ makers, builds the first **BARREL ORGAN**.

1773 London's Norris Street Coffee House is the first British eating house to serve **CURRY**.
•Anger over the British tax on tea leads to ships being turned away from American ports, while others have their cargo of tea thrown overboard; this is later known as the **BOSTON TEA PARTY**.
•English navigator and horologist John Harrison is awarded prize money for perfecting his marine **CHRONOMETER**, which revolutionized sea exploration; three years later, Captain Cook used one such apparatus to make accurate maps of Australia and New Zealand.

1774 Swedish chemist Carl Wilhelm Scheele discovers the reactive green gas **CHLORINE**.
•**OXYGEN** is discovered when British chemist Joseph Priestley observes the life-sustaining nature of plants, finding that a dying candle flame in a closed container is rekindled by the introduction of a sprig.

...NOW

THEN AND...

1771 English cricketer Thomas Shock White plays a match with a bat that is wider than the wicket. It is so difficult to get him out that a maximum width of 4½ in (11 cm) is decreed.

1779! The world's first **IRON BRIDGE** is built in Coalbrookdale across the Severn River in England.

AMERICA SOUNDS THE BATTLE DRUMS IN ITS FIGHT FOR INDEPENDENCE (SEE 1775)

1775 Birmingham inn owner Richard Ketley and others, establish Britain's first **BUILDING SOCIETY** to save money for purchasing and erecting housing for their own use.
•**ECCENTRIC** British dentist Martin Van Butchell's wife Mary dies; he has her body embalmed and glass eyes inserted, exhibiting her in a glass-topped coffin.
•The **AMERICAN REVOLUTION** begins with the Battle of Lexington in April, when a short spell of fighting between a company of American militia and 700 Royal troops is won by the British, with low casualties on both sides.

1776 The **DECLARATION OF INDEPENDENCE** on July 4th establishes the United States's independence from Britain, and makes the novel assertions that "all men are created equal" and that they have inalienable rights to "life, liberty, and the pursuit of happiness."
•The **BREECH-LOADING RIFLE** is designed by Scotland's Patrick Ferguson.
•The London-to-Edinburgh run between England and Scotland takes four days by a horse-drawn **FLYING COACH**.
•The first successful deployment of a **SUBMARINE** is at a battle in New York harbor, where David Bushnell's *Turtle* (named for its shape) is sent into action; the tar-covered oak vessel is driven by a hand-operated propeller; it submerges by taking in water and resurfaces by pumping it out again.
•Anne Seymour Damer becomes Britain's first **WOMAN SCULPTOR** when she turns professional after her husband commits suicide, leaving her to raise the funds to cover his gambling debts.

1777 The **CIRCULAR SAW** is invented in England by Samuel Miller; it will not become widely used until it is driven by steam power.
•The US adopts the **STARS AND STRIPES** as its official flag.
•French architect M. Bonnemain installs **CENTRAL HEATING** in the Château de Pecq, Saint-Germain-en-Laye.
•French chemist Antoine Lavoisier shows that **WATER** is a compound of hydrogen and oxygen.
•A 12-ft (3.7-m)-long pleasure boat made of **IRON** appears on the Foss River in Yorkshire, England, and takes up to 15 passengers.
•Imprisoned for drugging women, whom he dosed with a **LOVE POTION** made from the poison of Spanish flies – really a kind of beetle – the Marquis de Sade starts his writing career.

1778 William Wilkinson of England builds a railroad in France for the Indre **MUNITIONS FACTORY**.
•The first Asiatic **ORCHIDS** are brought to England from China.
•An Act of Congress bans importing **SLAVES** into the US.

1779 Italian biologist Lazzaro Spallanzani successfully crosses a spaniel with a hunting dog by **ARTIFICIAL INSEMINATION**, resulting in a litter of three crossbreeds.
•A **REPEATING RIFLE**, which fires 20 shots in succession, is manufactured by Vienna's Bartholomew Girandoni for use by the Austrian army.
•In Bohemia, the War of Bavarian Succession (which will be called **THE POTATO WAR**) between the Austrians and the Prussians comes to a halt when all the local supplies of potatoes have been eaten.
•English explorer Captain James Cook is stabbed and clubbed to death in **HAWAII** by locals, who had first thought him to be the reincarnation of Lono, their god of happiness and harvests.
•The **POINSETTIA** plant is named after American diplomat Joel R. Poinsett.

THE DEADLY "SPANISH FLY" (SEE 1777)

A love potion and wart remover rolled into one

EXTRA EXTRA! Steller's sea cow, a large marine mammal, is hunted out of existence by 1768.

1780 Luigi Galvani of Bologna, Italy, develops his theory of **ANIMAL ELECTRICITY** after watching a salt-watered frog's leg on a zinc dish twitch when his wife's scalpel touches it.
•Spaniard Sebastiano Carezo invents the **BOLERO** dance.
•**BENEDICT ARNOLD** betrays American plans to the British.
•Conductor Anselm Weber introduces the **BATON**, for beating time to the music and guiding the orchestra, at Germany's Berlin opera.

ANIMAL ELECTRICITY IS FOUND WHILE DISSECTING A FROG (SEE 1780)

1781 The planet **URANUS** is first observed from England by German-born William Herschel, a musician turned astronomer.
•**INFLUENZA** breaks out in China; at its height, 30,000 Russians die every day.
•British forces surrender to General Washington, ending **REVOLUTIONARY WAR** and securing US independence.

1782 Austrian chemist Franz Joseph Müller discovers the metallic element **TELLURIUM**; it will later be used in alloys and electronics.
•Slavery is **ABOLISHED** in Austria.

1783 The French **MONTGOLFIER** brothers demonstrate a hot-air balloon made of linen and paper and held together by buttons.
•Spaniards torture and execute **INCA** leader, Tupac Amaru II, for insisting that Spain promises to protect Indians.
•A **PIANO** with a "loud" pedal for sustaining notes and a "soft" pedal for dampening them is built by English cabinetmaker John Broadwood.

THEN AND NOW

1796 Inoculation is pioneered in England by Dr. Edward Jenner as protection against smallpox. He uses antibodies from cows, after his research finds that milkmaids rarely catch smallpox.
1980 The World Health Organization announces that smallpox has been eradicated worldwide, apart from laboratory stocks of the virus.

1784 Swiss inventor Aimé Argand invents an **OIL LAMP** with a circular wick that operates more efficiently than previous oil burners.
•Henry Shrapnel of England invents the **SHRAPNEL SHELL**, a hollow shell filled with musket balls which, when fired, explodes in midair, unleashing its contents on victims.
•English inventor Joseph Bramah offers a prize to anyone who can pick his new improved **SAFETY LOCK**; no one manages to win the prize until 1851.
•French astronomer Pierre-Simon Laplace predicts **BLACK HOLES** in space.

1785 Robert Ransome constructs the first cast-iron **PLOW**.
•New York outlaws **SLAVERY**.
•France's Jean Blanchard and England's John Jeffries cross the **ENGLISH CHANNEL** in a hydrogen balloon.
•The first mechanical **LOOM** is patented in Britain by the Reverend Edmund Cartwright, after a trip to a cotton mill.

1786 French queen Marie Antoinette and the Royal Court spend so extravagantly that they plunge France into **BANKRUPTCY**.

1787 A **METAL HULL BOAT** is invented by English armament manufacturer John Wilkinson.
•The US **CONSTITUTION** is written and adopted in Philadelphia.
•William Herschel discovers **OBERON** and **TITANIA**, moons of Uranus.
•The opera *Don Giovanni*, by Wolfgang Amadeus Mozart, is performed for the first time, in **PRAGUE**.
•Inventor John Fitch demonstrates the US's first steam-powered **PADDLEBOAT** on the Delaware River in Philadelphia.

1788 New York City becomes the temporary US capital when **YELLOW FEVER** sweeps Philadelphia.
•Thomas Whittle becomes the first white **AUSTRALIAN**, when he is born on board an English fleet ship in Sydney harbor.
•Political **UNREST**, directed against the monarchy, spreads throughout France.

1789 William Herschel discovers **ENCELADUS** and **MIMAS**, moons of Saturn; Enceladus is a mirror-like moon whose surface reflects back virtually all of the sun's rays that hit it.
•George Washington takes his first oath as president of the United States.
•The first **DAHLIA**, named in honor of Swedish botanist Anders Dahl, arrives in Europe from Mexico.
•French revolutionaries storm the **BASTILLE** prison in Paris; the National Assembly takes power, declaring in the Declaration of the Rights of Man (based on the Declaration of Independence of the US) that all men have equal rights.
•German chemist Martin Klaproth discovers **URANIUM**, a radioactive element later used in nuclear weaponry.

1790 **BENJAMIN FRANKLIN** dies at the age of 84; more than 20,000 mourners attend his funeral in Philadelphia, Pennsylvania.

1791 Austrian composer Wolfgang Amadeus **MOZART** dies at the age of 35 in Vienna, amid suspicion of poisoning by his rival Antonio Salieri; Mozart died so short of money that there was none to pay for his funeral, and he is given a pauper's burial.
•The US adopts the **BILL OF RIGHTS**.

EXTRA EXTRA! Karl Friedrich Meerwein of Austria builds a glider that is said to have made short hops, in 1781.

1792 The **GUILLOTINE**, named after Dr. Joseph Ignace Guillotin, is first used on Nicholas Jacques Pelletier, a French highwayman; the crowd, disappointed at its swiftness, bemoans the end of the gallows.
• The "one-horse flying **AMBULANCE**" is designed by Baron Dominique Jean Larrey, Napoleon's personal surgeon, to carry wounded men from the battlefield.
• Scots-born William Murdock succeeds in using **COAL GAS** to light his cottage.
• Although George Washington declares the US neutral in the European war, **THOMAS PAINE** arrives in Paris to support France's revolutionaries.

1793 American Eli Whitney invents the **COTTON GIN**; it separates cotton fibers from the seeds.
• **JEAN PAUL MARAT**, the leader of the French Revolution, is stabbed to death in his bath by Charlotte Corday; she is guillotined for her crime, as were Louis XVI and Queen Marie Antoinette the year before.

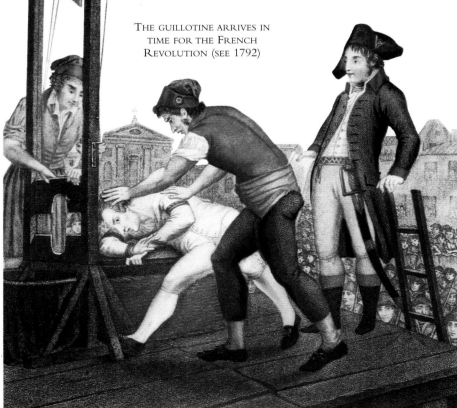

THE GUILLOTINE ARRIVES IN TIME FOR THE FRENCH REVOLUTION (SEE 1792)

• Blanchard and his passenger, a small black dog, make the first US **BALLOON FLIGHT** over Philadelphia; they are watched by George Washington.

1794 Poet and artist **WILLIAM BLAKE** captures the spirit of freedom and revolution in his poem, "Europe: A Prophecy," which is published in London, England.
• German scientist E. F. F. Chladni identifies **METEORITES** as lumps of metal or stone from outer space.
• English inventor James Six makes a maximum-minimum **THERMOMETER** to record temperature changes.

1795 A **HYDRAULIC PRESS** is built by the ingenuous inventor Joseph Bramah, a farmer's son.

1796 **CATHERINE THE GREAT**, who greatly expanded the power, territory, and wealth of Russia, dies in her summer palace.
• Germany's Aloys Senefelder invents the **LITHOGRAPHY** printing method.

1797 **CHROMIUM**, a hard metallic element, is discovered by Nicolas-Louis Vauquelin of France; it will be used in chrome plating.

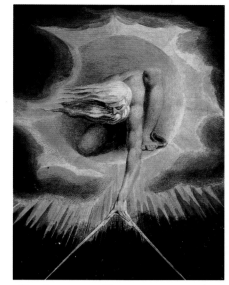

THE ANCIENT OF DAYS; AN ILLUSTRATION FOR EUROPE BY WILLIAM BLAKE (SEE 1794)

• French troops under Napoleon defeat Italy and stage a **COUP D'ETAT** at home.
• André-Jacques Garnerin gives the first public **PARACHUTE** demonstration; he leaps from a balloon 2,230 ft (678 m) above the Parc Monceau, Paris, France.

1798 English economist Thomas Robert Malthus forecasts **OVERPOPULATION**; he claims that famine, disease, and war keep world population (then at 800 million) at supportable levels; two centuries later Earth will hold seven times as many people, with overpopulation a huge threat to humans and the environment.
• The Austrian composer Joseph **HAYDN** finishes composing *The Creation*, his first oratorio, inspired by Handel.
• Henry Cavendish uses lead balls to reveal the **EARTH'S** weight and density.

1799 The **ROSETTA STONE**, a polished chunk of basalt inscribed with Greek characters and hieroglyphs, is discovered in the northern Egyptian town of Rosetta by French engineer Captain Boucard.
• After nine years of calculation and the careful measurement of a portion of the meridian between Dunkirk in France and Barcelona in Spain, **METRIC** measurement is introduced by the French Academy of Science.
• Napoleon **OUSTS THE GOVERNMENT** in France and takes control.
• George Washington, Pope Pius VI, and Chinese emperor Qianlong all die before the **NEW CENTURY**.

The foundation stone of the Capitol was laid by George Washington in 1793

THE AGE OF INDUSTRY

The newly created United States expands westward to the Pacific, while Spanish and Portuguese colonies in Central and South America gain independence. Industrialization gives rise to huge cities worldwide, while railroads and steamships give people the freedom to travel. European nations establish vast overseas empires to provide raw materials for their factories, and nationalism gains importance. By the end of the century, the balance of world power held by Britain and France passes to the United States – and then to Germany.

CENTURY STATISTICS

World population, 1800: 1.1 billion.
Bookmark: The most influential scientific work is Charles Darwin's *On the Origin of Species by Means of Natural Selection*, published 1859, in which he suggests that man and ape once had a common ancestor.
Landmark: Built as a temporary display piece for the 1889 Exhibition, the Eiffel Tower in Paris, France, stands at 985 ft (300 m).

1800 Physicist Alessandro Volta invents the **ELECTRIC BATTERY**, the first to be made of zinc and copper plates, in Pavia, Italy.
• The first **PASTA-MAKING MACHINE** is put into operation in Naples, Italy.
• British chemist Sir Humphry Davy describes the anesthetic properties of nitrous oxide, or **LAUGHING GAS**.
• US engineer Robert Fulton invents a cigar-shaped **SUBMARINE** (the *Nautilus*) propelled by a hand-crank, lit by two candles, and carrying oxygen supplies to last a crew of four up to three hours.
• England's William Cruikshank purifies water with **CHLORINE**.
• The **FLAT EARTH SOCIETY** is founded, sticking to the belief that Earth is flat.
• In Philadelphia, William Young makes the first shoes designed specifically for **LEFT AND RIGHT FEET**.

1801 The **UNITED KINGDOM** of Great Britain and Ireland is established; the Union Jack is its flag.
• The US goes to war with Tripoli (Libya) to protect US ships from **PIRACY**.

• Thomas Jefferson becomes America's third **PRESIDENT**; fellow Republican Aaron Burr becomes vice president.
• The despotic Russian emperor **PAUL I** is strangled in his bed by his own drunken palace guard.
• Italian astronomer Giuseppe Piazzi discovers the first and largest **ASTEROID**, Ceres, between Mars and Jupiter.
• A factory is set up to extract **SUGAR** from sugar-beet by Berlin chemist, Franz Karl Achard, in Germany.

1802 Swedish chemist Anders Gustaf Ekberg discovers a shiny silvery metal, **TANTALUM**, later used in electronics and cutting tools.
• German physicist Johann Wilhelm Ritter and British chemist William Hyde Wollaston independently discover **ULTRAVIOLET RAYS**.
• Napoleon Bonaparte is voted **CONSUL FOR LIFE** in France.
• All US states north of the **MASON-DIXON LINE**, except New Jersey, outlaw slavery.
• Swiss-born **MADAME TUSSAUD** opens a wax museum in London, England; during the Reign of Terror in Paris, France, she made wax death masks of famous guillotine victims.

1803 The first-ever **CHILDREN'S LIBRARY** is established in Salisbury, Connecticut, by bookseller Caleb Bingham, to give deprived children the chance to read.
• **CERIUM**, a gray metal named after the asteroid Ceres, is discovered by German chemist Martin Heinrich Klaproth in Berlin at the same time as two chemists in Sweden.

• A British Quaker chemist, John Dalton, presents the first **ATOMIC THEORY**.
• William Hyde Wollaston discovers palladium and rhodium, silvery white **METALLIC ELEMENTS**, which are later used in catalysts.
• British stationers fund the development of the Fourdrinier **PAPER-MAKING MACHINE**, invented by Bryan Donkin.
• **IRISH REBELLION** against the union with England is ruthlessly crushed.
• The US doubles its land area with the **LOUISIANA PURCHASE**.
• **HAITI** declares its independence.
• Russia occupies **EASTERN ALASKA** and the country of Georgia.

1804 **ALEXANDER HAMILTON**, former US secretary to the treasury, is killed in a duel by Aaron Burr, who had accused him of treason.
• Chemist Smithson Tennant discovers **OSMIUM**, the heaviest metal element, in Cambridge, England.
• The Père-Lachaise **CEMETERY** in Paris, France, is opened; its celebrity occupants later include actress Sarah Bernhardt, writer Oscar Wilde, lead singer of The Doors Jim Morrison, and wonder-dog Rin Tin Tin.
• In England, the first **STEAM ENGINE** to run on rails, the Penn-y-Daran, is constructed.
• John Stevens demonstrates the first **STEAMBOAT** to be driven by screw-propellers, his *Little Juliana*, in New York harbor.
• **UNIVERSITY EDUCATION** is made free in Russia under Tsar Alexander I.

Mission impossible: to reach the Pacific Ocean by canoe

EXPLORATION BY CANOE (SEE 1806)

EXTRA EXTRA! The last Pennsylvania bison is hunted to extinction for meat and leather, in 1802.

•Napoleon Bonaparte takes the title of Emperor of France. Upon hearing the news, **LUDWIG VAN BEETHOVEN** scribbles out the dedication to him on his Symphony No. 3 in E-flat Major.

1805 French engineer Claude Chappé, the inventor of the **SEMAPHORE** (or flag-signaling) system, is so stressed by his workload that he commits suicide.

•English artillerist Sir William Congreve invents an iron-shelled **ROCKET** full of gunpowder.

•Italian Luigi Brugnatelli pioneers an early form of **ELECTROPLATING**.

•**MOHAMMED ALI**, an Albanian tobacco merchant, becomes ruler of Egypt.

•British admiral **HORATIO NELSON** dies at the Battle of Trafalgar; his body, preserved in brandy, is returned to London for burial in St. Paul's Cathedral.

•**MORPHINE** (a powerful painkiller) is discovered by Friedrich Wilhelm Adam Sertürner, a German chemist.

•Napoleon becomes **KING OF ITALY** and crushes Russian-Austrian forces at Austerlitz in Czechoslovakia.

1806 American transcontinental explorers **MERIWETHER LEWIS** and **WILLIAM CLARK**, aided by Shoshone Indian **SACAJAWEA**, reach the Pacific Ocean safely with all expedition members from a 4,000-mile trek across largely uncharted territories: along the upper Missouri River, over the Rocky Mountains, and through the Columbia River basin.

•**MUNGO PARK**, Scottish explorer of Africa, is drowned in the Niger River.

•The **ARC DE TRIOMPHE** is erected in Paris, France; Napoleon commissioned it as a monument to his conquests, and it is modeled on the Triumphal Arch of the Roman emperor Septimus Severus, erected in AD 203.

•Joseph Grimaldi, father of **CLOWNS**, makes his first appearance as a clown in *Mother Goose* at the Drury Lane Theatre in London, England.

•**CARBON PAPER** is patented by Ralph Wedgwood in London, England; he invented this copying technique by applying a coating of carbon and oil to one side of a thin sheet of paper and then writing on the other side.

•**A COFFEE POT**, complete with metal sieve, is invented in Britain by the Count of Rumford, Benjamin Thompson, in the hope of persuading British workers to drink more coffee and less beer.

•"Twinkle Twinkle Little Star," by Jane Taylor, is published in *Original Poems for Infant Minds*, a collection by Jane and her sister Anne.

•The British take **CAPE COLONY**, in South Africa, from the Dutch.

•Napoleon declares the end of the **HOLY ROMAN EMPIRE**.

1807 Sir Humphry Davy discovers the elements **POTASSIUM** and **SODIUM**.

•American inventor Robert Fulton's *Clermont* is the first **STEAMBOAT** to travel a long distance, completing a 150-mile (240-km) journey along the Hudson River between New York and Albany at about 8 km/h (5 mph).

•Isaac de Rivez applies for the first patent for a gas-driven **AUTOMOBILE**.

•Scottish surgeon Charles Bell distinguishes between the sensory and motor **NERVES** in the brain.

•Britain's first **WOMEN'S PRISON** is established at Pentonville, London; it takes over a large mansion to accommodate up to 35 "fallen women."

•**SLAVE TRADING** is abolished throughout British territories.

•William Wordsworth's *Poems in Two Volumes* is published in England; it contains some of his most popular poems, including the famous "I Wandered Lonely as a Cloud."

•*Tales from Shakespeare*, a simplified version of Shakespeare's works for children, is written by Mary Anne **LAMB** and her brother Charles; plagued by insanity, they both lead a tragic and isolated existence after Mary stabs their mother to death.

•Vice President Aaron Burr is **ACQUITTED OF TREASON**.

1808 A massive **EXPLOSION** kills 230 people in Luxembourg; it is set off in a storm when a lightning bolt strikes a gunpowder storehouse.

•African **SLAVE IMPORTATION** is banned in the US.

•The first emergency **PARACHUTE JUMP** is made by Jordaki Kurapento to escape from his Montgolfier balloon, which is on fire over Warsaw, Poland.

•English chemist John Dalton creates the **PERIODIC TABLE OF ELEMENTS**.

•**A STEAM CIRCUS** is erected at London's Euston Square, as English engineer Richard Trevithick brings steam travel by rail to the public's attention.

•Germany's Johann Wolfgang **GOETHE** publishes his masterpiece, *Faust*.

JOSEPH GRIMALDI MAKES HIS CAREER FROM CLOWNING AROUND (SEE 1806)

1809 The head of Franz Joseph **HAYDN**, Austrian composer, is stolen by a grave robber; it is finally reunited with Haydn's body in 1984.

•Napoleon, in retaliation for being **EXCOMMUNICATED** from the Church, orders the arrest of Pope Pius VII and his secretary, Cardinal Pacca.

•The *Phoenix*, designed by Colonel John Stevens, becomes the first **STEAMBOAT** to travel on the open sea when Captain Moses Rogers takes it on a 13-day trip between New York and Philadelphia.

•A steel "metallic **WRITING PEN**" is patented by Peregrine Williamson in Baltimore, Maryland.

•By attaching a mini **HYDROGEN BALLOON** to his ornithopter, Jacob Degen of Switzerland succeeds in remaining airborne over short distances in a display that gives rise to a new sport of balloon-jumping.

•French naturalist and evolutionist Jean Lamarck publishes his theory on the **EVOLUTION OF ANIMALS**.

•A full-size **GLIDER**, with potential for carrying a person aloft, is flown unmanned by its inventor George Cayley; it is the first successful flight of its kind in the history of aviation.

•**SHAWNEE CHIEF** Tecumseh launches a campaign to unite diverse Indian tribes and stop the US expansion onto Indian lands west of the Mississippi.

HOMEOPATHIC
REMEDIES FOR
EVERY AILMENT
(SEE 1810)

"Treatment by the same" is the essence in homeopathic medicine

•Englishman William Hedley builds **PUFFING BILLY**, a steam locomotive named after the sound of its exhaust steam; it stays in service for the next 48 years, hauling wagons at a coal mine.

1814 German-born engineer Friedrich König's steam-powered **CYLINDER-PRESS** is installed in London, England, to print *The Times* at a rate of over a thousand sheets an hour.
•English inventor George Stephenson completes his first steam **LOCOMOTIVE**; although not very efficient, it convinces him that railways are the way forward.

1815 In Britain, two **MINERS' SAFETY LAMPS** are developed: "The Miner's Friend", by Humphry Davy, and "The Geordy", by George Stephenson.
•Napoleon returns from exile on Elba to begin his **HUNDRED DAYS'** rule; Louis XVIII flees his Paris throne.
•In one of the most important battles in history, Napoleon is defeated at the **BATTLE OF WATERLOO** (south of Brussels, Belgium) by British and Prussian forces led by the Duke of Wellington and General Blücher.
•**TAMBORA** volcano erupts in Indonesia, killing 10,000 islanders immediately, with another 82,000 subsequently dying

1810 **HOMEOPATHY**, a new system of medicine whereby mild doses are given to encourage rather than suppress symptoms, is devised by Dr Samuel Hahnemann of Leipzig, Germany.
•France's Nicolas Appert receives a prize of 12,000 francs from Napoleon for finding a way to preserve food using **TINS AND GLASS JARS**.

1811 John H Hall of America invents the **BREECH-LOADING RIFLE**, less cumbersome and faster to load than the musket.
•France's Bernard Courtois discovers the element **IODINE**; it will be used in medicines, dyes, and photography.
•*Sense and Sensibility, A Novel by a Lady*, is published anonymously in London, England; the author is later discovered to be **JANE AUSTEN**.

1812 Spencer Perceval becomes the only British Prime Minister to be **ASSASSINATED**; he is shot in the House of Commons by John Bellingham, who is later hanged for the crime.
•The first **STEAMSHIP** in regular service, Henry Bell's *Comet*, runs on the River Clyde in Scotland.
•The **BROTHERS GRIMM** of Hesse, Germany, publish what becomes known as *Grimm's Fairy Tales*, a collection of over 200 stories and legends, including *Rumpelstiltskin*, *Hansel and Gretel*, and *Snow White and the Seven Dwarfs*.
•A factory for **TINNED FOOD** (food in tin-coated iron cans) is set up in the UK.

1813 The Allied forces (Britain, Prussia, Austria, Sweden) defeat Napoleon at the **BATTLE OF THE NATIONS** in Leipzig, Germany.
•The first **STEAM-DRIVEN WARSHIP**, the *Demologos*, is designed by American Robert Fulton; it measures 43 m (140 ft) long and is equipped with 30 cannons.
•The dice gambling game **CRAPS** is introduced to New Orleans, USA, from France; the name comes from "Johnny Crapaud", a US term for a Creole person.

THEN AND NOW

1818 Jeremiah Chubb designs a lock mechanism that allegedly cannot be picked, to prevent burglaries at a local naval dockyard.
1986 An anti-theft electronic dog is invented by Dutchman A van de Haar; fitted with a built-in microphone, it "barks" whenever it detects a human presence.

STOP PRESS! Napoleon is exiled to the Mediterranean island of Elba, in 1814.

from disease and famine; the 1,700,000 tonnes (1,875,000 tons) of ash hurled into the atmosphere will affect the world's weather for the next year.

1816
SECATEURS (small pruning shears) are invented in France by the Marquis of Moleville.
•The **KALEIDOSCOPE** is invented by Scottish physicist Dr David Brewster.
•**SAMUEL TAYLOR COLERIDGE**, the penniless English poet addicted to the drug opium since 1803, initially dreams his famous poem *Kubla Khan*; when he comes to write it down he is interrupted, and cannot remember how it ends.
•**ENGLISH IMMIGRANTS** arrive in Canada and the USA in an effort to escape the economic crisis at home; next year, in Derbyshire, England, people riot against low wages.
•Frenchman Joseph Nicéphore Niépce invents the **IRIS DIAPHRAGM** to control light flow through the lens in his early photographic experiments; all modern cameras will utilize this principle.

1817
CADMIUM, a silvery metal later used in batteries, is discovered by German chemist Friedrich Stromeyer.
•The game of **SQUASH** is first played at Harrow School in England.
•**LITHIUM**, the lightest metallic element, is discovered by Sweden's Johann Arfvedson.

1818
Dr Thomas Blundell attempts the first **BLOOD TRANSFUSION**, at Guy's Hospital in London, England; it is unsuccessful.
•US paddle steamer, *The Savannah*, becomes the first **STEAMBOAT** to cross the Atlantic Ocean.
•Mary Shelley competes with her poet husband, Percy, and their friend, the poet Lord Byron, to write the best **GHOST STORY**. She wins, with *Frankenstein*.
•Jöns Berzelius, of Sweden, discovers the element **SELENIUM**.

1819
The era's most popular composer, **LUDWIG VAN BEETHOVEN**, whose health has been deteriorating, is now deaf.

•Switzerland's first **CHOCOLATE FACTORY** is opened by François Louis Cailler in Corsier near Lake Geneva.
•The USA gets its first show featuring a female **TIGHTROPE PERFORMER** when Madame Adolphe of Paris, France, appears at the Anthony Street Theater in New York City.
•Eleven people are killed and 500 injured in the **PETERLOO MASSACRE**, in England, when mounted cavalrymen charge an open-air meeting in which parliamentary reform is supported.

•Scottish engineer John MacAdam invents the **MACADAM** road surface, which consists of a layer of tiny stones.
•Thousands of Italians are killed when the cities of **GENOA** and **PALERMO** are destroyed by an earthquake.
•Madame Blanchard, French **BALLOONIST**, is killed in Paris, when fireworks set fire to her balloon.

The transport revolution steams ahead

PUFFING BILLY LEADS THE AGE OF STEAM (SEE 1813)

1820 Arthur Thistlewood, one of the five "Cato Street Conspirators," is the last person to be **PUBLICLY BEHEADED** in Britain.
•The **GALVANOMETER**, which measures electrical current, is invented by Johann Salomo Christoph Sweigger of Germany; it is named after Italian physiologist Luigi Galvani, the discoverer of animal electricity (or galvanism), who will also give his name to galvanizing (zinc plating to protect from rust).

1821 **CAFFEINE** is discovered by Pierre Joseph Pelletier at the Paris School of Chemistry, France.
•England's Michael Faraday builds the world's first **ELECTRIC MOTOR**.
•A **CENSUS** in Britain reveals that women live longer than men, and there are more of them.
•The **DIFFERENCE ENGINE**, a mechanical calculator (an early form of computer), is invented by Charles Babbage in England, but is never completed; other work takes priority.

1822 **MARIE TAGLIONE**, an eight-year-old Italian ballerina who achieves world renown, makes her debut performance in Vienna, Austria.
•Friedrich Buschman of Germany invents the **ACCORDION** (a year after he invented the harmonica).

THEN AND NOW

1821 Emperor Napoleon I of France dies while in exile on the island of St. Helena in the South Atlantic. When results from a detailed autopsy show traces of arsenic, murder by poisoning is suspected.
1993 Research reveals that the coloring that had been used in the wallpaper covering Napoleon's quarters contained high levels of arsenic. In the damp and moldy conditions in which Napoleon lived, this would have created a deadly gas, which is far more likely to have been the true cause of Napoleon's death than murder.

•The esteemed British **ASTRONOMER** Sir William Herschel dies; he believed the Sun is inhabited.
•Eleven-year old **FRANZ LISZT** makes his debut public performance when he plays the piano at Vienna, Austria.

•**A CYCLONE** hits the area around the mouth of the Ganges River in India; 50,000 people lose their lives.
•Britain's Dr. Gideon Mantell discovers the teeth of a gigantic **DINOSAUR**; he later names it *Iguanodon*, after the Central American iguana lizard.
•Boiling mud spews over the island of **JAVA** when the volcano Galung Gung erupts. Four days later the volcano is blown to pieces in another eruption, with the result that 100 villages and 4,000 people are lost.
•Louis J. M. Daguerre devises the **DIORAMA**, a precursor to the movies, in Paris, France; it is an entertainment based on large semitransparent painted linen screens, hung and ingeniously lit to create illusions of depth and movement.
•**PERCY BYSSHE SHELLEY**, English poet, drowns in a storm off the Italian coast.
•The five-shot **FLINTLOCK REVOLVER** is manufactured in London, England, by the American-born gunsmith Elisha Haydon Collier.

1823 The **SONG** *Home Sweet Home* is written by American dramatist John Howard Payne when he is homesick in Paris, France.

•Charles Macintosh of Glasgow, Scotland, patents a **WATERPROOF CAPE** made of rubberized cloth (later known as the "macintosh" or "mac").
•British pharmacists from Worcester John W. Lea and William Perrins set up shop; they later become famous for their **WORCESTERSHIRE SAUCE**, made according to a recipe from Bengal, India.

THE *IGUANODON* IS ONE OF THE FIRST DINOSAURS TO BE DISCOVERED (SEE 1822)

EXTRA EXTRA! British soldiers are issued their first pairs of trousers to replace their uniform breeches, in 1823.

•The game of **RUGBY** is born when William Webb Ellis, playing in a soccer match at Rugby School in England, picks up the ball and runs with it.
•Manufactured by German-born Johann Maelzel, **TALKING DOLLS**, which say "mama" and "papa," are sold in Paris, France, at ten francs each.

1824 Frenchman André-Marie Ampère, after whom **AMP** is named, invents his own galvanometer for measuring electrical current.
•**PORTLAND CEMENT** (named for its resemblance to limestone on the Isle of Portland, England) is patented by Yorkshire bricklayer Joseph Aspdin; he has made it out of limestone and clay.
•An important **STRIKE ACTION** in which US men and women collaborate, takes place when weavers protest in Rhode Island.
•The element **SILICON** is discovered by Sweden's Jöns Berzelius.

1825 America's first **STEAM ENGINE** to run on rails is tried out by its 76-year-old inventor John Stevens on a circular track in his back yard in Hoboken, New Jersey.
•Denmark's Hans Christian Oersted discovers **ALUMINUM**.

You can spot an Iguanodon by its three-toed prints

•French-born British engineer Marc Isambard Brunel starts work on the world's first **RIVER TUNNEL**, the Rotherhithe Tunnel under the Thames in London, England; it covers a distance of 1,500 ft (457 m) and its construction involves the use of the recently invented Portland cement; it is not completed until 1843.
•Professor Charles Wheatstone of London, England, invents the **CONCERTINA**, a variation on the accordion that works by pressing buttons, rather than keys on a keyboard.
•British inventor William Sturgeon invents a **MAGNET** that can lift 20 times its own weight.

1826 A **CHOLERA EPIDEMIC** begins in Europe; known in Britain as summer diarrhea, it will result in 900,000 deaths in five years.
•The first **GAS STOVE** is installed in the kitchen at the home of its inventor, James Sharp, assistant manager of the Northampton Gas Company in England.

1827 An **ELECTROMAGNET**, capable of lifting up to 14 lb (6.4 kg), is made by physicist Joseph Henry; he then makes one powerful enough to lift 2,880 lb (1,306 kg).
•Haitian-born **JOHN JAMES AUDUBON** begins *The Birds of North America*. Its 87 portfolios contain 1,065 engravings.
•Hammersmith Bridge, the world's first **SUSPENSION BRIDGE** to be made of stone and metal, is opened in London, England.

•Frenchman Joseph Nicéphone Niépce produces the earliest surviving **PERMANENT PHOTOGRAPH**, an extremely faint image of his home; it is the result of an eight-hour exposure.

1828 Italian Vittorio Sarti invents a **HELICOPTER** with blades that rotate in opposite directions, but it is never built.

AUDUBON'S PORTRAIT OF A VULTURE (SEE 1827)

•The **FIRST BONES** of the *Pterodactyl* dinosaur are discovered by Mary Anning, English paleontologist, who sells fossils to tourists in the town of Lyme Regis; the tongue-twister "she sells seashells on the seashore" is said to refer to her.

1829 The first **MODERN HOTEL**, where guests receive keys to private rooms, is the 170-room Tremont House in Boston.
•France's **LOUIS BRAILLE**, blind since he was three, invents a raised point printing system that can be read by touch.
•The first-ever **STEAM ENGINE** on an American railroad is the *Stourbridge Lion*, made at the Stephenson Engine Works; it runs the Carbondale-to-Honesdale route in Pennsylvania.
•France's Barthélemy Thimonnier invents the first-ever practical **SEWING MACHINE**.

•The sickly Reverend Sylvester Graham of Connecticut, nicknamed the "poet of bran," makes a wholewheat cracker later called the **GRAHAM CRACKER**.
•Frozen residents of **DANZIG** in Poland cling to church roofs for days awaiting rescue, after the icy Vistula River breaks through nearby dikes to flood the town.

1830 The horse-drawn cylindrical blade **LAWN MOWER** is invented in England by Edwin Budding.

•British Member of Parliament William Huskisson is the first person to be killed by a **MOVING TRAIN**, when the *Rocket* runs him down at the opening of the Liverpool-Manchester railroad.

•Joseph Smith publishes *The Book of Mormon*, claiming that it contains the word of God as revealed to him on buried gold tablets, and founds the Church of Jesus Christ of Latter-day Saints, the basis of the **MORMON** religion, at Fayette, New York.

•Augustus Siebe, a veteran of the Battle of Waterloo, invents a **DIVING SUIT** similar in principle to the modern suit.

ESSENTIAL DIVING HEADGEAR (SEE 1830)

Take a dive and see life on the ocean floor!

1831 Joseph Gillott, who cannot write, patents the first commercially successful steel pen nib in England.

•British Commander James Ross finds the location of the **MAGNETIC** North Pole, on a second Arctic expedition led by his uncle, Sir John Ross.

•Naturalist Charles **DARWIN** sails on an expedition of discovery to South America, New Zealand, and Australia aboard the HMS *Beagle*.

•The **ELECTRIC BELL** is invented by US mathematics teacher Joseph Henry.

•Nat Turner leads an uprising of slaves in the South, is captured, and hanged; now even tougher laws are enforced to control American **SLAVES**.

•British chemist and physicist Michael Faraday demonstrates his experiments on **ELECTROMAGNETIC INDUCTION**.

•French chemist Charles Sauria invents a **NEW MATCH** based on phosphorus, in an effort to eliminate the awful smell produced by British "Lucifers."

•**PARAFFIN** is produced by Germany's Baron von Reichenbach.

•England's King William IV and Queen Adelaide open the new **LONDON BRIDGE**; built by Sir John Rennie, it has five stone arches and is just along the River Thames from the old bridge.

1832 US wagon maker John Stephenson builds New York's first **STREETCAR**, which carries up to 30 passengers; it is pulled along tracks by horses.

•The body of eccentric philosopher Jeremy Bentham is **DISSECTED** by his friend, Dr. Thomas Southwood Smith, at a medical school in London, England; his head is later mummified and his skeleton, dressed in his clothes, is presented to University College, where it is still preserved and taken to meetings.

•The electric **DYNAMO**, fundamental to all future electricity generators, is shown in France by Hippolyte Pixii; it produces electricity by the hand rotation of a horseshoe magnet between two wire coils.

•Operagoers in Paris, France, can now don the collapsible silk **OPERA HAT**, designed by hatter Antoine Gibus.

1833 The first-ever book **DUST JACKET** is used to protect *The Keepsake* annual, which has been produced by Longmans booksellers in London, England.

1834 England's William H. Horner invents the **ZOETROPE**, an optical toy with a revolving drum into which are inserted paper picture strips depicting jugglers, dancers, and animals that give the illusion of movement.

EXTRA EXTRA! Using Biblical studies, American William Miller predicts the end of the world, in 1833.

JEREMY BENTHAM (SEE 1832)

•American-born Jacob Perkins invents an ice-making machine in England; it is the first to use vapor compression as a means of **REFRIGERATION**.
• The British **HOUSES OF PARLIAMENT** are destroyed by fire after stoves over-stuffed with wood rage out of control.
•Germany's Baron von Reichenbach extracts **CREOSOTE** from wood tar.
•The adhesive postage **STAMP** is printed by Scottish bookseller James Chalmers.
•**POKER**, a card game, is first described in America as a Mississippi riverboat game, in *Green's Reformed Gambler*.
•**SLAVERY** is abolished throughout the British Empire.

1835 France's Louis Daguerre produces the first **DAGUERREOTYPE** photograph, using his new process by which a permanent photograph is developed in 20 minutes.
•Germany's first **RAILROAD** is opened near Nuremberg; it uses a Stephenson steam engine driven by an Englishman.
•English printer George Baxter patents his **COLOR PRINTING** technique,

which uses a combination of wood blocks and steel and copper plates.

1836 The Battle of the Alamo is fought as American settlers struggle for independence from Mexico; the frontier hero **DAVY CROCKETT** is among the Americans killed by the 3,000 Mexican troops led by General Antonio de Santa Anna; only 30 women and children are left alive; from this event comes the famous battle cry "Remember the Alamo!"
•The primary cell, or **DANIELL CELL**, as it comes to be known, is invented by meteorologist and chemist John Frederic Daniell of London, England; it provides the first efficient electrical power supply.
•Both John Stevens and Swedish-born John Ericsson patent screw **PROPELLERS**, specifically designed to power ships.
•A **STEAM SHOVEL** is invented by Philadelphia's William Otis in response to America's demand for faster road-building and tunneling.

1837 A former science teacher, Switzerland's Frederick Wilhelm August Froebel, establishes the first **KINDERGARTEN** at Blankenburg in Germany; it is originally called a Kleinkindbeschäftigungsinstitut, or "small child occupation institute."
•American inventor Samuel Finley Breese Morse applies for a patent for his magnetic telegraph; it transmits messages as a series of dots and dashes and becomes known as **MORSE CODE**.
•British parachute pioneer Robert Cocking is killed in Kent, England, when his **PARACHUTE** disintegrates.
•Isaac Pitman, English schoolteacher, devises the first practical system of phonographic **SHORTHAND**; its worldwide spread is begun almost at once when his brother goes to Australia with 100 copies of *Stenographic Sound-hand*, in which the system is described.
•The **ELECTRIC TELEGRAPH** is patented in England by Sir Charles Wheatstone and Sir William Cooke; they took up the work begun by Russian diplomat Pavel Schilling, who died without completing his experiments with the electric telegraph in St. Petersburg.
•German publisher Tauchnitz issues the first **PAPERBACK** novels, in English – but for legal reasons they are sold everywhere except in England.

1838 The **STEREOSCOPE**, for viewing 3-D pictures,

is invented by physicist Sir Charles Wheatstone in London, England.
•German biologists Jakob Mathias Schleiden and Teodor Schwann make an outstanding discovery: that the basic makeup of plants is **CELLULAR**.

1839 American inventor Isaac Babbitt produces a bearing alloy made from tin, copper, and antimony in response to the need for better-quality metals for the production of bearings used in steam engines; it comes to be known as **BABBITT METAL**.
•**PRICKLY PEAR** is brought to Australia for use as hedging, but soon grows out of control, taking over huge areas of the Australian countryside.
•Scottish blacksmith Kirkpatrick MacMillan is the first man to build a kind of hobbyhorse, propelled by cranks and pedals; it is viewed by some as the predecessor of the modern **BICYCLE**.
•Charles Goodyear of the USA invents **VULCANIZED RUBBER** when he accidentally drops a combination of rubber and sulfur onto a hot stove; this method of curing raw rubber makes it strong and elastic and enables the manufacture of tires and associated products.
•The American publication *Musical World* notes the invention in Cincinnati of a "Porco-Forte," or **PIG ORGAN**. It is operated by pinching the tails of pigs housed in a partitioned box with their tails sticking out through a row of holes; this cruel idea was originally devised by the Abbot of Baigne, who designed the organ for King Louis XI of France.

THEN AND NOW

1839 Maria Ann Smith, born in Sussex, England, emigrates to Australia and achieves fame when her apples become known as Granny Smiths.
1995 To celebrate its bumper crop of Granny Smith apples, the Washington Apple Commission organizes the first *In search of Granny Smith* contest, designed to find "the world's best grandmother to represent the world's best apple."

EXTRA EXTRA! Proved wrong in 1833, William Miller revises his prediction for the end of the world to 1834.

81

1840 The **BINAURAL STETHOSCOPE**, a precursor of the modern stethoscope, with flexible tubing taking the sound to both ears, is introduced by George Philip Cammann of New York.

•With the closure of Eleanor Coade's factory in London, England, the secret formula for **COADE STONE**, a highly durable artificial cast stone used in architectural features and statues, is lost.

•Dr. John William Draper of New York takes a daguerreotype photograph of the moon in one of the earliest examples of **ASTROPHOTOGRAPHY**.

•In the grand redesign of Paris by French city planner Georges Eugène **HAUSSMAN**, 50 fountains are erected in the city's poorer districts.

•US child **PRODIGY** Zerah Colburn dies; once asked how many seconds had elapsed since the birth of Christ, Zerah instantaneously calculated in his head 57,234,384,000 (he was nine at the time).

•**OZONE** is discovered by Christian Friedrich Schhnbein, Professor of Chemistry at Basle in Switzerland.

•English-born fashion leader George "**BEAU**" **BRUMMELL** dies a pauper in a French asylum for the mentally ill.

•Austrian ballet dancer Fanny Eissler, of Vienna, dances the **POLKA** in America.

•Anna, Duchess of Bedford, instigates the English ritual of **AFTERNOON TEA**.

1841 **HYPNOSIS**, according to Dr. James Braid, can be produced by the maintenance of a confident air and fixed gaze, without any involvement of strange magnetic forces.

•**PAINT** in squeezable tubes is sold by artists' suppliers Winsor & Newton, using the collapsible metal tube recently invented by America's John Rand.

•The term **DINOSAURIA** (terrible lizards) is first used by paleontologist Richard Owen at a meeting of the British Association for the Advancement of Science, in Plymouth, England.

•Englishman William Henry Fox Talbot invents **CALOTYPE** photographs.

1842 America's Crawford Williamson Long performs the first surgical operation using **ETHER ANESTHESIA**, to remove a cyst.

•For 100 hours, **HAMBURG** in Germany is engulfed in flames; 100 die and one-fifth of the city's population is homeless.

•A **SUBMARINE CABLE** is laid by Samuel Morse in New York harbor; transmissions stop after just one day,

CHRISTMAS GREETINGS ARE SENT BY CARD (SEE 1843)

when a stretch of the insulated copper wire cable is cut by a ship's anchor.

1843 Two weeks before the statue of Lord Nelson is hauled to the top of **NELSON**'s Column in London, England, 14 men celebrate with a dinner of rump steak on the plinth, 166 ft (51 m) above the ground.

•Philadelphia small arms manufacturer Henry Deringer, Jr. makes a tiny pocket pistol; when one is used to assassinate President Lincoln, it becomes known as a **DERRINGER** (with an extra "r").

•One thousand printed **CHRISTMAS CARDS** are sent by Londoners, when British art critic and author Sir Henry Cole commissions the artist John Calcott Horsley to produce a Christmas card design; a central panel shows festive celebrations, and two side panels depict the poor being fed and clothed.

•The Great Comet that appears in the skies this year heralds the **END OF THE WORLD**, according to the Millerites, a religious sect founded by American prophet and farmer William Miller.

1844 English dye chemist John Mercer invents the process of toughening cotton and giving it a sheen; this process, which is named after him, is called **MERCERIZATION**.

•The constant sore throats and other illnesses of the servants at Britain's Windsor Castle is explained by the discovery of 53 overflowing **CESSPOOLS** beneath the castle.

•Joseph Smith, US presidential candidate and founder of the **MORMONS**, is imprisoned after vandalizing a rival's printing press and calling his followers to fight the oppression of the Gentiles; a mob breaks into the jail and Smith is lynched.

•Nitrous oxide (**LAUGHING GAS**) is used as an anesthetic by American dentist Horace Wells, who still manages to cause pain when he extracts his patient's tooth.

•The YMCA (**YOUNG MEN'S CHRISTIAN ASSOCIATION**) is founded by English social reformer George Williams, a dry-goods seller in London.

•Pickpockets Oliver Martin and Fiddler Dick are arrested in the English town of Slough, west of London, when police act on information received by wire from Paddington in central London; it is the first known use of the **TELEGRAPH** to aid in an arrest.

1845 A new pudding is concocted in the US by Peter Cooper, a New York steam engine manufacturer; it is a gelatin dessert made almost entirely of sugar, and in 50 years it will be manufactured as **JELL-O**.

•**LEUKEMIA** is described by Carl Virchow, a German pathologist.

•**ADHESIVE BANDAGES** are patented in New Jersey by Doctors William Shecut and Horace Harvel Day.

•Scottish engineer Richard Thomson patents the first **AIR-FILLED TIRE**, made from leather.

•The **TOILET** acquires the ball valve to control the cistern's water level, invented by England's Edward Chrimes.

1847! An inhaler is manufactured by British firm Attlee & Company for the purpose of administering ether during surgery.

•While drunk, William Lloyd stumbles into the British Museum in London, England, and smashes the priceless Roman glass **PORTLAND VASE**.

•**RUBBER BANDS** are patented in London, England, by rubber manufacturer Stephen Perry of Messrs Perry & Company.

1846 America's Elias Howe invents a **SEWING MACHINE**; it has a curved needle that makes stitches by being swung through the material on a mechanical arm.

•France's Bishop of Metz claims that the **FLOODING** of the Loire River is caused by not observing Sunday as a day of rest.

•French astronomer Urbain Le Verrier calculates the position of the planet **NEPTUNE** a year after the same discovery had been made by the self-taught American astronomer John Couch Adams did who could not persuade England's Astronomer Royal, George Airy, to take his findings seriously.

•In an effort to tackle Britain's drinking problem, the Prime Minister cuts import **TAX** on French wine in the hope that people will prefer wine over the crude spirits that are cheaply available to them.

•A collection of limericks and illustrations, written to entertain his employer's children, is published as *A Book of Nonsense* by English author and artist **EDWARD LEAR**; he trained his cat Foss to blot ink by rolling on it.

•**BELL-MEN** in London, England, who ring a bell to announce their arrival to collect people's outgoing mail for a penny a letter, are abolished when decent wages for letter carriers are introduced by the General Post Office.

•Adolphe Sax, Belgian instrument maker, patents the **SAXOPHONE**, named after him; despite his brilliance, he is unpopular in the trade because of his monopoly in instrument supply to the French army.

•A rotary **PRINTING PRESS** is invented by American Richard March Hoe; it reels off 18,000 sheets printed on both sides in one hour, and is first used to print the Philadelphia newspaper, *Public Ledger*.

1847 **CHLOROFORM** anesthetic is used by Scottish obstetrician Sir James Young Simpson to ease labor pains in childbirth.

•German chemist Christian Friedrich Schönbein discovers **NITROCELLULOSE**.

•Hungarian obstetrician Ignaz Philipp Semmelweis studies and prevents the transmission of **PUERPERAL FEVER** (childbed fever), in Vienna, Austria; he realizes it is contagious and brings in strict handwashing rules for doctors.

•Italian chemist Ascanio Sobrero makes **NITROGLYCERINE**, an oily explosive, but it is too dangerous to manufacture until a safer process is developed by Immanuel Nobel and his son Alfred.

•**CALIFORNIA** and **THE SOUTHWEST** become part of the United States.

• England's J. G. Ingram makes **TOY BALLOONS** from vulcanized rubber.

•**SALT LAKE CITY** is founded in Utah by the Mormons led by Brigham Young; they convert desert into land that can be successfully farmed.

1848 **HYPERION**, a satellite of Saturn, is discovered by US astronomer William Cranch Bond.

•The **SPEED OF LIGHT** is calculated by French physicist Hippolyte Fizeau.

•Linus Yale, Jr. patents a lock worked by pins within a revolving cylinder, which will become known as the **YALE LOCK**.

•A kind of **CHEWING GUM**, called "State of Maine Pure Spruce Gum," is cooked up by John Curtis in Maine.

•The Austrians conduct the first **AIR RAID** during the revolution sweeping Europe, when they

THEN AND NOW

1841 Thomas Cook starts a travel company, organizing the first-ever "package tour." He crams 570 members of an antialcohol society in Leicester, England, into nine open trucklike carriages without seats and takes them to a park in nearby Loughborough; here they play games and have afternoon tea before returning home.

1997 It is estimated that 613 million people – almost one in ten of the world's population – traveled as tourists to another country. Of these, more than half visited the top ten most-visited destinations: first is France with 66.8 million visitors, then the US, Spain, Italy, the UK, China, Poland, Mexico, Canada, and the Czech Republic.

attack Venice, Italy, with unmanned balloons carrying fire bombs.

•**A BATHING DRESS** with massive skirts and wide sleeves is designed – but it is difficult for the wearer to move in water.

•The **PRE-RAPHAELITE BROTHERHOOD** led by English poet and artist Dante Gabriel Rossetti is founded. Its aim is to return to naturalism, and the more serious approach to art that prevailed prior to Raphael.

1849 **LEVI STRAUSS** arrives in the US from Bavaria, Germany. One of many who flock to California in the Gold Rush, he begins to manufacture the jeans known by his name as durable wear for gold miners.

•**RAILROAD SIGNALS** are introduced on the New York and Erie Railroad; operated by hand, they are used to ensure that only one train can run on a given section of track at a time.

•America's earliest known **CHINESE RESTAURANT**, the Macao and Woosung in San Francisco, is set up by Norman Asing, an immigrant from China.

•The **SAFETY PIN** is designed by Walter Hunt of New York City after fooling around with a piece of wire.

•**CONDENSED**, or evaporated, milk is made by Gail Borden of America, after an ocean voyage in which rough conditions of the crossing made the cows too sick to be milked.

EDWARD LEAR MAKES NONSENSE RHYME (SEE 1846)

EXTRA EXTRA! The last surviving pair of flightless great auks are killed on behalf of an Icelandic collector, in 1844.

83

1850 French philosopher Auguste Comte proposes a 13-month **CALENDAR**, with each month commemorating an important historical figure, such as Moses, Aristotle, or Homer, and every day a celebration of a noteworthy member of the human race.
• Scottish-born James Harrison sets up an **ICE-MAKING PLANT** at Rodey Point, Victoria, Australia, where ice is produced by piping liquid ether through water.
• The first **BOWLER HAT** is made in the UK by hatmakers James Lock and Company, who name it the Coke, after a customer; later it is called the bowler, after one of the hatmaker's suppliers.

1851 American L. L. Langstroth discovers the **BEE-SPACE**, a small gap between frames of honeycomb that is left unbridged by the bees; his finding facilitates the movable frame bee hive, giving the bee keeper much more control.
• America's Isaac Merritt Singer patents his new lock-stitch **SEWING MACHINE** powered by a treadle; his partner, Edward Clark, initiates the first rental-purchase plan so that the machine can be paid for over a period of time; an army of door-to-door salesmen is sent out to market the sewing machine.
• **BLOOMERS** are promoted in America by Mrs. Amelia Bloomer, who gives her name to the outrageous new fashion of comfortable undergarments that become popular with women's rights activists.
• **GOLD** is struck in Victoria, New South Wales, Australia.
• The **OPHTHALMOSCOPE**, a tool for performing eye examinations, is made from a light, a mirror, and lenses by German physicist Hermann von Helmholtz of Prussia.
• The **AMERICA'S CUP** is first competed for when the English ask the Americans to send a yacht to take part in Royal Yacht Squadron regattas; the magnificent schooner *America* makes history when it wins the race ahead of all 17 British-built yachts.
• French physicist Léon Foucault swings a 200-ft (67-m) pendulum (later known as **FOUCAULT'S PENDULUM**) with a 62-lb (28-kg) ball from the dome of the Paris Panthéon providing scientific proof for the theory that Earth rotates.
• Ariel and Umbriel, satellites of **URANUS**, are discovered by British

astronomer William Lassell.
• The **CRYSTAL PALACE**, a vast glass conservatory designed by English architect and gardener Joseph Paxton, is constructed in London's Hyde Park to hold the Great Exhibition.

1852 The **SPARROW** is imported from Germany by the US government to reduce the increasing infestations of caterpillars that are depleting valuable crops.
• Three-year old Eliza Armstrong is the first patient at the UK's newly opened Great Ormond Street Hospital, the world's first **HOSPITAL FOR CHILDREN**.
• English scholar Peter Mark **ROGET** publishes his *Thesaurus of English Words and Phrases*, a classification of words in the English language; it will go into 28 editions during his lifetime.
• Frenchman Henri Giffard flies his steam-driven, hydrogen-filled **AIRSHIP** 17 mi (27 km) from Paris to Trappes.
• James Nye proposes a theory for **ROCKET-PROPELLED** airships.
• Germany's Butchers' Guild in Frankfurt introduces the **FRANKFURTER**.
• French housemaid Hélène Jegado, found guilty of murdering 23 people by arsenic poisoning, is **GUILLOTINED**.
• Léon Foucault invents the **GYROSCOPE**, a mechanical device by which he seeks to demonstrate the rotation of Earth; the gyroscope will be used in navigational and other aids.

1853 A railroad car with a **CORRIDOR** is introduced

CATERPILLARS MEET THEIR MATCH (SEE 1852)

by America's Hudson River Railroad; it has five compartments, a toilet room, and an 18-in (46-cm)-wide corridor.
• The first **POTATO CHIPS** are made by Native American George Crum, chef at the Moon Lake House Hotel, Saratoga Springs, New York, when asked for chips that are "thinner than normal French fried potatoes"; they become a fixture on the hotel menu and are called "Saratoga Chips."
• The **HYPODERMIC** syringe is invented by France's Charles Gabriel Pravaz.
• On New Year's Eve, 22 scientists dine

inside a **LIFE-SIZE MODEL** of an *Iguanodon* dinosaur before it is installed at the Crystal Palace in London, England.

1854 The **PENNY RED**, the first perforated stamp, is produced by the UK's Henry Archer, who had spent seven years perfecting his machinery.
• Bytown, Canada, named in honor of Colonel John By, changes its name to **OTTAWA**, a local Indian word.
• André Disdéri invents the **MULTIPLE-LENS CAMERA**, allowing many poses to be taken on a single plate; this discovery leads to his "carte-de-visite" (an early

"KANGAROO OFFICE" COINS CELEBRATE THE AUSTRALIAN GOLD RUSH (SEE 1851)

calling card, with details printed on the reverse side of a photograph of himself).
• **LIGHTNING** strikes a church storing gunpowder in Rhodes, Greece; 4,000 people die in the worst explosion ever.

1855 A **BARE-KNUCKLE** boxing match occurs in New South Wales, Australia; a record-breaking bout, it goes on for 186 rounds and takes 6 hours, 15 minutes.
• Dentist Arthur Robert of Philadelphia describes his **TOOTH-FILLING TECHNIQUE**, which makes use of the cohesive quality of gold foil.
• Jean-Baptiste Jolly sets up the first **DRY-CLEANING BUSINESS** in Paris, France, after spilling camphene onto a dress and the dress was magically cleaned rather than ruined.
• The **SAFETY MATCH** is invented by Sweden's Johan Edvard Lundström; it must be struck upon a special chemically treated surface to be lit.
• Scottish explorer David **LIVINGSTONE** discovers the 355-ft (109-m)-high

EXTRA EXTRA! Sir George Cayley's coachman resigns after being terrified by a ride in his master's glider, in 1853.

waterfall on the Zambezi River in Africa; originally known as the Mosi-oa-tunya ("the smoke that thunders"), it is renamed the Victoria Falls.

1856
"MAUVEINE," the first synthetic dye, is patented in Britain by 18-year-old chemistry student William Henry Perkin; the cloth industry is revolutionized by the dye and Perkin makes a fortune and gains a knighthood.

• A skull found in the Feldhofer Cave near Düsseldorf, Germany, is the first discovery of **NEANDERTHAL** man.

• London, England's **BIG BEN** bell is installed at the Houses of Parliament; it is named after Sir Benjamin Hall, Director of Public Works.

• To celebrate the end of the Crimean War, English confectioner George Bassett bakes a 9,767-lb (4,430-kg) iced cake, in a **PUBLICITY STUNT** for his firm.

• English inventor Henry **BESSEMER** patents his converter for steel manufacture, after discovering that the gun barrels of the day were not sturdy enough to fire his newly invented shells.

1857
US's Otis Steam Elevator Company installs its first passenger **ELEVATOR** in a store.

• **TOILET PAPER** is marketed in the US by Joseph Gayetty, in packs of individual sheets, which do not sell well; Americans would rather use old newspapers and catalog pages than waste good paper.

1858
A **WASHING MACHINE** is patented by Hamilton Smith of Pennsylvania; it is a wooden drum with a handcrank for rotating the wooden wringer.

• Ezra J. Warner of Connecticut patents the first **CAN OPENER**, a dangerous curved blade that is not popular with Americans.

• French Empress Eugénie and Napoleon III are traveling in a carriage in Paris when **ANARCHIST** Felice Orsini throws three bombs beneath it, killing ten and injuring 156; the Empress dismisses the incident as being "all part of the job."

• Henry Colden Harrison and Thomas Wills establish

NEANDERTHAL MAN REAPPEARS (SEE 1856)

THEN AND NOW

1856 An April Fool's joke persuades crowds of people to turn up for the nonexistent ceremony of lion-washing at the Tower of London. **1957** A TV documentary shown on April 1 convinces British viewers that spaghetti grows on trees.

AUSTRALIAN RULES football, an 18-a-side game, when Australia's Melbourne Football Club is founded.

• The first **BURGLAR** alarm is installed in the US; a spring-release action works when a door or window is opened, which in turn sets off a short-circuit reaction.

• During the English summer, London's Thames River becomes so **POLLUTED** with sewage it is called the Great Stink.

• US President Buchanan and England's Queen Victoria send each other greetings by telegram when the first **TRANSATLANTIC CABLE** is completed. The cable fails after only three months.

• US stationer Hyman L. Lipman becomes a millionaire after patenting a **PENCIL WITH AN ERASER** on the end.

• American tinsmith John Mason patents a jar with a zinc screw lid fitted with a rubber ring to make the jar airtight; the **MASON JAR** is still popular today.

• The first **AERIAL PHOTOGRAPH** is taken from a hot-air balloon over Paris by Nadar, the renowned French photographer.

1859
Gaston Planté of France invents the first **STORAGE BATTERY**, that will be crucial to the automobiles of the future.

• The **STEAMROLLER** is invented by France's Louis Lemoine.

• The first **OIL WELL** is drilled by Edwin L. Drake in Pennsylvania, striking oil at a depth of just under 70 ft (21 m).

• In North America, watched by a crowd of 5,000, **DAREDEVIL** Charles Blondin slings a 1,100-ft (335-m) tightrope 160 ft (49 m) above the Niagara Falls.

Neanderthal man lived 120,000 years ago!

LOCOMOTION

ALONGSIDE THE INDUSTRIAL REVOLUTION there was an amazing revolution in transportation. It began with the building of canals and surfaced roads in the late 1700s, then exploded with the coming of the railroad. For the first time ever, people were able to travel more than a few miles from home. As the mania for building spread around the world, millions of people suddenly began to move. By the time the car was invented in the 1880s, the world was a much smaller place.

CARRIAGE HEADLIGHT

RAILROADS

With the advent of the railroads in the 19th century, the world changed forever. As the rail network expanded across continents, goods and passengers could be carried vast distances overland for the first time ever, and cities grew as never before.

STEAM TRANSPORTATION

1769 Frenchman Nicolas Cugnot (1725–1804) builds the world's first **SELF-PROPELLED VEHICLE** – a large steam-powered three-wheel cart.

1804 English engineer Richard Trevithick builds the first steam-powered **RAILROAD LOCOMOTIVE**.
• US blacksmith Oliver Evans builds a **STEAM-POWERED CART** that can drive through rivers.

1813 In England, William Hedley (1770–1843) builds the first **SMOOTH-WHEELED** steam locomotive.

1823 The Stephensons begin to build railroad locomotives.

"ROCKET"
Built in 1829 by Robert Stephenson, Rocket was the locomotive chosen to operate on the new Liverpool and Manchester railroad.

RAILROAD LANDMARKS

HORSE-DRAWN passenger trains run in Britain from 1796.

FIRST STEAM FREIGHT SERVICE operates regularly on the Middleton line near Leeds, England.

WORLD'S FIRST STEAM RAILROAD to be open to the public goes into service in 1825 in England on the Stockton-to-Darlington track. Five years later, the Liverpool-to-Manchester line is opened.

FIRST REGULAR US STEAM SERVICE goes into operation in 1830. The trains are pulled by a locomotive called "The Best Friend of Charleston," which is the most successful steam locomotive to be built in the US.

FIRST EUROPEAN PUBLIC RAILROAD opens in 1835 in Nuremberg, Germany.

FIRST ACROSS AMERICA In 1863, the Union Pacific and Central Pacific begin building a line from opposite sides of the US. The lines meet in 1869 in Utah.

ORIENT EXPRESS Introduced in 1883, this train offers passengers luxury travel between London, Paris, and Constantinople.

GARE ST. LAZARE BY MONET
*The great railroad terminals
became the cathedrals of the age.*

THE AUTOMOBILE

The first powered vehicles date back to Cugnot's steam carriage of 1769, but it was Étienne Lenoir's invention in 1862 of the internal combustion engine, light and powerful, that was to open the way to the coming of the automobile.

FARES FAIR
Motorized, metered taxicabs were introduced in Germany in 1896.

London Electrical Cab Co.

DRIVING MILESTONES

1870 Engineer Siegfried Marcus is **BANNED** from driving his gas-powered car through Vienna, Austria, because of the terrible noise made by his invention.

1883 Gottlieb Daimler, a German engineer, develops a four-cylinder **INTERNAL COMBUSTION ENGINE** that is able to run on gas.

1885 Karl Benz builds the world's first car to be sold to the public, in Mannheim in Germany – a **TWO-SEATER TRICYCLE** powered by a gas engine.

1892 The **DIESEL ENGINE** is patented by Rudolf Diesel of Germany. He describes his invention as the "universal economical engine."

1895 Panhard Levassor puts the engine in front and builds the world's first **SEDAN**.

1908 Henry Ford opens his factory to make the **MODEL T FORD**, the world's first mass-produced car. The age of popular driving begins.

PUBLIC TRANSPORTATION

BUSES In 1662, Blaise Pascal begins a horse-drawn bus service. In 1827, Goldsworthy Gurney builds a steam coach, which runs a regular service from Cheltenham to Gloucester. The development of steam coaches is halted by a legal ban in Britain from 1831. Most buses are horse-drawn until 1904 when the London General Omnibus Company begins to run motor buses. Such buses also run in New York in 1904.

ELECTRIC TROLLEY Powered by overhead cables and run on inlaid rails, a double-decker trolley service starts in London, England, in 1901.

LEISURE TRAVEL

The revolution in transportation enabled the rich to travel in unbelievable splendor and the well heeled soon discovered the pleasures of tourism. On the seas, huge passenger steamships with swimming pools, palatial ballrooms, and elegant dining rooms plied between Europe and the United States. Wealthy rail travelers were no less pampered, traveling the world in trains equipped with first-class eating, sleeping, and dining facilities.

FIRST CLASS

1819 The *Savannah* is the first **STEAMSHIP** to carry first-class passengers across the Atlantic between Britain and the US.

1853 The Baltimore and Ohio Railroad is the first to serve **FOOD** on its trains.

1876 The European Wagons-Lit Company of Europe begins to run high-quality sleeping and **DINING CARS** on its trains.

N.Y.K. LINE

M
DESTINATION
M.S."
S.S.   MARU"
CLASS

BAGGAGE ROOM

LUGGAGE TICKET

THE GREAT ENGINEERS

ROLLS-
ROYCE
FIGUREHEAD

THE 19TH CENTURY was an age for engineers. There was a huge demand for construction on a grand scale – giant factories, mighty bridges, tunnels, roads, railroads, ships – and, for the first time, suitable materials (iron and brick) were being made in vast amounts. With little experience in construction on this scale, engineers were largely hard-bitten, practical men who learned by their mistakes.

BRIDGE BUILDERS

Hand in hand with the development of roads and railroads went achievements in the making of bridges, tunnels, aqueducts, and viaducts. Iron and brick were the favorite materials. Engineers like Pierre Trésaguet (1716–1796), Marc Séguin (1786–1875), Thomas Telford (1757–1834) and Isembard Kingdom Brunel (1806–1859) became the heroes of the age.

ENGINEERING ACHIEVEMENTS

1779 Abraham Darby III designs the world's first **ALL-IRON BRIDGE**, spanning the Severn River at Coalbrookdale, England.

1780 Pierre Trésaguet gives France the world's largest network of **PAVED ROADS**.

1819 Scotsman John McAdam (1756–1836) pioneers the use of a light, smooth **ROAD SURFACE**.

1826 Thomas Telford and Marc Séguin build the Menai bridge, the world's first iron-cable **SUSPENSION BRIDGE**.

1843 French-born Marc Brunel (1769–1849) completes the first **TUNNEL UNDER THE THAMES RIVER** (for pedestrians).

1859 Ferdinand-Marie de Lesseps (1805–1894) finally begins work on building the **SUEZ CANAL** to link the Mediterranean with the Red Sea.

1884 French engineer Alexandre Gustave Eiffel (1832–1923) builds the iron frame for the **STATUE OF LIBERTY**, designed for New York by Auguste Bartholdi (1834–1904). In 1889, Eiffel also builds Paris's **EIFFEL TOWER** from wrought iron.

SHIPS OF IRON AND STEAM

EARLY STEAM AND IRON Marquis d'Abbans sails the first steamboat on the Saone River in France in 1783. John Wilkinson sails the first iron boat on England's Severn River in 1787.

WILLIAM SYMINGTON sails the steam tug, *Charlotte Dundas*, on the Forth-Clyde Canal in 1801. Inspired, American Robert Fulton (1765–1815) builds the first successful commercial steamship *Clermont* in 1808.

THE SCREW Swedish-American John Ericsson (1803–1889) comes up with a successful design for a screw propeller to supersede the paddles used on earlier steamships.

S.S. GREAT BRITAIN is the biggest of the two great iron steamships built by Isambard Kingdom Brunel in the 1840s.

ISAMBARD
KINGDOM BRUNEL
(1806–1859)

MECHANICS

Great engineers with their grand designs were just one end of the scale. At the other were just as many inventive mechanics, creating all kinds of new machines – some to work in factories, like those of the early Industrial Revolution, but just as many for the growing numbers of people who wanted and could afford home machines, from sewing machines to typewriters.

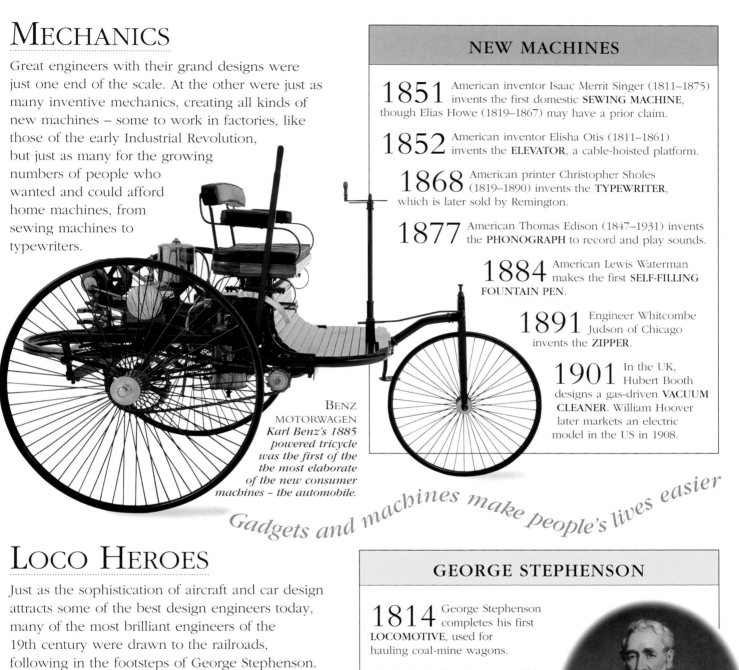

BENZ
MOTORWAGEN
*Karl Benz's 1885
powered tricycle
was the first of the
the most elaborate
of the new consumer
machines - the automobile.*

NEW MACHINES

1851 American inventor Isaac Merrit Singer (1811–1875) invents the first domestic **SEWING MACHINE**, though Elias Howe (1819–1867) may have a prior claim.

1852 American inventor Elisha Otis (1811–1861) invents the **ELEVATOR**, a cable-hoisted platform.

1868 American printer Christopher Sholes (1819–1890) invents the **TYPEWRITER**, which is later sold by Remington.

1877 American Thomas Edison (1847–1931) invents the **PHONOGRAPH** to record and play sounds.

1884 American Lewis Waterman makes the first **SELF-FILLING FOUNTAIN PEN**.

1891 Engineer Whitcombe Judson of Chicago invents the **ZIPPER**.

1901 In the UK, Hubert Booth designs a gas-driven **VACUUM CLEANER**. William Hoover later markets an electric model in the US in 1908.

LOCO HEROES

Just as the sophistication of aircraft and car design attracts some of the best design engineers today, many of the most brilliant engineers of the 19th century were drawn to the railroads, following in the footsteps of George Stephenson.

RAILROAD MEN

BOGIES – small wheels at the front of locomotives – are added by New Yorker John B. Jervis in the 1830s to keep them on the winding tracks of American railroads.

AIR BRAKES are introduced in 1869 by American George Westinghouse (1846–1914) to replace the guard's handbrake.

AN ELECTRIC TRAIN, made by Ernst Siemens (1816–1892) in Berlin, is driven by an engine taking a current from a live rail.

GEORGE STEPHENSON

1814 George Stephenson completes his first **LOCOMOTIVE**, used for hauling coal-mine wagons.

1823 Stephenson and his son Robert start a **LOCOMOTIVES FACTORY**.

1825 Stephenson builds the world's first passenger and freight **RAILROAD**.

1826 Despite opposition from canal owners and farmers, Stephenson wins approval to build a new railroad between Liverpool and Manchester. His locomotive *Rocket* is chosen to operate services on the line.

GEORGE
STEPHENSON

HARMLESS OR
POISONOUS?
(SEE 1861)

1860 The **WINCHESTER** repeating rifle is designed by B. Tyler Henry, who is employed by US manufacturer of guns and ammunition Oliver Fisher Winchester.
• **LINOLEUM** is made by the UK's Frederick Walton; the process involves cork dust, linseed oil, and resin, and it is the world's first practical floor covering that has been made synthetically.
• A revolutionary McKay **SHOE-SEWING** machine starts operation at William Porter & Sons' factory in Massachusetts; it chainstitches together the upper, lower, and inner parts of the shoe.

1861 A record 366 in (9,296 mm) of **RAIN** falls in one month in Cherrapunji, in northeastern India.
• The **PNEUMATIC DRILL**, invented by Germain Sommeiller of France, triples the work rate on the Mont Cenis rail tunnel project between France and Italy.
• Philadelphia stationer Hyman L. Lipman issues the first **POSTCARDS**, complete with an attractive border design.
• Pierre Michaux of France designs the "**BONESHAKER**" bicycle, the first to be propelled by pedals attached directly to the front wheel; its nickname comes from the steel tires and lack of springs.
• Henry Walter Bates, English naturalist and Amazon explorer, discovers that harmless edible creatures are protected from predators by resembling more deadly species; this phenomenon comes to be known as **BATESIAN MIMICRY**.
• French engineer Étienne Lenoir drives

a small car with a gas engine, a single cylinder, two-stroke system powered by exploding coal gas – the first practical **INTERNAL COMBUSTION ENGINE**.

1862 William Bruce Mumford is the first man to be hanged for **TREASON** in the US after ripping down the "old rag of the United States."
• The first modern **PLASTIC** is made from cellulose nitrate by British chemist Alexander Parkes.
• Captain Nathaniel Gordon is the first man to be hanged for **SLAVE-TRADING** in New York.
• The UK's James Glaisher ascends to a record height of 25,394 ft (7,740 m) in a **HYDROGEN BALLOON** over England.
• A law against **POLYGAMY** (being married to more than one person at the same time) is introduced in the US.
• An American hotel steam-cleans 100 articles of clothing in minutes, then dries them in a **CENTRIFUGAL MACHINE**.

1863 Midget Charles Sherwood Stratton, 40-inch "**GENERAL TOM THUMB**," marries 32-inch Mercy Lavinia Warren Bumpus in the US.
• **TNT**, the explosive with the full name of trinitrotoluene, is thought up by J. Wilbrand, a German chemist.
• The killing off of microorganisms by heating, later called **PASTEURIZATION**, is developed by France's Louis Pasteur.
• Russian writer Count Leo Nikolayevich **TOLSTOY** begins his epic philosophical novel *War and Peace* (to be completed in 1869), which follows the fates of three aristocratic families during the period when Napoleon invades Russia.
• French painter Édouard **MANET's** *Le déjeuner sur l'herbe* goes on display at the Louvre in Paris, but the shocking depiction of a naked woman with clothed male companions is deemed offensive and it has to be removed.
• The Confederate Army of the Southern States of America mourns the loss of one of its best generals, **THOMAS "STONEWALL" JACKSON**, who is shot in error by his own men just as they are achieving victory over the Union forces.

1864 **EQUESTRIANISM** becomes a sport when the first show-jumping competition is held by the Royal Dublin Society in Ireland.
• The **GENEVA CONVENTION** establishes rules for taking care of the sick and wounded in wartime.
• The first photograph using a **FLASH** is

taken of Sir Henry Roscoe in Manchester, England, where Professor Roscoe has just presented his paper on using the light of magnesium wire in photography.
• John Hanning Speke, British explorer who was the first European to find Lake Victoria in **AFRICA**, accidentally shoots himself while out partridge-shooting.

1865 Jules Verne's novel *From the Earth to the Moon* is published, telling the tale of four men who are fired from a huge **CANNON** on Cape Canaveral to the moon.
• Dr. Samuel Mudd is disgraced for life when he treats the broken leg of a stranger who turns out to be John Wilkes Boothe, **ASSASSIN** of President Abraham Lincoln; Mudd serves four years of a life sentence at Fort Jefferson in Key West, Florida before being pardoned.
• The first **TRAIN ROBBERY** in the US takes place in Ohio, when a train overturns near Cincinnati and thieves seize the opportunity to steal from it.
• British author **LEWIS CARROLL's** *Alice's Adventures in Wonderland* is published.
• **ANTISEPTIC** surgery is begun when Scotland's Joseph Lister applies carbolic acid to a compound wound; used during surgery, disinfectant will reduce deaths from a massive 45% down to just 15%.
• The **QUEENSBERRY RULES** for boxing with gloves are drawn up in the UK.
• A six-mile-long **OIL PIPELINE**, the first of its kind, is laid in Pennsylvania.
• The *Sultana* **PADDLE STEAMER**, built to take 376 passengers but carrying some 2,500 homeward-bound Union soldiers, explodes on the Mississippi River, killing about 1,450 people.
• The first known **PAY TOILETS** are installed in London, England; a penny a time is the charge for the convenience.
• Reinforced **CONCRETE** is first made in England, when concrete beams for us in house building are strengthened with wire rope; it will later make possible the erection of skyscrapers.
• The Stetson "**TEN-GALLON HAT**" is made for cowboys by the John B. Stetson Company in Philadelphia.

1866 Biologist Ernst Haeckel first uses the term **ECOLOGY** to describe environmental balance; he is the first German to promote Charles Darwin's theory of evolution.
• The first self-propelled **TORPEDO**, 14 ft (4 m) long with a warhead of 18 lb (8 kg) of explosive, is invented

1861! The Gatling machine gun is invented; it is cranked by hand and will fire up to 350 rounds per minute.

by British engineer Robert Whitehead.

•Quaker Richard **CADBURY** brings out Cadbury's Cocoa Essence, and the cocoa powder is the firm's biggest commercial success yet; the factory in Bournville, Birmingham, UK, has its own model town to accommodate the workers.

•J. Ousterhoudt of New York brings out food cans opened by **KEYS**.

•The laying of the Atlantic **TELEGRAPH CABLE** between the US and UK, masterminded by American Cyrus Field, is successfully completed.

•The explosive **DYNAMITE** is invented by Swedish chemist Alfred Nobel.

1867 The first **BELMONT STAKES** is run over a 1.5-mi (2.4-km) course at Belmont Park, New York; it becomes one of the most important horse races in America.

•American Alphonso Dabb patents his invention of **BARBED WIRE** for fencing.

•Switzerland's Henri Nestlé makes evaporated **MILK POWDER** and markets it successfully as a baby product.

•American Christopher Sholes comes up with a basic design for a **TYPEWRITER**; the Remington Model I will be the first commercially viable typewriter.

•**DIAMONDS** are discovered near the Orange River in Cape Province, South Africa, triggering a rush to the area.

•**FANNY ADAMS** is murdered and her body cut into tiny pieces; Britain's Royal Navy, with grim humor, adopts her name to refer to a ration of canned meat.

1868 In one of the first **ENDOSCOPIES**, a sword swallower has an inflexible tube passed into his stomach by German physician Adolf Kussmaul, who sees nothing because the tube is not lit well enough.

•The old game of shuttlecock is introduced to society when it is played at a weekend party at Badminton Hall, Gloucestershire, home to England's Duke of Beaufort; from now on the game will be known as **BADMINTON**.

•An **ELEVATED STREET RAILROAD**, named the "El," is constructed by Charles T. Harvey in New York.

•The British Post Office sanctions the appointment of three **OFFICIAL CATS** on a wage of one shilling (about 33 cents) a week between them; cats have been on the payroll ever since.

•The skeleton of an ancient inhabitant of Europe, the **CRO-MAGNON** man of the Upper Paleolithic age, is found by France's Louis Lartet.

QUEEN VICTORIA'S PUBLIC ROOM, DECORATED TO HER MAJESTY'S TASTE (SEE 1869)

1869 QUEEN VICTORIA boosts the popularity of the railroads with her lavish furnishings on the Royal Train. She chooses maple wood for the furniture and white-quilted silk for the ceiling of her public room.

•The first **TRANSAMERICAN RAILROAD** is completed after five years, when construction workers who started at opposite ends of the track meet in Utah.

•France's first Paris-to-Rouen velocipede race is won by British-born Dr. James Moore on an early **BICYCLE**.

•Francis Peters and George Clem of Cincinnati, Ohio, patent their **ROTATING TOILET SEAT**, to prevent people from standing on the seat.

•Russian chemist Dmitri Mendeleyev states that "the properties of the elements are in periodic dependence upon their atomic weights," and draws up the **PERIODIC TABLE** of the elements.

•Henry John **HEINZ** and L. C. Noble found H. J. Heinz & Company in the US. They sell clear bottles of processed horseradish to rival the green bottles of their competitors, which disguise that the contents are bulked out with turnip.

•France's Hippolyte Mège-Mouriès develops **MARGARINE** as an alternative to butter, which is in short supply; he makes it from pulverized beef suet, cow's udder, and warm milk.

•The game of soccer is brought to the water in England when a new game of **WATER POLO** is invented.

•The **SUEZ CANAL** is completed, allowing ships to sail from the Mediterranean to the Far East; to celebrate this feat, Italian composer Giuseppe Verdi's new opera *Aïda* is performed in Cairo, Egypt.

•England's Dante Gabriel **ROSSETTI** reopens his wife's coffin to retrieve his poems buried with her seven years ago.

•The first cog or "rack-and-pinion" railway opens on the slopes of Mt. Washington, USA. The locomotive has a gear wheel that meshes with a toothed rack between the rails so it does not slip.

THEN AND NOW

1864 Founded by Jean Henri Dunant of Switzerland to eliminate unnecessary suffering on the battlefields, the Red Cross is awarded neutrality by the Geneva Convention to tend the wounded and sick during wartime. **1901** Dunant receives the first Nobel Peace Prize for founding the International Red Cross.

EXTRA EXTRA! The Rev. Etham Smith of Poultney, Vermont, declares that the world will end, in 1866.

91

1870 Britain's first all-metal bicycle goes into mass production; it is called the Ariel Ordinary bicycle, or **PENNY-FARTHING**.
• During the Prussian army's Siege of Paris, France, diners eat horses, cats, dogs, rats, and even Castor and Pollux, the two **ELEPHANTS** in the Paris Zoo.
• Balls of **CHEWING GUM**, made from chicle, the dried sap of the sapodilla tree, are sold for a penny each at a drugstore in New Jersey.
• Austrian engineer Siegfried Marcus drives his **GAS**-powered car through Vienna; the police ban him from driving because of the noise of his invention.
• Jules Léotard, famous French trapeze artist, dies of smallpox; he is remembered for inventing the **LEOTARD**.
• US inventor Thomas Edison develops a **TICKER-TAPE** machine, to provide stock market information; later, New York "ticker-tape" parades will shower famous heroes with confetti-like paper tape.
• America's modern **CAN OPENER**, invented by William W. Lyman, scores an immediate hit; it has survived with only one notable modification to date: the introduction, in 1925, of a serrated "feed" wheel.

THEN AND NOW

1877 The first Lawn Tennis Championships (comprising just the Gentlemen's Singles) are held at The All-England Croquet and Lawn Tennis Club in Wimbledon, England. The Wimbledon Championships become one of the four major tennis tournaments known as the "Grand Slam."
1969 During the first-round match of the men's singles, US players R. A. Gonzales and C. M. Pasarell play a record-breaking total of 112 games.

1871 When **FIRE** breaks out in the Shanghai Theater in China, 900 people perish in one of the worst such incidents in history.
• Harrison Weir, an artist noted for his animal paintings, organizes the first-ever **CAT SHOW** in London, England.
• A steam-powered industrial **VACUUM CLEANER** is invented in the US.
• The world's first **WIND TUNNEL** is constructed in Britain.
• A **FOREST FIRE** in Wisconsin claims 2,682 lives.

1872 A cable-drawn **MONORAIL** is designed for transporting people at the Lyons Exposition in France.
• **WOMEN'S RIGHTS** protestors are arrested in Rochester, New York, when they try to vote in the November elections.
• At age 15, Milton **HERSHEY** becomes an apprentice in a candy store in Pennsylvania; in the 20th century, his Hershey Chocolate Corporation will have the world's largest chocolate plant.

ELEPHANTS ARE OFFERED A LA CARTE IN PARIS (SEE 1870)

• America's George Brayton builds a two-stroke, gas-powered **INTERNAL COMBUSTION ENGINE**.

1873 To stop the large number of injuries to cyclists in downhill accidents, British cyclist John Keen invents bicycle **BRAKES**.
• Scottish missionary **DR. DAVID LIVINGSTONE** dies in Africa; his body is taken to England, but his heart is buried in Africa.
• Belgian engineer Zenobe Gramme demonstrates that his electric dynamo can convert mechanical energy, produced by water or steam, into electricity; his design works equally well in reverse, converting electrical current into mechanical energy. Thus he create the first efficient **ELECTRIC MOTOR**.
• A **FIRE ALARM** is invented; it has a flashing light and a bell set off by significant rises in room temperature.
• France's Frédéric Kastner invents the **PYROPHONE**, a musical instrument that is played by applying flames to glass tubes of various lengths.
• Norwegian bacteriologist Armauer Hansen discovers the **LEPROSY** bacillus; from then on, it is known medically as Hansen's Disease.

1874 Britain's Dr. Percy invents **ABSORBENT COTTON** to filter the air in London's Houses of Parliament.
• Joseph F. Glidden of Illinois receives the first of his several patents for **BARBED WIRE**.
• Rugby is blended with soccer, in a game between Harvard University (Massachusetts) and McGill University (Montreal), when the visiting Canadians introduce running with the ball. In the first half the game is played by Harvard's rules, in the second by McGill's; the Americans are impressed by the idea of running with the ball, and the beginnings of modern **FOOTBALL**, as it will be played in the US, are established.
• US physician Andrew Still develops **OSTEOPATHY**; he believes that illness can be cured by spinal massage – the body will naturally heal itself if the spine is healthy and able to circulate its own curative fluids.
• Dichloro-diphenyl-trichloroethane, or **DDT**, is discovered by Austrian chemist Othmar Ziedler; it will become the world's most widely used insecticide.

1875 French aeronaut Gaston Tissandier is the sole survivor when *Zenith*, a coal gas-fueled balloon, makes a record-breaking ascent to 27,593 feet; the flight ends in tragedy.
• England's Captain Matthew Webb is the first person to **SWIM** the English Channel, crossing it in 21 hrs 45 min.
• George F. Green of Michigan patents the electric **DENTAL DRILL**.
• English illusionist John N. Maskelyne exhibits his windup robot, **PSYCHO**, in London; it can nod, shake hands, smoke, perform tricks, and even play cards.
• **MEASLES** wipes out a third of Fiji's population; 40,000 die when their king brings back the disease from Australia.
• Mark Twain (real name Samuel Langhorne Clemens) publishes his exciting tale, *The Adventures of Tom Sawyer*; Clemens's pseudonym, adopted during the Civil War, means being "two fathoms deep."
• The All-England Croquet Club builds the first **TENNIS COURTS** at Wimbledon.
• Fishermen enjoy the delights of canned **BAKED BEANS**, specially prepared for them to eat at sea, by the Burnham & Morrill Company, Portland, Maine.
• One of the world's greatest storytellers, Danish children's author **HANS CHRISTIAN ANDERSEN**, dies.
• **SNOOKER**, a type of pool, is first played in Jubbulpore, India, when the British game of Black Ball is adapted by adding more colored balls.

1876 Scottish-American speech therapist Alexander Graham Bell patents the **TELEPHONE** while looking for a way of helping deaf children to talk.
• H. J. Lawson builds a "safety" **BICYCLE**, which has two wheels of equal size and a chain to transmit the power of the pedals to the rear wheel.
• The **CARPET SWEEPER** is invented by Melville R. Bissell, china shop proprietor in Michigan, for clearing up straw packing in which the china is delivered.
• US inventor Elisha Gray is beaten by Bell when he tries to patent his own telephone; undaunted, he invents the "telautograph," an early **FAX MACHINE**.
• General **CUSTER'S LAST STAND** occurs at the Battle of Little Big Horn, Montana, when he and his Cavalry are wiped out by the Sioux.
• Bankrupted by a failed crop deal, American Henry John Heinz relaunches his business with the manufacture of bottled tomato **KETCHUP**.

• English politician Sir Samuel **PLIMSOLL** introduces the "Plimsoll line" (legal load line for international freighters); the canvas shoes, later known as plimsolls (sneakers in the US), resemble the Plimsoll line in the way that the upper part of the shoe is joined to the sole.

1877 The first **WIMBLEDON** tennis championships are held in Wimbledon, England. The tournament continues to take place in June each year, and has become the world's longest-running tennis event.
• The US's Charles Cuttris and Jerome Redding, and, separately, Germany's Ernst Werner von Siemens develop the dynamic **MICROPHONE**.
• US astronomer Asaph Hall discovers Phobos and Deimos, moons of **MARS**.
• English-born Eadweard Muybridge produces the first successful **SEQUENCE** photographs when he records a trotting horse; he is said to achieve an exposure rate of a thousandth of a second.
• US physicist Thomas Alva Edison, who is deaf, invents the **PHONOGRAPH**; he shouts out the words of "Mary had a little lamb" down a tube as he turns the handle of his new invention, using a tinfoil cylinder to make the first-ever recording of the human voice.

1878 Henry Tate of London, England, begins production of **SUGAR CUBES** at his refinery.
• Robert A. Chesebrough applies the trademark **VASELINE** (from German "wasser" for "water," and Greek "elaion" for "olive oil") to the petroleum jelly which he first invented in 1859.
• Coal miners at Bernissart in Belgium discover the bones of 39 *Iguanodon* dinosaurs 1,056 ft (322 m) underground, where dinosaur corpses had fallen on one another in what was once marshland.
• America L. O. Colvin invents the **MILKING MACHINE**, a boon for dairy farmers everywhere.
• **CLEOPATRA'S NEEDLE**, a 68.5-ft (20.8-m)-high granite obelisk weighing 187 tons (190 tonnes), is erected on the Victoria Embankment in London, England, after being transported from Egypt in a specially designed iron pontoon; a time capsule buried beneath it contains four Bibles in different languages, morning newspapers, coins, photographs of 12 beautiful English women, and a railroad guide.
• America's Thomas Alva Edison invents the **MEGAPHONE**, to aid the deaf.

EDISON'S WALL-MOUNTED TELEPHONE (SEE 1879)

• English engineer James Wimshurst builds a static electricity **GENERATOR**.
• Sweden's Gustav de Lava invents the **CREAM SEPARATOR**; it takes over the old method of skimming cream by hand.

1879 US inventor Thomas Edison introduces the wall-mounted telephone, fitted with his own-design microphone and receiver.
• American saloon keeper James Ritty of Ohio patents the **CASH REGISTER**, as a solution to the thievery of his bartenders.
• Germany's Karl von Linde invents the first domestic **REFRIGERATOR**; steam-powered, it uses a cooling cycle of compressing and evaporating ammonia.
• On New Year's Eve, 3,000 people flock to see Thomas Edison's display of **ELECTRIC ILLUMINATIONS**, which he calls "the eighth wonder of the world."
• Benjamin B. Oppenheimer of Trenton, Tennessee, designs a new method of **FIRE ESCAPE**: jumping out of the window with a parachute attached to the head and wearing cushioned shoes.
• The rules for the modern sport of **TUG-OF-WAR** are laid down by the New York Athletic Club.
• The first roll of **PERFORATED TOILET PAPER** is produced in Britain by Walter Alcock, whose idea fails despite a ten-year fight to have it accepted by the stuffy Victorians – they find the subject too disgusting to be discussed.
• America's first **MILK BOTTLES** are made by a dairy in New York City.

EXTRA EXTRA! The last Falklands Island wolf is killed, in 1876.

93

1880 American inventor **THOMAS ALVA EDISON**'s electric lightbulb, which burns for about two days, is granted a patent in the US.
•The Lambert Pharmaceutical Company of St. Louis makes **LISTERINE**, the first mouthwash; it is named in honor of antiseptic pioneer Sir Joseph Lister.
•In the US, a **HEARING AID** is patented by Francis D. Clarke and M. G. Foster.
•The first chain-driven safety **BICYCLE** is designed by Thomas Shergold, a shoemaker from Gloucester, England.

WORK STARTS ON GAUDI'S DREAM CATHEDRAL, *SAGRADA FAMILIA* (SEE 1883)

One hundred years on and the building is still not finished

•Wabash, Indiana, is the first town to be illuminated by **ELECTRICITY**.

1881 Women are first allowed to **VOTE** in parliamentary elections on Britain's Isle of Man.
•American health food guru **W. K. KELLOGG** introduces Granola cereal.
•**TSAR ALEXANDER II**, Russia's ruler, is assassinated by Nihilist terrorists in St. Petersburg.
•French microbiologist Louis Pasteur develops an **ANTHRAX VACCINE**.
•Ebenezer Burr and William Thomas Scott, from London, England, patent the first **ELECTRIC FLASHLIGHT**, a portable lamp powered by a wet-cell battery.

1882 **JUDO** is invented in Japan by Dr. Jigoro Kano.
•The first electrically lit **CHRISTMAS TREE** is put up by Edward H. Johnson, an associate of Thomas Edison.

•An early **FUNGICIDE**, which will prove invaluable to the French vineyards, is discovered by Professor Millardet of Bordeaux University when he notices that mildew is held off by spraying grapes with copper sulfate.
•**JESSE JAMES**, a notorious outlaw, is shot in the back for reward money by fellow gang member Robert Ford at Saint Joseph, Missouri.
•Louis Pasteur develops another vaccine, this time for **RABIES**.

1883 The first public **ELECTRIC TRAINS** are opened; they are the Volk's Electric Railway at Brighton in England and the Giant's Causeway Railway in Northern Ireland.
•In Wisconsin, Anglo-American inventor William Horlick introduces malted milk, later known as **HORLICK'S**.
•Work starts on the **SAGRADA FAMILIA**, a cathedral designed by Antonio Gaudi in Barcelona, Spain; the building is still under construction today.
•UK's Joseph Swan invents a **RAYON FILAMENT** for his electric lightbulb.
•**BROOKLYN BRIDGE** is completed in New York; some 20 workmen have been killed during its construction.
•Mark Twain's *Life on the Mississippi* is the first-ever **TYPEWRITTEN** book.
•The **GARBAGE PAIL** is invented by Paris Prefect of Police Eugène Poubelle.

• The loudest noise ever known to man is heard 3,000 miles away when the volcanic island of **KRAKATOA** explodes; the resulting tidal waves kill 36,000 people on Java and Sumatra.

• **STANDARD TIME ZONES** (Eastern, Central, Mountain, and Pacific) are established in the US.

• Work starts on the Home Insurance Building in Chicago; it is the first true "**SKYSCRAPER**."

1884 Lewis E. Waterman patents the **FOUNTAIN PEN**.

• The first photograph of **LIGHTNING** is taken by W. C. Gurley in Ohio.

• The first **ROLLER-COASTER**, the Switchback, is opened at Luna Park in New York's Coney Island.

• The US's first commercial **ELECTRIC STREETCAR** opens in Cleveland, Ohio.

• Inspired by the cash prize offered by New York newspapers for an invention that will speed up the process of setting printing type, Ottmar Mergenthaler introduces **HOT METAL TYPE**.

1885 The **STATUE OF LIBERTY** arrives in New York City, a gift from France to commemorate the US's 100th year of independence; the 252-ton (229-tonne), 151-ft (46-m) statue is set on a 155-ft (47-m) granite platform donated by the Americans and erected on Bedloe's (later Liberty) Island.

• British General Charles George Gordon is speared to death in the **SUDAN**.

• **SODA CRACKERS** are first made by William Jacob of Dublin, Ireland.

• Nikola Tesla of the US invents the **INDUCTION MOTOR**, a new type of electric motor working on principles of electromagnetic induction discovered by Faraday; today, induction motors used in industry account for some 95% of the total output of electric motors.

• The Washington Monument is completed; at 585 ft (178 m) high, it is the world's tallest **STONE MONUMENT**.

• **SALMONELLA** (a bacteria causing food poisoning) is named after US scientist Daniel Elmer Salmon.

• Austrian physician Sigmund Freud begins **PSYCHOANALYSIS** with the publication of *Studien über Hysterie*.

• The first **SUNGLASSES** go on sale in Philadelphia, Pennsylvania.

• Gottlieb Daimler and Wilhelm Maybach build the first **MOTORCYCLE** with twist-grip handlebar accelerator, in Germany.

• The first **SELF-SERVICE CAFETERIA** in the US opens in New York.

• The first US **APPENDECTOMY** is performed in Iowa.

1886 Dutch physician Christiaan Eijkman conducts a study into **BERI-BERI**, a disease currently wiping out many Indonesians, and finds the lack of an essential nutrient (later called thiamine, vitamin B_1) is the root cause.

• Scottish novelist Robert Louis Stevenson writes the horror story, *Dr. Jekyll and Mr. Hyde*.

• The first **COCA-COLA**, made by the US's John S. Pemberton, goes on sale.

• The Canadian Pacific Railway, running from Montreal to Vancouver, the first **TRANS-CANADA RAILWAY**, is completed.

• Chemist Clemens Alexander Winkler names his new discovery, the element **GERMANIUM**, after his country.

• England's Dan Albone invents the **TANDEM BICYCLE** and six years later the Ivel farm tractor.

1887 **ESPERANTO**, an artificial language, is invented in Poland.

• The first **FEMALE TYPISTS** start work at Britain's Inland Revenue Office.

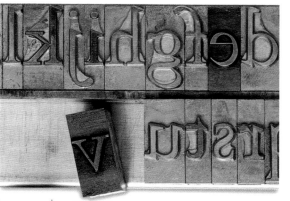

COLD METAL TYPE, WHICH NEEDS TO BE SET BY HAND, GOES OUT OF FASHION (SEE 1884)

• Glass **CONTACT LENSES** are invented by Switzerland's Dr. Eugen A. Frick.

• The **GRAMOPHONE** is invented by Emile Berliner in the US.

• The first **MOTOR RACE**, organized by the cycling journal *La Vélocipède*, is held along the Seine in Paris, France.

1888 George Eastman, American photographic genius, patents the **KODAK CAMERA**, the first camera to use flexible film.

• Scottish-born veterinary surgeon Dr. John Boyd Dunlop makes the first rubber **AIR-FILLED TIRES**.

• American Marvin Chester Stone invents the waxed paper **DRINKING STRAW**.

• The first **ELECTRIC CAR**, a battery-powered tricycle, is built in the US.

• The first **SEISMOGRAPH** (an instrument detecting and recording earthquakes) is demonstrated at the Lick Observatory, California.

• The **REVOLVING DOOR** is patented by Theophilus Van Kannel of Pennsylvania.

1889 The dish **CHOP-SUEY** is first created in San Francisco.

• France introduces the first **BABY INCUBATOR**.

• Gustave Eiffel builds the **EIFFEL TOWER** for the Paris Exposition in France.

• The first electric **ELEVATOR** is designed in the US by the Otis Co.

• **TABLE TENNIS** is played by James Gibb, an English engineer and athlete.

• The **ELECTRIC DRILL** is patented by Arthur Arnot of Melbourne, Australia.

• William Gray of Connecticut patents the coin-operated **PHONE BOX**.

• The first **JUKEBOX** is installed in a San Francisco hotel, the Palais Royal.

THEN AND NOW

1888 The first disk record player, playing music reproduced from a master disk, is invented by Emile Berliner in the US.

1925 The first electronically recorded disk is released by the US's Victor Talking Machine Company; this new electronic method makes it possible to record entire orchestral works.

1890
The first **AMPHIBIOUS AUTOMOBILE** is created by Monsieur Ardidékeon in France.
•An **AIR HAMMER** is invented by Charles Brady King of Michigan.
•Scotland's Forth Rail Bridge is opened; it is a **CANTILEVER BRIDGE** designed by English engineer Sir Benjamin Baker.
•William Kemmler, alias John Hart, axe murderer, becomes the first criminal to be **ELECTROCUTED**, in New York.

1891
The US's shortest **RAIL TUNNEL** is 30 ft (9 m) long, on the Louisville-to-Nashville Railroad.
•Thomas Edison and William Dickson, invent the kinetograph camera, an early version of **MOVING PICTURES**.
•Canadian minister and physical education teacher Dr. James A. Naismith invents **BASKETBALL** at the International YMCA College in Massachusetts.
•The **ZIPPER** is invented by Whitcomb L. Judson for a dancer in Chicago.
•Marcellus Berry of American Express invents the modern **TRAVELER'S CHECK**; his employer's son, William Fargo, is the first person to cash one for the sum of $50, in Leipzig, Germany.

1892
An electric **ESCALATOR** is built in New York.
•Russian biologist Dmitri Ivanovsky proves the existence of **VIRUSES**.
•The **DIESEL ENGINE**, running on cheaper fuel than gas, is built and patented by Germany's Rudolf Diesel.
•Alexander Grant creates the **DIGESTIVE BISCUIT** as an aid for indigestion.
•British physicist Sir James Dewar invents the **THERMOS FLASK**, as a way initially of insulating laboratory gases.
•A. Kwiatkowski of Germany applies for a patent for a bizarre coffin to prevent **PREMATURE BURIAL**. If the occupant should happen to wake up, a chimney sweep's brush shoots up a tube, attracting the attention of passers-by.

1893
The great Russian composer Peter Ilyich **TCHAIKOVSKY** dies of cholera.
•What will become *Happy Birthday to You* is written by sisters Mildred and Patty Hill from Kentucky; it begins as a song to start the school day.
•Canadian Governor-General Lord Stanley of Preston makes the first presentation of the **STANLEY CUP**, which will be competed for by Canadian ice hockey teams until the present day.
•**SHREDDED WHEAT** breakfast cereal is invented by a lawyer in Colorado.

1894
The world's first-ever car **RALLY** is run in France.
•Drought and famine lead to a major outbreak of **PLAGUE** in China and Hong Kong, and 100,000 people perish.
•An underwater vehicle called the *Argonaut Junior* is built in New York; it is powered by a hand crank and is taken to a depth of 20 ft (6 m).
•**ARGON** (Greek for "lazy"), an inert gas, is discovered in the air by Britain's Sir William Ramsay and Lord John William Rayleigh through spectroscopic analysis.
•Paul Nipkow of Germany comes up with the first idea for **TELEVISION**, when he suggests that a revolving disk with a spiral of holes might be used to scan an illuminated image.

•Irish-Italian Guglielmo Marconi, the pioneer of practical radio transmission, begins experiments with **WIRELESS TELEGRAPH MESSAGES** and next year will succeed in sending a message to his brother Alfonso, situated on the other side of a hill from him.
•Percival Lowell, American astronomer, founds the **FLAGSTAFF OBSERVATORY** in Arizona, to study the planet Mars.

1895
John Wesley Hardin, American **GUNFIGHTER**, is shot in the back of the head while playing poker in El Paso, Texas.
•Daniel D. Palmer, a grocer from Iowa, invents **CHIROPRACTIC**, a therapy for treating ailments by spinal manipulation.
•The **SOUSAPHONE**, a deep-sounding, tubalike instrument, is invented by John Sousa, US conductor and composer.
•The Lumière brothers Auguste and Louis open their **CINEMATOGRAPH** in France, and enthralled audiences watch lifelike moving pictures on a screen.
•Medical diagnostic techniques take a huge leap forward with the discovery of **X RAYS** by German physicist Wilhelm Conrad Roentgen.
•The Michelin brothers enter a Peugeot car, the first four-wheeled vehicle with **AIR-FILLED** tires, in a race in France.
•**HELIUM**, a colorless inert gas, is isolated by England's Sir William Ramsey and separately by P. T. Cleve and N. A. Langlet in Uppsala, Sweden.
•The game of **VOLLEYBALL** is devised by William George Morgan at the Young Men's Christian Association in Holyoke, Massachusetts.

1896
A STEAMSHIP ON WHEELS is launched in France.
•The world's **SHORTEST** war, between Britain and Zanzibar, lasts 38 minutes.
•Traveling on New York's Third Avenue train, American Henry J. Heinz sees a sign advertising "21 Styles" of shoes; he adapts it as his slogan, "**57 VARIETIES**."
•The **NOBEL PRIZE** is established when Swedish scientist Alfred Bernhard Nobel dies; he leaves a substantial trust fund to award prizes for excellence in physics, chemistry, medicine, international peace, literature, and, later, economics.
•The first modern **OLYMPIC GAMES** are staged at Athens in Greece.
•The first **ARMORED CAR** is built by American-born E. J. Pennington in England; the 16-horse-power, four-seater car comes complete with steel armor and two machine guns.

ARGONAUT JUNIOR EXPLORES THE SEABED (SEE 1894)

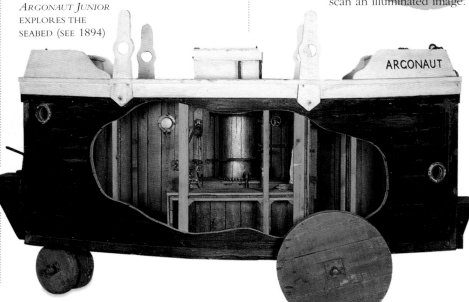

- England's Brian Gamlin invents a new numbering system for **DARTS**.
- The first **DIAL TELEPHONES** come into operation at Milwaukee City Hall.
- Italian-born Italo Marcioni brings the **ICE CREAM CONE** to America.

1897
Irish author Bram Stoker's *Dracula*, a Gothic horror novel inspired by the legendary 15th-century Prince **VLAD THE IMPALER**, is sold wrapped in brown paper.
- The first motorist convicted of **DRUNKEN DRIVING** in Britain is taxi driver, George Smith, who is fined £1.
- The Great Assam Earthquake spares lives but sends **SHOCK WAVES** through an area the size of Europe; it causes widespread nausea and Earth's crust rises and falls some 20 in (51 cm).
- A **SHOWER** driven by pedal power, the *Vélo-douche*, is exhibited at the Paris Bicycle Exhibition in France.
- The Boston Marathon, the world's oldest annual **MARATHON**, is run by 15 competitors and won by John J. McDermott of the Pastime Athletic Club in New York City.
- The first **WILDLIFE PARK**, the Umfolozi Game Park, is founded in South Africa.
- English art teacher William Harbutt concocts **PLASTICINE**, as a solution to students' problems with dried-out clay; he uses a garden roller to press it flat.
- Georg Lüger of Austria invents a new **AUTOMATIC PISTOL** for the Swiss army.
- Fifteen-year old Walter Lines of London, England, invents the **SCOOTER**.

1898
British physician Sir Ronald Ross discovers that the female mosquito is responsible for the transmission of **MALARIA**; previously it had been thought that the disease was caused by bad smells, the word "malaria" meaning "bad airs."
- US astronomer William Pickering discovers **PHOEBE**, a satellite of Saturn.
- British author H. G. Wells's science fiction classic, *The War of the Worlds*, is published; it helps maintain the belief that there is life on the planet Mars.
- France's Madame Laumaille is the **FIRST WOMAN TO TAKE PART IN A CAR RACE**; she comes in fourth in the run from Marseilles to Nice, on her De Dion tricycle, a kind of three-wheeled car.
- After experimenting for several years at their health resort at Battle Creek, Michigan, brothers Will Keith and Dr. John Harvey Kellogg develop a new cereal called **CORNFLAKES**.

THEN AND NOW

1899 The first American driver arrested for speeding is Jacob German, who is prosecuted for performing the "breakneck speed" of 12 mph (19 km/h) in an electric taxi along Lexington Avenue in New York City.
1997 At the US's Black Rock Desert, Englishman Andy Green driving *Thrust SSC* becomes the first person to break the sound barrier in a land vehicle, reaching a speed of 763.04 mph (1,227.99 km/h).

- The *Holland* submarine is launched at Elizabeth, New Jersey, the first-ever submarine to be powered by internal combustion engines on the water surface and electric motors for submarine travel; it is built by John Philip Holland, father of the modern **SUBMARINE**, whose basic design will be followed until the advent of nuclear power.
- **RADIUM**, a soft silvery radioactive metallic element, is discovered by Pierre Curie and Marie Curie in Paris, France.
- Denmark's Valdemar Poulsen, age 20, invents the first **TAPE RECORDER**, but his demonstration of the machine at the Paris Exhibition in France does not receive an enthusiastic response.
- The first **WORLD SPEED RECORD**, the forerunner to the Land Speed Record, is set by France's Comte Gaston de Chasseloup-Laubat; he manages to take his Jeantaud electric car up to a speed of 39.24 mph (62.78 km/h).
- Neon and krypton, colorless, odorless gases obtained from liquid air, are discovered by Sir William Ramsay and M. W. Travers in London, England; **NEON** will be used in decorative lighting displays.

1899
ASPIRIN is patented and sold in powder form, by the German Bayer company; its usefulness in pain relief was rediscovered by an employee, chemist Felix Hoffman, who treats his father's rheumatism with it; its name comes from "a" for acetyl, "spir" from the Latin for meadowsweet flower, and "in" which was a popular ending for drug names.

- Martha M. Place is the first woman to be electrocuted, at **SING SING** prison in the state of New York, for murder.
- US writers Ernest Hemingway and Hart Crane are born on the same day. Both will commit **SUICIDE**: Crane falls from a ship and Hemingway shoots himself.
- US dentist Dr. George F. Grant patents the **GOLF TEE**; an avid golfer, he has the idea of a wooden peg with an indented top for the golf ball to balance on, instead of dirtying his hands shaping a heap of earth or sand, as other golfers or their caddies do until his invention catches on.
- Germany's Herr Bunse invents a life-saving trunk, as a **PORTABLE FIRE ESCAPE**, with a rope attached to the window frame by which the suitcase, with escapee inside, is lowered to safety.
- Camile Jenatzy establishes a new **LAND SPEED RECORD** of 65.79 mph (105.26 km/h).

The first sousaphone is heard

THE SOUSAPHONE
JOINS THE BAND
(SEE 1895)

1892! The first stories about Sherlock Holmes, the fictional detective created by Sir Arthur Conan Doyle, are published.

The 20th-century Sydney Opera House symbolizes modern Australia

THE AGE OF TECHNOLOGY

At the start of the 20th century, European empires dominate the globe. However, conflicts within Europe cause two world wars, more terrible than any before. After World War II the empires gradually break up, giving rise to independent nations in Africa, Asia, and the Pacific. Tensions develop between the superpowers of the US and the Soviet Union, until the Soviet bloc breaks up in the 1980s. As the century ends, incredible advances in communications constantly change the world – yet overpopulation and limited resources cause concern for the future.

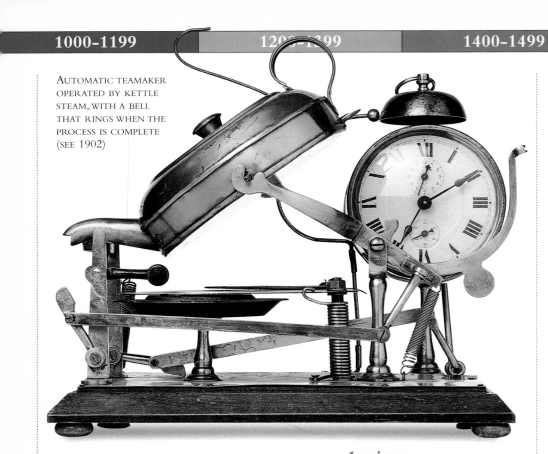

AUTOMATIC TEAMAKER OPERATED BY KETTLE STEAM, WITH A BELL THAT RINGS WHEN THE PROCESS IS COMPLETE (SEE 1902)

Early morning tea is now being served

1900 Germany's Count Ferdinand von **ZEPPELIN** flies his first airship, LZ1, taking five passengers on a 20-minute journey.
• The **DAVIS CUP** is contributed by Dwight F. Davis, American tennis player, and is competed for by national teams.
• The first practical **RADIO TELEPHONE** is invented in the US.
• Frank Brownell's **BROWNIE** camera makes photography accessible to all.

1901 The first **TRANSATLANTIC WIRELESS** message is sent from England to Newfoundland, Canada.
• Englishman Frank Hornby patents **MECCANO**, a kit for children that allows them to explore construction.
• Austrian scientist Karl Landsteiner's discovery of three blood groups, A, B, and C (later O), will save many lives by allowing safer **BLOOD TRANSFUSIONS**.
• The world's first **MULTISTORY** garage is erected in London, England.

1902 American Willis Carrier develops a system of **AIR CONDITIONING**, which works by circulating air through cold water. This method is still in use today.

• America's **WRIGHT BROTHERS** construct their third glider; it is a huge success and will fly nearly 1,000 times.
• French novelist Emile **ZOLA** dies from carbon monoxide poisoning.
• A spring-wound alarm clock **TEAMAKER** is invented in England.
• Inspired by the performing bears seen at a traveling circus, German toymaker Margarete Steiff makes the first **TEDDY** bear, with movable arms and legs.

1903 Orville Wright is the first man to fly a heavier-than-air, powered **AIRCRAFT**; he remains airborne for some 12 seconds, traveling a distance of 120 ft (36.5 m) in the *Flyer* built by him and his brother Wilbur.
• Britain's Emmeline **PANKHURST** starts the Women's Social and Political Union, which becomes increasingly militant in its Votes for Women campaign.
• The **ELECTROCARDIOGRAPH** (ECG), which measures the heart's electrical activity, is invented by Dutch physiologist Willem Einthoven.
• French chimney sweep Maurice Garin wins the first **TOUR DE FRANCE** bicycle race. He is one of 21 riders to complete the 1,510-mile (2,428-km) course.

• Paul **GAUGUIN**, the French painter who developed a new "savage" style in art, dies in the Marquesas Islands.
• The first baseball **WORLD SERIES** is won by the Boston Red Sox.

1904 A new land speed record is set by **HENRY FORD** of the Ford Motor Company, who achieves a skidding speed of 91.37 mph (146.19 km/h), when he races his 16.7 liter car across a frozen lake.
• A **CATERPILLAR** (crawler tractor) is invented by America's Benjamin Holt.
• The first mass-produced double-sided phonograph **DISKS** are sold in Germany.
• The first **CRASH HELMET** is worn in an auto race at France's Parc des Princes.
• Charles D. Perrine discovers Himalia, a distant moon of **JUPITER**, and Elara, another satellite of Jupiter.
• The Waimangu **GEYSER** in New Zealand erupts to a record height of 1,509 ft (460 m).
• **REVOLUTION** stirs in Russia after the Bloody Sunday massacre at the Winter Palace in St. Petersburg.
• **BRASSO**, a liquid polish for cleaning metal, is offered for sale in Britain.
• The first real **HYDROFOIL** is invented by Enrico Forlanini of Italy.
• American **MILLIONAIRE** George A. Kessler throws a party at London's Savoy Hotel. He has the courtyard flooded and guests are seated in gondolas; an elephant brings in the birthday cake, but the swans that are supposed to swim among the diners are poisoned by blue dye in the water and float feet up.

1905 The first car **BUMPERS** are attached by Frederick R. Simms to his Simms-Welbeck cars.
• Albert **EINSTEIN** first proposes the General Theory of Relativity, which will offer a new system of mechanics.

CENTURY STATISTICS

World population, 1900: 6,000 million
Bookmark: Quotations from the Works of Mao Tse-tung, Chairman Mao's *Little Red Book*, which it was once compulsory for all Chinese people to own, and which sold an estimated 800 million copies.
Landmark: Built in 1997, the Petronas Towers in Kuala Lumpur, Malaysia boast 96 floors and soar to a world-record height of 452 m (1,482 ft).

CHINESE GOOSEBERRY
NAMED KIWI
(SEE 1906)

1906
American Lt. Frank Lahm wins the world's first international **BALLOON RACE**, taking off from Paris, France, bound for England.
•The **KIWI FRUIT**, or Chinese gooseberry, discovered in 1845, is brought to New Zealand from China. Local farmers are the first to cultivate it commercially in orchards; they later export the fruit, naming it after the national flightless bird, the kiwi.
•The Automatic Entertainer, the first successful preselecting **JUKE BOX** record player, is produced in the US.
•The land **SPEED RECORD** is broken by the *Rocket*, which hits 121.7 mph (194.51 km/h) at Daytona Beach, Florida.
•The world's first **CARTOON FILM**, by J. Stuart Blackton, features animated rolling of eyes and cigar-smoking.
•The wireless distress signal, Save Our Souls, is introduced; the letters **SOS** are chosen because they are the simplest to convey in Morse code, by three dots, three dashes, and three dots.

1907
A. F. Gaudron flies a huge hydrogen **BALLOON** 721 miles (1,160 km) across the North Sea from England to Lake Vänern in Sweden.
•**IN VITRO** cultivation is achieved by American Ross G. Harrison, who grows animal cells and tissues outside of their natural environment.
•The first untethered **HELICOPTER** flight is made in France by Paul Cornu, who achieves a height of 1 ft (0.30 m) and stays off the ground for 20 seconds.
•Color photography takes off after Louis and Auguste **LUMIÈRE**, French movie pioneers, develop the first successful three-color process.
•The **ELECTRIC SUCTION SWEEPER** is patented by an asthmatic American, James Murray Spangler, and sold to manufacturer William Henry Hoover.
•The first hand-operated car windshield **WIPERS** are introduced in France.
•Belgian-born Leo Baekeland invents **BAKELITE**, a heat-resistant rubber substitute that will revolutionize the pan handle and electric plug industries.
•**CHEMOTHERAPY** is developed by German bacteriologist Paul Ehrlich, who pioneers research into disease-curing chemicals that do not damage human cells.

1908
Lt. Thomas Selfridge, a passenger in an aircraft piloted by Orville Wright, becomes the first-ever victim of an **AIRPLANE CRASH**.
•**CELLOPHANE** is invented by Swiss chemist Jacques Brandenberger; "cello" is for "cellulose" from which it is made, and "phane" means "show through."
•The **GEIGER COUNTER** for measuring levels of nuclear radiation is designed by German physicist Hans Geiger.
•The disposable **PAPER CUP** is invented.
•The All Alaskan Sweepstake, the first official **SLED DOG RACE**, is held; it covers a distance of 408 miles (657 km).
•The first successful **FILTER COFFEE POT** is invented in Germany, when Mrs. Melitta Bentz of Germany places a circle of blotting paper between the two sections of the traditional brewing pot.

1909
US navy officer and Arctic explorer Robert Peary leads a team of men to the **NORTH POLE**; he is the first man to stand upon the icy northernmost point of the world.
•On a **SEA CROSSING** from Australia to England, the Blue Anchor Line's SS *Waratah* and its 211 passengers mysteriously vanish after making a stopover in Durban, South Africa.
•English Lord Brabazon straps a pig into a basket attached to his Short **BIPLANE**, with the sign, "I am the first pig to fly."

Men and husky dogs share the long haul in the race to the Pole

ROBERT PEARY REACHES
THE NORTH POLE (SEE 1909)

1910
The Paris Hippodrome in France holds the first international **ROLLER HOCKEY** tournament; an English team wins.
•**BATHROOM SCALES** are invented by the Jas Ravenol company in Germany.
•Vitamin B$_1$ is found in unpolished rice by Polish biochemist Casimir Funk; he introduces the word **VITAMINE**.
•American writer Mark **TWAIN** dies, believing his death is linked to the appearance of Halley's comet, which was previously seen at his birth.
•James Atkinson of Leeds, England, invents a spring-operated **MOUSETRAP**.
•The first **AIRPLANE** to take off from a ship is flown by American Eugene B. Ely from the USS *Birmingham*.

1911
Franz Richelet, Austrian **BIRDMAN**, falls to his death from the Eiffel Tower in Paris, France.
•Playwright and humorist William Schwenk **GILBERT** dies while rescuing a drowning woman; best known for creating operettas with his partner composer Sir Arthur Sullivan, Gilbert ended the partnership when they argued over the cost of a new carpet.
•Auto racing's first **INDIANAPOLIS 500** takes place in the US.
•Leonardo da Vinci's masterpiece, the *Mona Lisa*, is stolen from the **LOUVRE MUSEUM** in Paris, France, by an Italian waiter who simply strolls out of the museum with the painting under his arm; during its two-year absence, the *Mona Lisa* is copied by master forger Yves Chaudron, who produces six replicas and sells them at great profit.
•Ted "Kid" Lewis is the first boxer to make regular use of a **GUM SHIELD**.
•The first long-distance **MONTE CARLO** car rally takes place in France.

THE *TITANIC* GOES DOWN (SEE 1912)

•Britain's first railroad **ESCALATOR** is installed at Earl's Court in London, England. To demonstrate its safety, "Bumper" Harris, who has a wooden leg, is paid to walk up and down the escalator all day long; this stunt proves so successful that train passengers soon get off at the station just to take a ride on the new installation and then catch the next train to continue their journey.
•Roald Amundsen, Norwegian polar explorer, races his English rival, Robert Scott, to the **SOUTH POLE**. By starting his overland journey 60 miles (96 km) nearer to the Pole, Amundsen is first to reach his destination; he completes the round trip in just 99 days.
•British polar explorer **ROBERT SCOTT** and his companions die after reaching the South Pole; he had set out with 59 men, 3 motorized sleds, 19 ponies, and 34 sled dogs; as conditions worsened, the ponies were killed for food, the dogs were returned to the base camp, and a team of just five men completed the last stage of the journey.

1912
The world's longest-surviving **ROLLER COASTER**, the Scenic Railway, is opened at Luna Park in Melbourne, Australia.
•The world's largest and fastest ship of its time, the *Titanic*, sinks on her **MAIDEN VOYAGE** when it hits an iceberg off Newfoundland, Canada; of the 1,316 passengers and 891 crew, only 705 people survive, having been saved by the ship's lifeboats, of which there are not enough to carry everyone to safety. The event brings about an international agreement for ice patrols to be carried out between March and June every year, when shipping routes in the North Atlantic are most prone to icebergs.

1913
The first **CROSSWORD** puzzle, created by English-born Arthur Wynne, is published in the *New York World*.
•Determined to draw the government's attention to the growing demand of votes for women, **SUFFRAGETTE** Emily Davidson throws herself under the King's racehorse during the English Derby and is killed outright.
•The first pilot to **LOOP THE LOOP** is a Russian, Lt. Peter Nesterov, over Kiev.
•Britain's Harry Brearley invents **STAINLESS STEEL** in Sheffield, England.
•US scientists discover **VITAMIN A**, both at Yale University and at Wisconsin Agricultural Experiment Station.
•Swedish-American Gideon Sundback patents his first improved **ZIPPER**.

1914
Archduke Ferdinand, Austro-Hungarian heir to the Austrian throne, is assassinated at Sarajevo by Bosnian nationalists, triggering the start of **WORLD WAR I**.
•The **DODGE** brothers set up their Dodge car business in Detroit, Michigan, the first successful manufacture of all-steel cars.
•The **ALUMINUM FOIL** milk bottle top is produced in Sweden by Josef Jonsson.
•The first electric red and green **TRAFFIC LIGHTS** are installed in Cleveland, Ohio.
•Dr. Bunting renames his Sunburn Remedy **NOXZEMA** after one of his customers tells him that the cream has cured his eczema.
•A **BOXING** match held in London, England, between French champion Georges Carpentier and Britain's George Mitchell lasts a mere 95 seconds.
•The 50-mile (80-km) **PANAMA CANAL** between the Atlantic and Pacific Oceans is completed by the Americans.
•American astronomer Seth Nicholson discovers **SINOPE**, a satellite of Jupiter.
•Russia's capital since 1712, the port city of St. Petersburg, is renamed Petrograd; in 1918 the **CAPITAL** will be Moscow.
•The **LEICA** 35-mm film camera is invented by Germany's Oskar Barnack.
•The 761-ft (232-m), 55-story Woolworth Building in New York is the world's tallest building and the world's first **SKYSCRAPER**.

1915
A **POCKET BIBLE** saves the life of Private W. Hacket, who at Armentières, France, is hit by a bullet. It passes through from the back cover to the front without injuring him.

1910! The Avro Triplane, invented by British engineer Alliot V. Roe, flies for the first time.

•Edith Cavell, a Belgian **NURSE** working at a Red Cross hospital, is executed by a German firing squad for helping 200 Allied soldiers escape from captivity.
•German-US physicist Albert **EINSTEIN** presents his startling Special Theory of Relativity, which suggests that the universe is not infinite; his revolutionary style of thinking and use of mathematics helps to reshape contemporary views of space and time.

1916 Grigory **RASPUTIN**, the Russian "mad monk" who wins the favor of the Tsar's wife

•The **SUN** falls from the sky and plunges into a crowd, claim 70,000 people in Fatima, Portugal; a total eclipse of the sun is likely to be the true explanation.
•The first **ELECTRIC RAZOR** is patented by American Jacob Schick.
•A new island, **ANAK KRAKATAU** (which means child of Krakatau), emerges in Indonesia; it is a relic of the island of Krakatua which was blown apart by volcanic activity in 1883.

Total eclipse of the sun wreaks havoc!

THE DAY THE SUN FELL FROM THE SKY (SEE 1917)

but is hated by the public, is poisoned, stabbed, shot, and drowned.
•Clarence Saunders' Piggly Wiggly **SELF-SERVICE STORE** in Memphis, Tennessee, is the first store to do away with counter service; it is the forerunner of modern supermarkets.

1917 Prince Ras Tafari (later known as Haile Selassi I) becomes ruler of **ETHIOPIA**; he is regarded as the Messiah of the black race, and his name is given to the Rastafarian religion from the West Indies.
•America's Ford Motor Company begins manufacture of the **FORDSON**, the first mass-produced tractor.
•The **ROLLER TOWEL** is patented in the US by George Steiner of the American Linen Supply Company in Salt Lake City, Utah.

THEN AND NOW

1919 Britain observes the first two-minute silence in remembrance of the casualties of World War I; a red poppy becomes the symbol of the lives lost during war, recalling the poppy fields of Flanders where thousands of soldiers died.
1991 A folded, pinned red ribbon is adopted as symbol of support for the fight against AIDS.

•The **OCTOBER REVOLUTION** takes place in Russia on November 7, when the Bolsheviks seize the capital of St. Petersburg and overthrow capitalism.

1918 The **RED BARON**, Manfred von Richthofen, German air ace responsible for shooting down 80 Allied aircraft since 1916, is killed when hit by a single shot in the chest.
•US **MAGICIAN** Chung Ling-Soo is shot dead on stage in London, England, when a trick goes drastically wrong.
•Legendary American movie star **HUMPHREY BOGART** is hit in the face by a handcuffed prisoner while he is serving in the US Navy; his upper lip is almost ripped away by the blow, and from now on he will speak with a lisp.
•An **ELECTRIC CLOCK** is designed by Henry Ellis Warren in the US.
•**YUGOSLAVIA** becomes an independent nation, covering the areas of Serbia, Slovenia, Montenegro, Croatia, Dalmatia, and Bosnia-Herzegovina.
•The first commercially successful electric domestic **REFRIGERATOR**, the Kelvinator, is designed by Nathaniel Wales and manufactured in the US.
•The sport of **ORIENTEERING**, using maps and a compass to find one's way on a cross-country run, is invented by Major Ernst Killander of Sweden.
•The **POP-UP ELECTRIC TOASTER** is patented by Charles Strite in the US.

1919 Muslin **TEA BAGS** are made in San Francisco, California, for caterers; they take 16 years to become popular with the general public.

•Eleven people die in the US when a 50-ft (15-m) tall tank of **MOLASSES** bursts, sending a flood of over two million gallons of molasses down Boston's Commercial Street at 35 mph (56 km/h) in a wave of devastation some 15–30 ft (5–9 m) high.
•Britain's John Alcock and Arthur Whitten Brown make a historic **TRANSATLANTIC FLIGHT** in *Atlantic*, a specially modified, twin-engined Vickers Vimy bomber; they take off somewhat precariously from Newfoundland, Canada, and land in a bog at Clifden near Galway, Ireland.
• "Shoeless Joe" Jackson and seven other players for the Chicago White Sox baseball team are **BANNED FOR LIFE** under suspicion of having conspired to deliberately lose the World Series to the Cincinnati Reds; the famous words "Say it ain't so, Joe" are spoken to Jackson by a disappointed fan.
•Tired of being "owned" by the Hollywood film studios, actors Charles Chaplin, Douglas Fairbanks, Mary Pickford, and director D.W. Griffith set up the **UNITED ARTISTS** film company in the US to gain more independence.
•American comedian Harold **LLOYD** loses his right thumb and forefinger when what he had thought was a fake bomb explodes in his hands during a publicity shoot for *Haunted Spooks*.
•British-American Alexander Graham Bell designs a high-speed, cigar-shaped **HYDROFOIL** that breaks the world water speed record, the first hydrofoil to do so; it traveled at 70.86 mph (114.03 km/h).

EXTRA EXTRA! Incas, the last known Carolina parakeet, dies in the Cincinnati Zoo, in 1918.

103

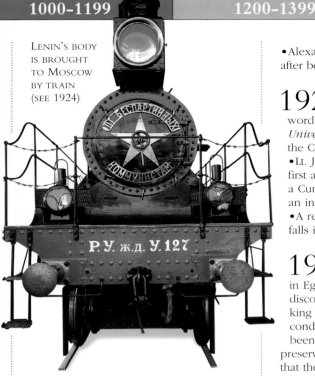

LENIN'S BODY IS BROUGHT TO MOSCOW BY TRAIN (SEE 1924)

Р.У. ж.д. У.127

1920 The first **PRIX DE L'ARC DE TRIOMPHE** is run at Longchamp, France; this popular horse race continues to be run every year on the first Sunday in October.

•**PROHIBITION** is introduced as an experiment in the US; the production and sale of strong drinks is forbidden, but illegal drinking carries on at places known as "speakeasies."

•**ESKIMO PIE**, the first chocolate-ice bar, is marketed by Christian K. Nelson, a candy store owner in the US; his product is inspired by a young boy who finds its difficult to choose between chocolate and ice cream.

•Alexander, King of Greece, dies after being bitten by his **PET MONKEY**.

1921 Czech playwright Karel Capek introduces the word **ROBOT** in his new play *Rossum's Universal Robots*; robot is derived from the Czech word *robota*, meaning work.

•Lt. John B. Macready carries out the first aerial **CROP-DUSTING** from a Curtiss JN6 light aircraft, to treat an insect-infested grove in Ohio.

•A record 76 in (1,870 mm) of **SNOW** falls in a day at Silver Lake, Colorado.

1922 After carrying out 30 years of archaeological surveys in Egypt, Englishman Howard Carter discovers the tomb of XVIII Dynasty king **TUTANKHAMUN**, in near-perfect condition; the mummified body had been surrounded by wines and preserved foods together with items that the king had used during his life, including clothing, toys, walking sticks, chariots, and weapons.

•The first advertisement to be heard on **RADIO** promotes apartments in Jackson Heights, New York.

•**WATERSKIING** is invented by 18-year old Ralph Samuelson of Minnesota; he first tries to use snow skis on water but finds more success with his own pinewood water skis, whose tips are curved by the steam from a boiler.

•**VITAMIN E** is discovered by Americans Herbert McLean Evans and K. S. Bishop.

•The first **AUTOMATIC DOORS** are installed on the Piccadilly subway in London, England.

1923 New Zealand's Johnnie Hoskins establishes **MOTORCYCLE SPEEDWAY** racing in New South Wales, Australia.

•Auto racing's first **LE MANS 24-HOUR RACE** is won by André Lagache and René Leonard at Sarthe, France.

•A cloud measuring 300 miles (500 km) long by 100 miles (150 km) wide and composed entirely of **LOCUSTS** destroys all vegetation in its path in Montana.

•Soccer's first Wembley **FA CUP FINAL**, in England, is won by Bolton, who beat West Ham before an official crowd of 126,047 (more get in without paying).

•The Russian-born "father of television," Vladimir Zworykin, invents the world's first **TELEVISION CAMERA** in the US.

•J. H. Fabre's *Social Life in the Insect World* claims that **PRAYING MANTIS** trap their victims by pretending to be ghosts.

•In Japan, 143,000 people die after an earthquake hits Tokyo and Yokohama during the midday meal; overturned household braziers (for grilling food) start a blaze that virtually destroys the cities and becomes known as the **GREAT TOKYO FIRE**.

•America's Clarence Birdseye is the first to mass-produce **FROZEN FOOD**, having observed on a trip to the Arctic that frozen fish could be stored for months and still be fresh when thawed.

TUTANKHAMUN'S MIDDLE MUMMY CASE HELD A SOLID GOLD INNER CASE (SEE 1922)

The tomb of 18-year-old king Tutankhamun is opened

EXTRA EXTRA! After careful studies of the Great Pyramid, Colonel J. Garner calculates that the world will end in 1920.

1924

More than 700,000 people come to pay their respects to the embalmed body of **LENIN** (born Vladimir Ilich Ulyanov), the leader of the Russian Revolution. His funeral train is preserved as a memorial to him and his decaying body undergoes constant secret revamping such that his hair becomes thicker than it was in the prime of life. His brain is later taken out and sliced into 34,000 segments for analysis.

• *Alice in Cartoonland* is the first cartoon film by **WALT DISNEY**; it features a live actress playing Alice in a world of drawings.

• Chanel No. 5 perfume is brought out on the fifth day of the fifth month by French fashion designer **COCO CHANEL**, whose lucky number is five.

• The world's first **HIGHWAY** opens in Italy, covering 13 miles (21 km) from Milan to Varese.

• Motorcycling's first scrambles race, or **MOTO-CROSS**, is held on a dirt circuit over rough terrain in Surrey, in the UK.

• An electric **WASHING MACHINE** with spin dryer is manufactured in New York by the Savage Arms Corporation.

1925

The Archbishop of Naples blames an earthquake at Amalfi, Italy, on the outrageous fashion for **SHORT SKIRTS**.

• Notorious gangster **AL CAPONE** takes over the Chicago bootlegging (liquor-smuggling) business; his empire covers gambling houses and dance halls.

• The first **MOTEL**, called the Motel Inn, opens in San Luis Obispo, California.

• The first **IN-FLIGHT MOVIE**, *The Lost World*, is shown on a continental flight from London, England.

1926

Rolex's "Oyster," the world's first **WATERPROOF WATCH**, is made in Switzerland.

• US magician **HARRY HOUDINI**, who boasted that he could survive a punch in the stomach, dies in Montreal, Canada, after a blow to the stomach from amateur boxer Joselyn Whitehead; Houdini was a talented escapologist, who had even managed to break free from ropes while contained inside a weighed-down sack and dropped into an ice-covered river.

• John Giola of New York dances the Charleston nonstop for a **RECORD-BREAKING** 22 hours and 30 minutes. Originally from Charleston, South Carolina, the dance involves twisting the knees in and out while swinging the heels outward.

• The **AEROSOL** is patented by Erik Rotheim, an engineer from Norway.

• The first liquid fuel **ROCKET** is fired into the atmosphere in Massachusetts by physicist Robert H. Goddard.

1927

The first American **TELEVISION** pictures of a moving object are transmitted by Charles Francis Jenkins.

• British chemist William Walker Hunter invents a tasty glucose drink to aid the recovery of his jaundiced daughter, and names it **LUCOZADE**.

• X rays taken of the wooden *Madonna and Child* in the style of Giovanni Pisano reveal 20th-century nails; the piece turns out to have been produced by the brilliant Italian forger Alceo Dossena, whose **FAKES** are displayed in the world's finest art collections.

• **ISADORA DUNCAN**, an American dancer who was famous for her distinctive style of performing barefoot and wearing long flowing fabrics, is strangled in Nice, France, when her scarf catches in one of the wheels of the Bugatti car in which she is a passenger.

• In a **FOOTBALL** match between two Kansas high schools, Haven records a 256-0 victory over Sylvia.

• American **CHARLES LINDBERGH** is the first to fly solo across the Atlantic, in his *Spirit of St. Louis* monoplane.

• Dialogue is finally heard at movies showing *The Jazz Singer*, the first **TALKIE**, or feature film synchronized with sound recorded on disks.

• The Roxy Theater opens in New York City; nicknamed "The Cathedral of Motion Pictures," it is the world's largest and most expensive **MOVIE THEATER**, boasting an audience capacity of 5,920.

• Using a pair of vacuum cleaners, American Philip Drinker of Harvard University constructs an **IRON LUNG**, a mechanical breathing apparatus.

1928

Spanish painter **SALVADOR DALI** goes to Paris, France, and joins the Surrealists, becoming one of the movement's principal members; Dali is also a pioneer of "Futurist" cooking, which offers such original dishes as mashed herrings and raspberry jam, mortadella sausage with nougat, pineapple with sardines, and cooked salami immersed in hot black coffee, flavored with Eau de Cologne.

• US animator Walt Disney waits for the arrival of synchronized sound with film before introducing his famous

THEN AND NOW

1926 Britain's John Logie Baird presents the first television set in London, England; it is constructed out of cardboard, cans, and knitting needles stuck together with glue and sealing wax.

1996 Equipment manufacturers Fujitsu and ICL combine the personal computer with the television to form the PC/TV, an all-in-one media system for the home.

character, **MICKEY MOUSE**, in a cartoon called *Steamboat Willie*.

• When British novelist **THOMAS HARDY** dies, his ashes are buried in Westminster Abbey, but his heart is said to have been devoured by his sister's cat.

• *White Shadows in the South Seas* is the first talking film in which Leo, the trademark lion of the **MGM** film company, is heard to roar; apart from Leo, there is music and sound effects such as breaking waves – but only one word of dialogue, "Hello."

• **ELASTOPLAST**, an adhesive bandage, is made by T. J. Smith & Nephew Ltd. at Hull, UK; the American version, Band-Aid, is produced by Johnson & Johnson.

• **VITAMIN C** is isolated from citrus fruits by Hungarian biochemist Albert von Nagyrapolt Szent-Györgyi at the University of Cambridge in the UK.

1929

US research technician Richard Drew invents "**SCOTCH**"-brand adhesive tape, which is first tested by car-body builders for screening off areas of bodywork that need to be painted in a second color.

• **YO-YO** fever sweeps across America, when the yo-yo (Filipino for "come-come") is manufactured by Donald F. Duncan, a Chicago toy-maker.

• In the ongoing gang warfare to win control of the trade in illegal alcohol, gangster Al Capone is blamed for the **ST. VALENTINE'S DAY MASSACRE** in Chicago, Illinois, in which seven members of the gang run by his rival "Bugs" Moran are brutally slaughtered.

• Germany's Dr. Fritz Pfleumer patents magnetic sound **RECORDING TAPE**.

1926! The first edition of *Winnie the Pooh* by A. A. Milne is published; it becomes a world children's classic.

1930
King Kullen Market, the first **SUPERMARKET**, is opened on Long Island in New York.
•Sir Henry Segrave is killed while breaking the **WATER SPEED RECORD** on Lake Windermere in England.
•**PLUTO**, the farthest planet from the sun in our solar system, is discovered by US astronomer Clyde Tombaugh.
•In soccer's first **WORLD CUP** home-team Uruguay beats Argentina 4–2.

TIFFANY STANDARD LAMP
(SEE 1933)

•Americans Charles Beebe and Otis Barton construct a **BATHYSPHERE**, taking them to a depth of 3,000 ft (914 m) off the coast of Bermuda.
•The first **BRITISH EMPIRE GAMES** (later known as the Commonwealth Games) are held at Hamilton, Canada.

1931
German physicists Ernst Ruska and Max Knoll invent the **ELECTRON MICROSCOPE**.
•A board game based on word construction is first devised by an unemployed American, Alfred Butts of New England, to amuse himself; originally called Criss-Cross, the game is later renamed and patented as **SCRABBLE**, to become one of the most successful board games ever.
•Nicknamed the "Empty State Building" because only a few floors have been leased when it opens, New York's 102-story steel-frame **EMPIRE STATE BUILDING** is completed. Reaching a height of 1,250 ft (381 m), it is topped with a mooring mast for zeppelins, and, on a clear day, visitors to the outdoor observation decks have a 78-mile (124.8-km) panoramic view of the city.

1932
Plennie L. Wingo finishes his journey in Istanbul, Turkey, having **WALKED BACKWARD** all the way from Santa Monica, California.
•American Karl Jansky picks up static from beyond the solar system to initiate **RADIO ASTRONOMY**.
•American Forrest Mars sets up a factory in Slough, England, to produce the **MARS BAR**.
•American aviator Amelia Earhart becomes the first **WOMAN TO FLY SOLO** across the Atlantic when she repeats the 1927 voyage made by Charles Lindbergh, from Canada to Ireland in her Lockheed Vega plane.

1933
American glassmaker and Art Nouveau designer **LOUIS COMFORT TIFFANY** dies in the US; an example of his classic designs for leaded-glass lamps, after the invention of the electric lightbulb, is to be found in most fashionable homes.
•**BAUHAUS**, the radical German school of design, is closed down by the new Hitler regime, which is opposed to progressive art.
•In an attempt on the life of President **FRANKLIN DELANO ROOSEVELT** in Miami, Florida, a would-be assassin's bullet misses him but kills Anton Cermak, the Mayor of Chicago, Illinois.
•The telephone **SPEAKING CLOCK** begins service in France.
•America's Edwin H. Armstrong develops **FM RADIO**, which uses frequency modulation and is less prone to interference.

Art Nouveau brings style to modern homes

•**DAYGLO** fluorescent colors are invented by brothers Joe and Bob Switzer in Los Angeles, California.
•**VITAMIN B$_2$** is discovered by Austrian chemist Richard Kuhn, Hungarian biochemist Albert von Nagyrapolt Szent-Györgyi, and Austrian neurologist Julius Wagner von Jauregg.

1934
The trail of robberies and murders committed by the gangsters **BONNIE AND CLYDE** is brought to a sudden end when the couple is shot dead by six Texas Rangers in northern Louisiana.
•Richard Hollingshead sets up the first **DRIVE-IN CINEMA**, in New Jersey.
•The Cunard shipping company is obliged to swiftly rename its new liner *Queen Victoria* as *Queen Mary*, after a misunderstanding by England's King George V; Cunard's chairman had said that the liner was to be named "after one of England's most noble queens"; assuming this to be a compliment to his wife, the king replied "Her Majesty will be so pleased."
•A **DUST BOWL** storm deposits 12 million tons of dust on Chicago when the combination of a drought and poor farming techniques turns the fertile Great Plains to dust; winds whip up "black blizzards" in a disaster that drives half a million people from their homes.
•UK road repairman Percy Shaw invents the **CATSEYE** reflective road stud; the idea comes to him when he brakes suddenly in thick fog to avoid a cat, whose glowing eyes pierced the gloom.
•J. F. Cantrell's Washeteria at Fort Worth, Texas, is the US's first **LAUNDROMAT**.

1935
George Gallup founds the American Institute of Public Opinion and initiates the **GALLUP POLL**; by canvassing people selected at random to obtain their views, he is able to correctly predict the result of the 1936 presidential election.
•English soldier **LAWRENCE OF ARABIA**, who led the Arabs in their revolt against Turkey, is killed in a crash on a motorcycle given to him by Irish playwright George Bernard Shaw.
•American seismologist Charles Richter invents the **RICHTER SCALE**, which measures the intensity of earthquakes.

EXTRA EXTRA! The last Schomburgk's deer vanishes from Thailand, in 1932.

•**PARKING METERS** are invented by Carlton Magee in Oklahoma City.

1936 *Australopithecus*, the oldest known **HUMAN REMAINS**, are found in Africa.
•The **SPANISH CIVIL WAR** breaks out between the elected government and the rebel forces of General Francisco Franco.
•German leader Adolf Hitler commissions Dr. Ferdinand Porsche to produce a car for the masses; Porsche designs the **VOLKSWAGEN BEETLE**; by the 1970s, it becomes the world's most-manufactured car.
•The world's biggest dam, the **BOULDER DAM** on the Colorado River, begins to generate electricity.

1937 An **EXPLOSION** caused by a gas leak kills 297 children and teachers at a Texas school. The explosion is later found to be deliberate.
•The **HINDENBERG**, the huge German-built airship, bursts into flames while landing in New Jersey; 35 of the 97 passengers on board are killed.
•**BESSIE SMITH**, the black American blues singer, is hurt in a car crash and taken to a nearby whites-only hospital, which allegedly refuses to admit her and she dies from her injuries.
•Walt Disney's *Snow White and the Seven Dwarfs*, the first full-length animated film in **TECHNICOLOR**, is released in the US.

THEN AND NOW

1935! The Monopoly board game is devised by Charles B. Darrow of Philadelphia; initially dismissed by manufacturers as boring and too complicated, it has become the best-selling copyrighted game ever. **1999!** Three new Monopoly pieces, the first in 40 years, are introduced: a sack, a biplane and a piggy bank.

1938 **PANIC** sets in when a radio broadcast of H. G. Wells's science fiction classic *The War of the Worlds* convinces listeners that they are hearing a genuine news bulletin.
•Hungarian-born brothers Laszlo and Georg Biro invent the **BALLPOINT PEN**.
•The first issue of Action Comics, which features **SUPERMAN**, is published.
•The **SPLITTING OF THE ATOM** is described by German chemist Otto Hahn and Austrian physicist Lise Meitner in their findings on nuclear fission.
•A 500-ton **METEORITE** crashes to Earth, narrowly missing Pittsburgh, Pennsylvania.

1939 **WORLD WAR II** begins when German forces invade Poland; Hitler says he will not wage war against women and children, and has ordered his air force to restrict itself to military targets.
•"Puss" of Clayhidon, Devon, UK, the **OLDEST CAT** on record, passes away on the day after his 36th birthday.
•MGM launches its most expensive film to date, *The Wizard of Oz*, a **FANTASY MUSICAL** filmed in Technicolor; Buddy Ebsen, the first actor to play the Tin Man, has to be hospitalized after breathing in large quantities of aluminum dust from his costume.
•Eugene Weidmann is the last person to be publicly **GUILLOTINED** in France.
•British archaeologist Howard Carter, who discovered Tutankhamun's tomb, dies after a mosquito bite, establishing the **CURSE OF TUTANKHAMUN**.
•Oregon wins the first NCAA **BASKETBALL** Championships in the US.
•The epic film of the **CIVIL WAR**, *Gone with the Wind*, is released.

Originally called the KdF-wagen, the Beetle brings driving to the people

THE ETERNALLY POPULAR VOLKSWAGEN BEETLE (SEE 1936)

EXTRA EXTRA! Following a forest fire and a virus, the heath hen is wiped out on Martha's Vineyard, Massachusetts, in 1932.

GLOBAL WAR

THE 20TH CENTURY WAS the century of war. Before the century was half over, the world had suffered two great World Wars, each killing more people than all the previous wars in history, while much of the second half has been dominated by the fear of a third global war, even more terrible than the first two. In such a warlike century, it is not surprising that many of the key technological breakthroughs have been linked to, or even demanded by, military need.

LONG-RANGE SHELLS
Filled with gas or pieces of shrapnel, these long-range shells were used to attack frontline troops in World War II.

PRODUCTS OF WAR

Both World Wars forced the pace of technological developments dramatically. Weapons developed most, of course. But some less warlike inventions such as rockets, instant coffee, insect sprays, tupperware, radar, and computers were also by-products of war.

KILLING MACHINES

MACHINE GUNS firing multiple streams of bullets automatically come to the fore in World War I and are now the standard weapon for soldiers.

TANKS are developed in 1915 in France and Britain to break through the German trenches. Now they are the standard battlefield assault vehicles.

BALLISTIC MISSILES In 1944, the Germans develop the world's first ballistic missiles, the V-1 and V-2 flying bombs, to deliver warheads to distant targets. Now "cruise missiles," armed with nuclear or conventional warheads, are the standard method of remote attack.

GERMAN WORLD WAR I MACHINE GUN USED IN TRENCH WARFARE

MAJOR WARS

1914 **WORLD WAR I** (1914–1918) begins when Austrian Archduke Ferdinand is assassinated and the European alliances break down. War on a huge scale, including mass slaughter in opposing trenches, claims the lives of over 20 million.

1939 **WORLD WAR II** (1939-1945) begins with the invasion of Poland by Hitler's Nazi Germany. This war engulfs the whole world, lasts for six years, and claims over 50 million lives.

1945 After World War II, Europe is split between the USSR-backed East and the US-backed West in a standoff called the **COLD WAR**.

Both sides race to build up nuclear weapons until each has enough to destroy the world many times.

1965 The US, along with Australia, sends troops to South **VIETNAM** to fight the communist North. Growing protests at home eventually lead to a US withdrawal.

1980 Iran and Iraq fight each other in what is the heaviest of the wars that have raged across the Middle East in the second half of the 20th century.

WAR ART
War inspires many works of art, such as this 1916 painting of a World War I battle by German artist Ludwig Putz.

MEDICAL ADVANCES

1920 The world's first voluntary **BLOOD DONOR** service is established when four British Red Cross Society members give blood at London's King's College Hospital, in the UK.

1921 Canadian physiologist Frederick Banting, who had discovered a practical means of extracting insulin from the pancreas, conducts successful trials of **INSULIN** for the treatment of diabetes.

1928 **PENICILLIN**, a powerful antibiotic, is accidentally discovered by Scottish bacteriologist Alexander Fleming. A practical method of producing penicillin is developed in 1939.

1931 Professor Sergei Sergeivitch Yukin at Moscow's central emergency service hopsital, sets up the world's first **BLOOD BANK**.

FIRST–AID BAG
The red cross is now a familiar symbol.

CASUALTIES OF WAR

In wartime, surgeons had no shortage of casualties on whom to develop new techniques. Governments boosted medical research to save troops from diseases such as cholera. It was during World War II that penicillin was used for the first time.

MEDICAL AIDS

WHEELCHAIR The casualties of World War I spur American engineer Harry Jennings to design a folding wheelchair in 1931.

PLASTIC EYES When export of glass eyes from Germany ceases in World War II, American doctors make an unbreakable alternative in 1944.

KIDNEY DIALYZER Sausage skins are used as membranes in the development of the first artificial kidney during the 1940s.

SKY'S THE LIMIT

The two World Wars were a major spur to aircraft development. Prior to World War I, for instance, flying machines were only for brave pioneers. But the war saw them developed into such practical machines that the first passenger services soon follow.

Wartime technology inspires many great inventio.

COCKPIT OF A 1917 VICKERS VIMY BOMBER

FLYING HIGH

1919 The Vickers Vimy, designed for long-range bombing, makes the first **TRANSATLANTIC FLIGHT**, piloted by Alcock and Brown.

1941 **JET ENGINES** are invented simultaneously in Germany by Pabst von Ohain and in England by Frank Whittle. It is, however, the demand for fast planes during World War II that makes them a practical reality, and it is during the wartime period that the greatest advances in jet-engine technology are made.

HEROES AND HEROINES

AGAINST A BACKGROUND of global conflicts and political oppression, many men and women of the twentieth century have demonstrated incredible heroism, not only in war, but also in movements toward peace and human rights. Others have displayed their heroism in sports, art, music, and many other fields.

THE POWER OF PROTEST

Many of the most courageous and principled acts of heroism were inspired by protest movements. At the start of the century the focus was on the female suffragettes who fought for women to get the vote. Other heroes stood up against the German Nazis in the 1930s. More recently, many black people successfully fought to overturn the apartheid system in South Africa.

JESSE OWENS
The success of black American athlete Jesse Owens in the 1936 Berlin Olympics offends Nazi leader Adolf Hitler who storms out in protest.

FIGHTERS OF OPPRESSION

NELSON MANDELA (b. 1918)
In 1964, South African lawyer Nelson Mandela is imprisoned for 26 years on Robben Island for leading the black people of South Africa in their struggle against the apartheid system. In 1994, as leader of the ANC (African National Congress party) he becomes South Africa's first black president.

MAHATMA GANDHI (1869–1948)
Insisting on nonviolent protest, Gandhi leads India in its struggle for independence from British colonial rule. By imposing hardship on himself and never showing anger, he slowly wins over his enemies.

CHÉ GUEVARA (1928–1967)
In 1959, this Latin American freedom fighter overthrows the Cuban dictator Batista. He is killed opposing oppression in Bolivia.

MARTIN LUTHER KING, JR. (1929–1968)
In the 1950s and 1960s, King leads a movement fighting for the rights of American blacks. In 1963, in an inspiring speech he proclaims, "I have a dream that one day this nation will rise up and live out the true meaning of its creed: We hold these truths to be self-evident; that all men are created equal." He is assassinated in 1968.

AUNG SAN SUU KYI (b. 1945)
This courageous woman leads the movement for human rights in Burma (Myanmar).

PEACEFUL PROTESTS

1901 The first **NOBEL PEACE PRIZE** is awarded jointly to the founders of the International Red Cross and of the French Society of the Friends of Peace. The prize is named after Swedish inventor of dynamite Alfred Nobel, whose money funds the award.

1932 The first conference to reduce the world stockpile of weapons is held.

1934 The **PEACE PLEDGE UNION**, a pacifist organization, is founded; in two years it gathers more than 100,000 signatures from people who pledge to renounce war as a way of resolving disputes between nations.

1958 The **COMMITTEE FOR A SANE NUCLEAR POLICY** is founded in the US.

WAR HEROES

BARON VON RICHTOFEN (1882–1918) The German "Red Baron" is one of the greatest fighter pilots of World War I.

WILFRED OWEN (1893–1918) One of the greatest-ever wartime poets brings home to people what life is like for a soldier in the trenches in World War Î.

DOUGLAS BADER (1910–1982) In World War II, British fighter pilot Bader becomes a hero when he loses both legs in action.

DOUGLAS MACARTHUR (1880–1964) is the most famous of all American generals in World War II.

ETERNAL FLAME FOR THE UNKNOWN SOLDIER

SPORTS HEROES

Sports have become incredibly important to the average person during the century – especially since the coming of television – and billions of people tune in to watch great sports events such as the World Cup or the Olympic games. No wonder, then, that sports stars have become among the best known and often the most popular heroes of all.

GIANTS OF TRACK AND FIELD

MICHAEL JORDAN (b. 1945) The most famous basketball player ever is renown for the height he jumped – and scoring over 32 points a game for Chicago Bulls.

MUHAMMAD ALI (b. 1942) Born as Cassius Clay in Kentucky, Ali becomes US world heavyweight boxing champion in 1964.

DONALD BRADMAN (1908–1998) Australian cricketer Bradman is one of the best batsmen of all time.

JESSE OWENS (1913–1980) This champion black American athlete's Olympics success offends Hitler.

PELÉ (b. 1942) Brazilian Pelé may be the best-ever soccer player.

GIRL POWER

The 20th century finally saw women gaining the same rights as men in many places. By the end of the 1920s, women had won the right to vote in Australia, Canada, Finland, Germany, Britain, Sweden, the US and many other places. The world wars gave many ordinary women the chance to show they could cope with all kinds of jobs, such as office work, driving, and even farming, as well as men. In the 1960s, the feminist movement began to fight for equal opportunities. These are just some of the women who have made their mark.

FEMALE BOXER *In the 20th century, women begin to compete in traditionally "male" sports, such as boxing.*

FEMALE FIRSTS

EMMELINE PANKHURST and her daughter Christabel lead the British suffragette campaign for votes for women, 1903–1918.

MARIE STOPES is the Scottish founder of the first birth-control clinic in London, UK.

AMY JOHNSON is the first woman to fly solo from Britain to Australia. In 1930, her 10,000-mile (16,000-km) flight takes her 19 days to complete.

AMELIA EARHART, an American aviator, is the first woman to make a solo transatlantic flight in 1932.

SIRIMAVO BANDARANAIKE of Sri Lanka becomes the world's first-ever female Prime Minister in 1960.

VALENTINA TERESHKOVA, a Russian cosmonaut, is the first woman in space in 1963. Her flight in *Vostok 6* lasts 3 days.

1940 About 4,500 Polish officers are massacred and their bodies buried in a mass grave in the **KATYN FOREST** near Smolensk (then in the USSR), on the orders of the Soviet dictator Joseph Stalin; the victims are taken from among the 14,500 Poles imprisoned during the Soviet invasion of Poland; the remaining 10,000 captives probably met with a similar fate.

•**LEON TROTSKY**, Russian revolutionary and founder of the Red Army who has been expelled from Russia for plotting against the State, is assassinated with an ice pick in Mexico; the involvement of Stalin's secret police is suspected.

•**PLUTONIUM** is discovered by American nuclear chemist Glenn Seaborg; it is eventually used in atomic weapons and in nuclear reactors.

•**NYLON STOCKINGS** are introduced to the US by Du Pont of Delaware.

•Robert Pershing Wadlow, the world's **TALLEST MAN**, dies; the length of his coffin is 10 ft, 9 in (3 m, 25 cm).

• *For Whom the Bell Tolls*, US novelist Ernest Hemingway's classic tale set in the **SPANISH CIVIL WAR**, is published.

FIRST USED FOR EXECUTION IN 1890, THE ELECTRIC CHAIR PROVIDES A HOT SEAT FOR CRIMINALS (SEE 1941)

1941 **AMY JOHNSON**, record-breaking British aviator, vanishes during a flight over the Thames Estuary, east of London, England.

•The **FOUR FREEDOMS** are set out by four-time US President Franklin Roosevelt in his State of the Union Message; they are the freedom of speech and expression, freedom of worship, freedom from want, and freedom from fear of war.

•As a mark of defiance, UK radio listeners are advised to whistle the opening notes of Beethoven's Symphony No 5 in the presence of German soldiers, because it shares the same rhythm (three dots and a dash) as the Morse code signal for **V** (for victory). The four notes are added to the chimes of the Big Ben bell in the tower of the UK Houses of Parliament.

•**TEFLON** is patented by the Du Pont company in the US, after its accidental discovery by research chemist Roy Plunkett; the product is kept secret throughout World War II while its military potential is tested, and is not used in cookware until the 1960s.

•A law is passed in Germany ordering all Jewish people over the age of six to wear a **YELLOW STAR OF DAVID** on their clothing, for display when they are in public; they are also forbidden to leave the areas in which they live.

•Two murderers are executed by **ELECTRIC CHAIR** at the Florida State Prison; their names are Willburn and Frizzel.

•Within three hours of a surprise air raid by Japanese warplanes on **PEARL HARBOR**, Hawaii, the US declares war on its aggressor.

1942 US air ace Edward Vernon Rickenbacker crashes into the Pacific and spends 23 days **ADRIFT** on a makeshift raft before he is rescued.

•The *Queen Mary* **LUXURY LINER**, pressed into service as a troop carrier, slices through her escort ship, the *Curaçao*, killing more than 300 sailors.

•The South Atlantic island group of Tristan da Cunha, with its tiny community descended from a group of 19th-century shipwrecked sailors, is commissioned as **HMS ATLANTIC ISLE**, and a radio and weather radio station is set up, providing its only contact with the outside world.

•A 35 mph (55 km/h) **SPEED LIMIT** is imposed on US roads.

•The **T-SHIRT**, previously worn as underwear, becomes standard issue in the US Navy.

1943 The *Shooting Star* is the first US **FIGHTER PLANE** to fly at more than 500 mph (800 km/h).

•America's first zone improvement plan (**ZIP CODES**) are introduced by the US Post Office in Pittsburgh, Pennsylvania.

•A peasant farmer in Parangaricutiro, Mexico, notices, while plowing, that the soil is hot against the soles of his bare feet; the next day there appears a mound of earth 25 ft (8 m) tall; within six months it measures 1,500 ft (450 m); the farmer has witnessed the birth of a **VOLCANO**, Paricutin, whose eruption halts in 1952, just as abruptly as it started and without any loss of life.

•In London, England, a woman trips down a staircase when entering an air-raid shelter; the crowd of 300 behind her cannot stop moving forward and more people fall; 173 people, including 60 children, are crushed to death in the **HUMAN AVALANCHE**.

•The **AQUALUNG** is invented by Jacques Cousteau, who is a commandant in the French Navy. It is the first successful lightweight underwater breathing apparatus and uses compressed air cylinders that are strapped to the backs of "frogmen," who will be employed in World War II to undertake unseen raids on enemy ships.

1944 The first **KIDNEY DIALYSIS** machine, a filter made out of cellophane immersed in water, is connected to a patient's bloodstream by Dutch-American physician Willem Kolff.

•Mary Chase's award-winning play, *Harvey*, opens at the 48th Street Theater in New York; its star is a 6-ft (1.8-m) **INVISIBLE RABBIT** called Harvey.

•The **AUTOMATIC SEQUENCE-CONTROLLED COMPUTER** is built by a team led by Professor Howard H. Aiken at Harvard University; it adds numbers 100 times faster than a manually operated calculator.

•The first prefabricated homes go on display in London, England; intended for demobilized servicemen and bombed-out families, it is claimed that a **PREFAB** can be erected in a few hours.

1945 Irish-born **FRANCIS BACON** becomes the most notorious artist in Britain following the exhibition of his *Three Studies of Figures at the Base of a Crucifixion* at the Tate Gallery in London; his critics claim that he depicts the human form as though it were simply meat in a butcher's shop.

• The atomic bomb "Little Boy," carried by the American B-29 Superfortress *Enola Gay*, is dropped on the Japanese city of **HIROSHIMA**, leaving the city devastated and 80,000 people dead.

• George Orwell's *Animal Farm* is finally published, after being rejected 23 times; a satirical **TALE OF REVOLUTION**, it is set on a farm where the animals stage a rebellion against humans, but the pigs establish an equally tyrannical regime.

• **ADOLF HITLER**, whose first job was painting picture postcards, marries Eva Braun in an air-raid shelter in Berlin, Germany, and, on the same day, they commit suicide together.

• A B-25 bomber plane flying too low becomes lost in the fog and crashes into the 78th floor of New York's **EMPIRE STATE BUILDING**; the impact plunges an elevator 79 floors to the basement but the operator inside is saved by the emergency brakes.

• Jerome **NAPOLEON BONAPARTE**, a member of Emperor Napoleon's family, trips over his wife's dog's leash in Central Park in New York City and dies.

• British science fiction writer **ARTHUR C. CLARKE** suggests the idea of space satellites in an article that appears in *Wireless World*.

• The electronic numerator, integrator, analyzer, and calculator (ENIAC), the first all-purpose fully **ELECTRONIC DIGITAL COMPUTER**, is completed by John Eckert and John Mauchly at the University of Pennsylvania; a true monster of a machine, it weighs 30 tons (30.5 tonnes), occupies 1,500 sq ft (140 sq m) of floor space, and can perform 5,000 simple calculations per second; its 19,000 valves use as much electricity as 200 electric heaters.

• The US company Raytheon patents the world's first **MICROWAVE OVEN**; it was discovered by chance that microwaves could be used in cooking when a bag of corn was turned into popcorn.

1946 Albanian king Ahmed Bey Zog I dies, age 23, a regular smoker of 240 cigarettes per day.

• The first **ESPRESSO COFFEE** machine is invented in Italy by Achille Gaggia, and it becomes a worldwide success.

• **H. G. WELLS**, English author, dies of cancer of the liver ten minutes after dismissing his nurse with the words "Go away, I'm all right." Originally an enthusiast about the possibility of space travel and new technology, Wells campaigned for world peace and an understanding of the evils of war. His optimism was so crushed by World War II that he predicts a disastrous end for the human race.

• The **BIKINI** two-piece swimsuit is revealed by French designer Louis Réard to an amazed audience at his Paris fashion show; its name comes from the South Pacific atoll of Bikini, site of the atomic bomb tests, in the hope that its impact will be similarly explosive.

1947 The **SOUND BARRIER** is broken by US Air Force Captain Charles E. Yeager when he flies his Bell X-1 rocket plane from a base in California; he is the first person to fly beyond the speed of sound.

• The *Dead Sea Scrolls*, the earliest known **BIBLICAL TEXTS**, are discovered in Jordan by Muhammad ad-Dibh, a Bedouin shepherd, in clay jars in a cave close to the Dead Sea.

• The American flying boat *Spruce Goose* – the world's **LARGEST AIRCRAFT** – makes its one and only flight; it is piloted by millionaire Howard Hughes, who had designed it as an international troop carrier.

• George Ellery Hale sets up a 200-in (500-cm) **REFLECTOR TELESCOPE** on Palomar Mountain in California; known as the Hale Telescope, it is the largest optical telescope in the world.

• The **TRANSISTOR** is invented by US physicists William Shockley, Walter Brattain, and John Bardeen at the Bell Telephone Laboratories. Made from a small piece of the chemical germanium, the device is able to increase the strength of a signal 100 times over; it is later used for computers and electronic devices.

1948 Mohandas Karamchand Gandhi is assassinated by a Hindu nationalist in Delhi, just ten days after a previous attempt on his life; better known as **THE MAHATMA** (meaning "great soul"), Gandhi had played an important role in securing India's independence from Britain by means of nonviolent protest.

• The first 12-inch 33⅓ rpm microgroove **LONG-PLAYING (LP) VINYLITE RECORDS** with 23-minute-per-side capacity are introduced by the Columbia Record Company in the US.

• The US's John Grimek becomes the world's first-ever **MR. UNIVERSE** when he wins the contest in London, England.

• The first **McDONALD'S** hamburgers are sold by Richard and Maurice McDonald at their new self-service restaurant in San Bernardino, California; salesman Ray Kroc visits the store to take an order for eight milkshake mixers and is so impressed with the operation that he decides to buy the franchising rights. Within 20 years he opens 4,000 restaurants and buys his own baseball team, the San Diego Padres.

• Swiss mountaineer Georges de Mestral, inspired by the irritating prickly balls of thistle that stick to his clothing while hiking in the Alps, comes up with the idea of **VELCRO**; the tape consists of two nylon strips, one containing thousands of miniature hooks, the other with matching eyes.

• The first **NONSTOP AROUND-THE-WORLD** flight is completed by Captain James Gallagher and his US Air Force crew; they fly a Boeing B-50A Super Fortress out of Fort Worth, Texas, and arrive back 94 hours and 1 minute later; they refuel four times in midflight.

• The "instant" photograph is invented in the US; Edwin H. Land's **POLAROID** Land camera can produce a black-and-white print within 60 seconds of the picture being taken.

• **MARGARET MITCHELL**, American author of *Gone with the Wind*, is struck and killed by a speeding car.

1949 Paddle rackets, a game played with a shortened tennis racket, is invented by Joe Sobek in the US; today's **RACQUETBALL** is derived from this original game.

• The world's first jet airliner, the British **DE HAVILLAND COMET**, is flown by Group Captain John Cunningham.

• Paddipads, the first-ever **DISPOSABLE DIAPERS**, are introduced in Britain.

HENRY MOORE'S
KING AND QUEEN
(SEE 1953)

Abstract modern art becomes respectable

1952 The US company Gibson begins production of the first solid-body **ELECTRIC GUITARS**, designed by musician Les Paul.

•**SMOG** claims more than 4,000 lives in London, England, as the weather conditions trap heavily polluted air.

•Philippe Piché patents the revolving fork for eating **SPAGHETTI**.

•Germany's Godfried Büren "proves" that the Sun is hollow; **SUNSPOTS**, he claims, are brief breaks in the Sun's surface fires, allowing glimpses of the cool, vegetation-covered globe within.

1953 The fundamental structure of life, known as **DNA**, is discovered by the UK's Francis Crick and American James Watson.

•UK abstract artist **HENRY MOORE** completes his latest sculpture, *King and Queen*. A former teacher, Moore is now able to support himself as a full-time sculptor as his work gains critical acclaim.

1950 The biggest-ever soccer crowd (203,500 spectators) watches Brazil play Uruguay in the **WORLD CUP FINAL** held in Brazil.

•American George Jorgensen travels to Denmark to become Christine in the first-ever **SEX CHANGE** operation; it is performed by Dr. Christian Hamburger.

•Italy's Giuseppe Farina wins the first World Championship **MOTOR RACING** event, the British Grand Prix.

•The world's first **CREDIT CARD**, the Diner's Club Card, allows members to dine on credit at 27 restaurants in New York City; the idea comes from the "plastic cash" identity cards issued by oil companies to their customers.

•Elevator attendants fear for their jobs when the first elevator with **AUTOMATIC DOORS** is installed by Otis at the Atlantic Refining Building in Dallas, Texas.

1951 In New York City, CBS starts up the first regular **COLOR TELEVISION** service.

•Mary Reeser **BURNS TO DEATH** in her armchair at home in Florida; the fire that kills her reaches the ferocious heat of 3,000°F (1,649°C) and yet not a scorch mark is made on the chair in which she is sitting, nor anywhere else in the room.

•France's first throwaway pen, the **BIC** ballpoint, is invented by Baron Marcel Bich, whose manufacturing process allows them to be made at very low cost.

•The **SAMARITANS**, the world's first telephone helpline, is set up in Britain by the Reverend Chad Varah after his sad experience of burying a young girl who had committed suicide.

•American children are inoculated with the first effective **POLIO VACCINE**, developed by Jonas E. Salk of Pittsburgh.

•Edmund Hillary from New Zealand and Tenzing Norgay, his Sherpa guide, share cake at the top of the highest mountain in the world, Nepal's **MOUNT EVEREST**, 29,078 ft (8,853 m) above sea level, which they have just conquered.

•The Chevrolet **CORVETTE** is the first car to have fiberglass body panels.

1954 The world's **BIGGEST WARSHIP**, the 59,650-ton (60,607-tonne) USS *Forrestal* aircraft carrier, sails from Newport News.

•The **4-MINUTE MILE** is broken by Britain's Roger Bannister at the Iffley Road Sports Ground, Oxford, England, in a time of 3 minutes, 59.4 seconds.

•The US's National Cancer Institute proposes that **LUNG CANCER** may be linked to smoking.

•The USS *Nautilus*, the world's first **NUCLEAR SUBMARINE**, is launched; it later travels under the polar ice cap from the Pacific to the Atlantic ocean.

•At **LE MANS** in France, Pierre Levegh's Mercedes racing car hits a wall and explodes in midair; 82 people are killed by showering wreckage.

•The US enters the age of jet air transportation when the **BOEING 707** makes its maiden flight from Seattle in the state of Washington.

•The first **NUCLEAR REACTOR** to generate power for general consumption is installed in Russia.

•Gregory Pincus of Massachusetts and John Rock produce a contraceptive pill that proves to be one of the most effective methods of **BIRTH CONTROL**.

1955 **DISNEYLAND** opens on a 244-acre (98.7-hectare) site in Anaheim, California; it becomes the world's most popular theme park.

•The **HOVERCRAFT** is patented by the UK's Christopher S. Cockerell; it is the first practical amphibious vehicle, propelled on an air cushion about 9 in (23 cm) above ground, or water surface.

•**LEGO**, a construction game for children, is invented in Denmark by Godtfred Christiansen; his "automatic building brick" derives its name from the Danish *leg godt*, meaning "to play well."

•**RADIOCARBON DATING** is developed by Willard F. Libby at the University of Chicago; it allows organic matter such as bone or wood to be dated by studying the radioactive isotopes present in the matter; it becomes a particularly valuable tool for archaeologists.

•US manufacturer General Electric produces the first **ARTIFICIAL DIAMONDS** by heating carbon to a very high temperature; used in industry, the tiny black diamonds are so time- and labor-intensive to create, that they are more expensive (and less attractive) than natural diamonds.

•Police are called in when English teenage audiences go out of control at the first showing of the **ROCK 'N' ROLL** music movie, *Rock Around the Clock*.

1956 The first **TRANSATLANTIC TELEPHONE CABLE** is successfully completed in a joint venture between companies from France, Britain, and Canada.

1954! A plague of desert locusts in Morocco destroys $14 million worth of citrus crops in just six weeks.

- ELVIS PRESLEY records the classic song *Heartbreak Hotel* at the age of 21.
- American actor George Reeves, the first film SUPERMAN, is shot dead.
- Art Ingles builds a prototype GO-CART, using a lawn-mower engine; the vehicle soon catches on and the first go-carting event is held in a nearby shopping center car park in California.
- The largest known ICEBERG, covering an area of more than 12,000 sq miles (31,000 sq km), is spotted in the South Pacific Ocean by the USS *Glacier*.
- The Ampex VR 1000, introduced by Ampex of California, is the first commercially produced VIDEO RECORDER; it is a massive machine using 2,600-ft (800-m) reels of tape.
- The first taped TELEVISION program is broadcast from Hollywood, California, three hours after its live broadcast in New York City.
- JACKSON POLLOCK, American action painter who pioneered the drip painting technique, is killed in a car crash.

1957 A serious accident causes an escape of RADIATION at the Atomic Energy Authority's Windscale nuclear plant in northwestern England.
- The USSR's *Sputnik 1*, the first man-made SATELLITE, orbits Earth.
- LAIKA (meaning "barker" in Russian) becomes the first dog in space when it is sent up on a life support machine in the USSR's *Sputnik 2* satellite; sadly, Laika dies shortly after going into orbit and the satellite disintegrates upon reentry to Earth's atmosphere.
- The US Navy's *Vanguard* SPACE ROCKET lifts just 4 ft (1m, 20 cm) off its launch pad before exploding into flames; it is renamed "Kaputnik" and "Stayputnik" by the press.
- The word FRISBEE first appears in print in *Newsweek* magazine; it originates from the Frisbie bakery in Bridgeport, Connecticut, where employees hurl pie tins during their breaks; ten years later, the Wham-O Manufacturing Company patents its "Improved Frisbee."

1958 Britain's James Gorman complains of serious STOMACH PAINS; during an emergency operation at a County Durham hospital, doctors remove 366 half-pennies, 11 pennies, 26 sixpenny pieces, 4 one-shilling pieces, and 27 pieces of wire.

- A craze for the HULA HOOP sweeps across the US; concerned doctors issue health warnings because participants who are out of shape are thought to be in danger of collapsing from heart failure; "hula" refers to a traditional Hawaiian dance in which the hips are gyrated.
- SKATEBOARDS are invented by father-and-son team Bill and Mark Richards, who run the Val Surf Shop at Dana Point, California; they design and sell wooden boards attached to skates that have been cut in two.
- The first SILICON CHIP is designed by US's Jack Kilby of Texas Instruments and Robert Noyce of Intel; silicon chips contain thousands of integrated circuit components within a few millimeters.

THEN AND NOW

1952 Dr. Paul M. Zoll implants a pacemaker under the skin of a 72-year-old patient; the pacemaker sends a constant flow of tiny electric shocks to the heart, stimulating it to beat regularly. **1967** The first successful human heart transplant is performed by South Africa's Dr. Christiaan Barnard on Louis Washkansky at Groote Schuur Hospital.

- Belgium, France, Germany, Italy, Luxembourg, and the Netherlands form the EEC (European Economic Community) when they sign the Treaty of Rome; the member nations will form a common market for trade and industry.
- RADIATION BELTS are mapped around Earth using data from Geiger counters sent on *Explorer 1*, the US's first space satellite; they are called Van Allen Belts after their discoverer, J. A. Van Allen.

1959 The world's first automatic PHOTOCOPYING machine, the Xerox 914, is introduced in New York by the Haloid Company. Haloid spent $12.5 million on research; it will generate over $1 billion in sales revenue within the next eight years.
- The IDENTIKIT system for identifying crime suspects is first used, in California, to apprehend a man wanted for robbing a liquor store; the idea of constructing a photographic likeness based on witness descriptions of individual facial features was the idea of Los Angeles police detective Hugh C. McDonald.
- The SNOWMOBILE, or "Ski-Doo," is invented and marketed by Canadian mechanic J. Armand Bombardier.

EXTRA EXTRA! The last two Euler's flycatchers are killed when Hurricane Janet hits Jamaica, in 1955.

115

1960 An early form of **WINDSURFING** becomes popular in Brazil using a fishing raft, or Jangada, to skim across the sea.

• An effective **VACCINE** against measles, the deadly childhood disease, is developed by American bacteriologist John Enders.

• The USS *Triton*, a **NUCLEAR-POWERED SUBMARINE**, travels underwater around the world in 84 days.

• **ALUMINUM CANS** for drinks are introduced, but many people prefer the taste of products sold in glass bottles.

• A digital **FLIGHT SIMULATOR**, which allows pilots to train on the ground, is built at the University of Pennsylvania.

RIDING THE WAVES IN BRAZIL (SEE 1960)

• The Digital Equipment Corporation brings out the **PDP-1 COMPUTER**. It takes up just four 6-ft (1.8-m)-high cabinets and is the first to cost less than one million US dollars.

• Off the coast of Florida, the first **POLARIS MISSILE** to be fired from a submerged submarine is launched from the USS *George Washington*.

1961 As the Cold War continues between the Soviet bloc and the Western powers, East Germany erects the **BERLIN WALL**, closing the border between East and West Berlin. Built from concrete blocks and heavily guarded by East German soldiers, it prevents East Germans from trying to escape from the Communist regime.

• The **GOLFBALL** electric typewriter, which prints characters from a revolving ball, is manufactured by the IBM company in the US.

• "Pick and pluck" **INDUSTRIAL ROBOTS** are introduced in the US by Unimation; they are used on car assembly lines.

• The USSR sends the first man into space on April 12; **YURI GAGARIN** orbits the Earth in *Vostok 1*.

• US heart specialist Albert Starr and aircraft engineer M. Lowell Edwards invent the first reliable **HEART REPLACEMENT VALVE**, a plastic ball in stainless steel caging.

1962 The *Telstar* **COMMUNICATION SATELLITE** is launched from Cape Canaveral, Florida; within hours television pictures are being screened live across the Atlantic Ocean.

• The Amphicar, an **AMPHIBIOUS CAR**, is built by Germany's Hans Trippel.

• US **FROGMAN** Fred Baldasare swims the English Channel underwater.

1963 The first compact audio **CASSETTE TAPE** is produced by Philips in Holland.

• High levels of **RADIOACTIVE FALLOUT** are detected in cows' milk; it results from cattle feeding on contaminated grass after nuclear weapons tests were carried out by both the USSR and the US.

• Russia's **VALENTINA TERESHKOVA** is the first woman in space, orbiting Earth 48 times in the space capsule *Vostok 6*.

• President **JOHN F. KENNEDY** is shot dead in his open-topped limousine in Dallas, Texas; the alleged assassin, Lee Harvey Oswald, despite being under police guard, is himself shot dead two days later, in front of the TV cameras.

• *Whisky-A-Go-Go* in Los Angeles is the world's first **DISCOTHEQUE**.

• **MARTIN LUTHER KING, JR.**, delivers his legendary speech to the largest-ever civil rights demonstration, a crowd of more than 200,000 gathered in Washington, DC; he calls for racial harmony, drawing on the truth that all men are created equal: "I have a dream that one day this nation will rise up and live out the true meaning of its creed."

• Dutch astronomer Maarten Schmidt is the first to identify a **QUASAR**, a source of immense energy; he estimates it to be two billion light-years from Earth.

1964 In Peru, 320 people die in **RIOTS** after a disputed result in a Peru vs. Argentina soccer match.

• The USSR's *Voskhod 1* space capsule is the first to send back live **TELEVISION PICTURES FROM SPACE**.

• GI Joe is introduced by Mattel of Hawthorne, California; the world's first **ACTION MAN** toy stands 12 in (30 cm) high in World War II uniform, and has a battle-scarred face.

• BASIC (Beginners All-purpose Symbolic Instruction Code) **COMPUTER LANGUAGE** is devised at Dartmouth College in New Hampshire, to help students learn programming.

1965 World-famous and most successful pop group ever, **THE BEATLES** perform before a record 55,600 fans at Shea Stadium, home of the New York Mets baseball team. To ensure their safe arrival, they are driven to the stadium in a Wells Fargo armored truck.

• The world's **LARGEST CUSTARD PIE**, 36 in (91 cm) across and weighing 18 lb (8 kg), is baked at Clayton Secondary Modern School in Oxford, England.

1968! Czech students in Prague protest against invasion by the USSR, placing flowers down Soviet gun barrels.

THEN AND NOW

1961 Amnesty International is launched in 1961 by British lawyer Peter Benenson, after publishing a worldwide appeal. He receives more than 1,000 offers of support for an international campaign to defend human rights.

1990 After worldwide concern about the abuse of human rights in South Africa, where apartheid – the separation of racial groups – is practiced, the government bows to international pressure and repeals the discriminatory laws that force black and white people to lead separate lives.

•Radical Black Muslim leader **MALCOLM X** is shot dead in New York City at a rally in Harlem.
•The first-ever **SPACEWALK** is made by Soviet astronaut Alexei Leonov when he makes a ten-minute tethered excursion from his *Voskhod 2* capsule.

1966 The Chinese leader **MAO TSE-TUNG** instigates the Cultural Revolution, spearheaded by students organized into bands of Red Guards; armed with copies of his *Little Red Book*, students tour the country reciting Mao's thoughts on communism.
•The first **TIDAL POWER STATION** in the world starts generating electricity for Electricité de France (EDF) on the estuary of the Rance River in Brittany.
•A world record is set for **GUNPOWDER-POWERED MISSILES** when the US Defense Department uses a HARP gun to fire a 185-lb (94-kg) projectile to a height of 110 miles (180 km).
•A live-virus **VACCINE** against rubella (German measles) is developed by Harry H. Meyer and Paul D. Parkman; because unborn babies are at risk, the vaccine is targeted at pregnant women.
•The **GIANT AFRICAN SNAIL** is brought to Florida by an 8-year-old boy; the 8-in (20-cm)-long snail is equipped with 80,000 teeth and can consume a head of lettuce in a matter of hours; within three years these snails become a serious menace to food crops.

•At the Standard Telecommunications Laboratories in the UK, **OPTICAL FIBERS** made of strands of glass are first used to carry telephone calls; the transmitted signal is sent as a series of light pulses and is decoded by the end receiver.

1967 USSR astronaut Alexei Leonov finds himself the target of an **ASSASSINATION ATTEMPT** when a gunman fires three shots into the limousine in which he is traveling; it proves to be a case of mistaken identity – the bullets were intended for Soviet president Leonid Brezhnev.
•The first **NEUTRON STAR**, the dense remains following the supernova explosion at the end of a star's life, is discovered by English astronomer Antony Hewish with Jocelyn S. Bell Burnell; they detect its pulsating signal while researching quasars.
•A **SPACE CAPSULE FIRE** aboard *Apollo 1* kills astronauts Edward White, Gus Grissom, and Roger Chaffee during testing at Cape Canaveral, Florida, for the launch of the new *Saturn 1B* rocket.
•**FOOT-AND-MOUTH DISEASE** breaks out in the UK; the germ is carried by humans on their footwear and clothing and by animals and birds; more than 100,000 cattle have to be slaughtered to prevent further infection.
•Donald Campbell is killed when his boat *Bluebird* crashes at Lake Coniston in England during a failed attempt to raise his own world **WATER-SPEED RECORD** to over 300 mph (483 km/h); only his helmet, shoes, oxygen mask, and teddy bear mascot are recovered from the lake.
•The rock musical *Hair* opens in New York; it is the first time that **NUDITY** has been seen in a legitimate US theater.
•The first Football **SUPER BOWL** is won by the Green Bay Packers, who beat the Kansas City Chiefs 35–10.
•Car manufacturer Saab introduces the **TURBOPRESSOR** in its cars, allowing engines to produce supercharged power.

THE BEATLES MAKE POP HISTORY (SEE 1965)

1968 Martin Luther King, Jr., US civil rights leader, is shot dead in Memphis by **JAMES EARL RAY**, who is sentenced to 99 years in jail.
•The first **FLIGHT AROUND THE MOON** is made by US astronauts Frank Borman, James Lovell, and William Anders in *Apollo 8*; TV pictures of Earth taken from 250,000 miles (400,000 km) away, are broadcast on Christmas Eve.
•**YURI GAGARIN**, the first man in space, is killed when his MiG fighter plane crashes north of Moscow in the USSR.
•Paris is brought to a standstill when 30,000 students **PROTEST** the US involvement in the Vietnam War.

1969 Advertised as "the greatest outdoor party since the miracle of the loaves and fishes," the **WOODSTOCK** Music and Art Festival, held at Max Yasgur's farm near Woodstock, New York, attracts 400,000 hippies, a term to describe the latest look for young people who grow their hair long and reject conventional society.
•The first home **VIDEO RECORDER**, the CV-2000, arrives in US stores.
•The world's **FIRST SUPERSONIC AIRLINER**, the Tupolev Tu-144, is demonstrated by the Russians.
•**ANTIWAR PROTESTS** sweeping the US against the country's military involvement in Vietnam culminate in massive demonstrations; on November 15, 250,000 peaceful demonstrators march in Washington, DC; another 200,000 people gather in San Francisco's Golden Gate Park, singing "all we are asking is give peace a chance."
•The **INTERNET**, linking computers by telephone to allow scientists and engineers to communicate with one another, is set up in the US.
•US astronaut Neil Armstrong is the first man to **WALK ON THE MOON**; as he steps down from the *Eagle* module he says, "That's one small step for man . . . one giant leap for mankind."

1970 US chemist Linus C. Pauling claims that a large daily dose of **VITAMIN C** protects against colds.
• The US sends the NOAA **WEATHER SATELLITE** into polar orbit with a camera programmed to constantly take pictures.
• The Boeing 747, the first **JUMBO JET**, enters regular service across the Atlantic.
• The USSR's *Lunokhod 1*, the first remote-controlled **LUNAR VEHICLE**, collects soil samples on the Moon.
• In the US, IBM launches the **FLOPPY DISK**, a flexible, magnetic disk in an outer case, for computer data storage.
• The largest recorded **HAILSTONE** is found at Coffeyville, Kansas; it weighs 1.67 lb (758 g) and measures 7 1/2 in (190 mm) wide.
• The supersonic airliner **CONCORDE**, jointly developed by Britain and France, travels at twice the speed of sound for the first time.

• US integrated circuit manufacturer Intel is asked by a Japanese company to supply the main components of a computer on just one circuit for use in its new calculator; the result is the Intel 4004, the first **COMMERCIAL MICROCHIP**.
• Texas Instruments make the first **POCKET CALCULATOR**; it weighs over 2.5 lb (1 kg) and costs $150.
• **GREENPEACE**, which campaigns worldwide on environmental issues, is founded.

1972 The award-winning computerized axial tomography (CAT) **SCANNER** revolutionizes medical investigative techniques; it can find a brain tumor, for example, by creating an image from a series of X rays.
• The theory of **BLACK HOLES** (collapsed stars) is supported by data recorded by the *Uhuru* satellite's X-ray telescope.

• The **COMPACT DISC** is developed by Philips in Holland and Sony in Japan; capable of holding more than 75 minutes of digital music, it encodes sounds in binary form in a series of 0s and 1s.
• Lewis R. Toppel of Wisconsin, USA, patents the **COUGHING CIGARETTE PACKAGE**, which makes a noise like a hacking cough when picked up; it serves as a reminder of the side effects of smoking.

• Michelangelo's **SCULPTURE**, *Pietà*, is attacked with a hammer in the Vatican in Rome, Italy.

1973 The **HIGHEST OFFICE BUILDING** in the world, the twin-towered World Trade Center, is completed in New York, its towers standing 1,368 ft (417 m) and 1,362 ft (415 m) tall.
• US astronauts Gerald Carr, Edward G. Gibson, and William R. Pogue spend a record 84 days in space when visiting the US Skylab 4 **SPACE STATION**.

Exploring every nook and crater by remote control

LUNOKHOD 1 MAKES HOLES IN THE MOON (SEE 1970)

1971 Director **FRANCIS FORD COPPOLA** shoots *The Godfather*, a film about a secret criminal society; after mass demonstrations and bomb threats, the filmmakers agree with the Italian-American Civil Rights League to make no mention of the Mafia.
• The first liquid crystal displays (LCDs) are developed by Hoffman-La Roche of Switzerland.

1975! Leonard McMahon gulps down 501 live goldfish in four hours at Oakland, California.

•The first **MOUNTAIN BIKES** appear in California, when Marin County's Canyon Gang customize their bicycles to ride up the steep sides of the canyon.
•**SYDNEY OPERA HOUSE** in Australia opens; designed by Danish architect Joern Utzon, it is nicknamed "the peeled orange" and "the stranded whale."

1974 Richard Nixon becomes the first US president to resign, after his involvement in a break-in at **WATERGATE**, the headquarters of the Democratic party in Washington, DC.
•Japan's Lt. Hiroo Onoda surrenders in the Philippines,

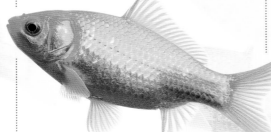

29 years after the end of World War II; he had not realized the war was over.
•*Earthquake* is the first film to be made in **SENSURROUND**, wherein vibrations are felt by the audience.
•America's **STREAKING CRAZE** spreads to Europe: 11 naked people cycle around the Eiffel Tower in Paris, France.
•Chlorofluorocarbons, or **CFCs**, used in aerosols and refrigeration, are found to be a threat to the ozone layer, exposing Earth to the sun's harmful radiation.
•The **TRIATHLON** is devised in the US; this tough test of endurance combines cycling, long-distance swimming, and running in one competition.
•The Swedish band **ABBA** wins the Eurovision Song Contest with *Waterloo* and becomes one of the most successful pop groups of all time; the band's name is an acronym of its members' initials: Agnetha, Benny, Björn, and Anni-Frid.
•The three-million-year-old remains of our ancestor, "**LUCY**," are found at Hadar in Ethiopia.

1975 Excavations in the Shensi province, China, uncover the **TERRACOTTA ARMY**, 6,000 life-sized terracotta soldiers guarding the tomb of Shi Huangdi, the first Emperor of China. The bodies of the workers who had built the original tomb were also found walled up inside.

•The last US troops are evacuated from **VIETNAM**; the war ends with the conquest of Saigon by North Vietnam.

1976 At an American Legion meeting in Philadelphia, 29 members die from a mystery illness, known as **LEGIONNAIRE'S DISEASE**.
•When American billionaire **HOWARD HUGHES** dies, 40 wills quickly surface.
•Chuck Peddle designs the 6502 8-bit microprocessor, which will be used for the **APPLE II** by Stephen Wozniak and Steve Jobs in the US.
•UK punk rockers, **THE SEX PISTOLS**, release their first single, *Anarchy in the UK*. Led by Johnny Rotten, the group shows little musical talent but is an instant hit with rebellious teenagers.

1977 The acknowledged King of rock 'n' roll, **ELVIS PRESLEY**, age 42, dies from a heart attack in his Graceland mansion in Memphis, Tennessee.
•The classic science fiction movie, *Stars Wars*, is released; its spectacular **SPECIAL EFFECTS** are achieved with a relatively small budget of $11 million.
•The first US **SPACE SHUTTLE** is strapped to a Boeing 747 jet and released for gliding trials; against the wishes of NASA, it is named the *Enterprise* by President Ford at the request of 100,000 *Star Trek* fans.
•Two Boeing 747s crash into each other in thick fog on the Los Rodeos Airport runway in Tenerife, killing 579 people in the world's **WORST AIR ACCIDENT**.
•American millionairess Sandra West of San Antonio, Texas, is buried alongside her husband; as a condition of her $2.8-million will, she is buried wearing her satin and lace nightdress, seated at the wheel of her blue Ferrari.

1978 Weighing in at 1,410 lb (640 kg), John Minnoch of Seattle, Washington, becomes the world's **HEAVIEST-EVER HUMAN**.
•Georgi Markov, a Bulgarian defector, is assassinated in London, UK, with a poisoned ball-bearing shot from an umbrella by a Bulgarian secret agent.
•Item 271 in an auction in London, UK, is described as the skull of Swedish philosopher Emanuel **SWEDENBORG**; it is sold and taken to Uppsala, Sweden, to be reburied with Swedenborg's body, which is found to already have a skull.
•**POISONING** is suspected when Pope John Paul I dies after 33 days in office.

THEN AND NOW

1978 Based on the wooden-cased Apple I computer, the Apple II becomes the first personal computer made for the mass market; users do not need to know electronics or programming to be able operate it.
1984 Less powerful but easier to use than the popular IBM PC, the first Apple Macintosh computer is launched with emphasis on its ability to be used as a one-stop graphics and printing machine; it becomes the standard tool for the publishing and design industry.

•The world's first **TEST-TUBE BABY**, Louise Brown, is born in Oldham District Hospital, England, following the development of *in vitro* fertilization.
•James Jones, cult leader, dies in Guyana with 912 followers, in the largest **MASS SUICIDE** of modern times.
•James Walter Christy at the US Naval Observatory in Arizona discovers that Pluto has a moon; it is named **CHARON** after the underworld ferryman; nearly half the size of Pluto, its existence makes Pluto a "double planet."

1979 A **POCKET TELEVISION** with an LCD flat screen is patented by Matsushita in Japan.
•A series of labor union strikes cuts power supplies, causing the UK's **WINTER OF DISCONTENT** during which blackouts occurred nationwide.
•**SPACE INVADERS**, an extremely successful video game, is produced by Bally in the US and designed in Japan.
•Margaret Thatcher, leader of the Conservative Party, becomes the UK's first **WOMAN PRIME MINISTER**.
•The **EUROPEAN SPACE AGENCY** (ESA) launches the *Ariane* rocket from French Guiana; the ESA was formed in 1975 by 14 European countries to pursue peaceful scientific objectives.
•The longest-lasting **RAINBOW** appears for three hours above the coast of North Wales in the UK.
•The first **SONY WALKMAN** portable audio cassette player goes on sale.
•Hungarian Erno Rubik's ingenious invention makes him a multimillionaire. **RUBIK'S CUBE** consists of 27 cubes in six different colors; the aim is to turn the sections so each side is a single color.

EXTRA EXTRA! American Paul MacCready flies the first successful human-powered aircraft, *Gossamer Condor*, in 1977.

119

THEN AND NOW

1985 The Compact Disk Read-Only Memory (CD-ROM), which records images in digital form and is read by laser, is introduced for computers. **1997** The ability of new high-density Digital Video Disk (DVD) to store two layers of data outshines CD-ROM.

RAIN FORESTS' PLIGHT COMES TO LIGHT (SEE 1983)

1980

An international crisis is narrowly avoided when a US computer error falsely indicates a USSR **MISSILE ATTACK**.

• *Voyager 1*, the US **SPACE PROBE**, travels deep into the solar system and discovers six more moons of Saturn.

• The UK's Nigel Short, age 14, is the youngest-ever International **CHESS MASTER**.

1981

IBM markets its first **PERSONAL COMPUTER** using MS-DOS (Microsoft disk-operating system), which will become the dominant system for all PCs.

• **POPE JOHN II** is shot and seriously injured in an assassination attempt in St. Peter's Square in Rome, Italy; the gunman, Mehmet Ali Agca, is sentenced to life imprisonment.

• **AIDS** (Acquired Immune Deficiency Syndrome) is recognized by the US Center for Disease Control.

• The MacCready *Solar Challenger* is the first **SOLAR-POWERED AIRPLANE** to fly across the English Channel, maintaining an average speed of 35 mph (56 km/h).

• NASA launches *Columbus*, the first **SPACE SHUTTLE**.

• The **LONDON MARATHON** is run for the first time; this UK event attracts 7,055 entrants, 6,418 of whom complete the course.

EXTRA EXTRA! Professor A. Gagin and his Israeli team pelt the clouds with silver iodine filings to induce rainfall, in 1984.

1982 The vast **THAMES BARRIER** is completed across the Thames Estuary at Woolwich Reach in England; it has four main steel shipping gates towering 67 ft (20 m) above the riverbed, and six minor gates; the Barrier will safeguard London from tidal floods.
• Hans Thostrup and Larry Perkins travel 2,538 mi (4,084 km) in *Solar Trek 1*, a **SOLAR-POWERED CAR**, from Perth to Sydney in Australia.

1983 The **COMPUTER MOUSE** and pull-down screen menu are introduced by Apple Computer.
• The **AMERICA'S CUP** is won by the Australian yacht *Australia II*; it is the first time the US has lost the race since it was founded in 1870.
• **RAIN FOREST DESTRUCTION** brings ozone layer warnings.

1984 **INDIRA GANDHI**, Prime Minister of India, is shot dead by her Sikh bodyguard.
• **GENETIC FINGERPRINTING** is pioneered by the UK's Alec Jeffreys, making it possible to identify a suspect from traces of blood, hair, or skin.
• After a **LETHAL GAS LEAK** at the Union Carbide plant in Bhopal, India, 2,500 people die, 200,000 are injured.

1985 The unseeded West German tennis player, 17-year-old **BORIS BECKER**, makes history when he becomes the youngest Wimbledon Men's Singles Champion.
• Holland's Philips and Japan's Sony introduce the **CD-ROM** (Compact Disk Read-Only Memory).

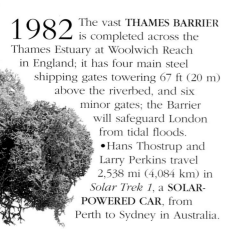

GREENPEACE FIGHTS TO SAVE THE PLANET (SEE 1985)

• A **48-GAME CHESS MATCH** between world champion Anatoly Karpov and Gary Kasparov, both of the USSR, ends after five months due to Karpov's exhaustion; Karpov eventually loses his title to the 22-year-old Kasparov.
• One person is killed when the **GREENPEACE** ship *Rainbow Warrior*, in the South Pacific to disrupt French nuclear tests, is sunk by an explosion in Auckland, New Zealand; two French secret service agents are later found guilty of manslaughter and sabotage.
• The Nevado del Ruiz **VOLCANO** erupts in Colombia, killing some 25,000 people.

1986 The USSR's *Mir* **SPACE STATION** is launched; the aim is to keep it permanently manned.
• **SPACE SHUTTLE FLIGHTS** are suspended in the US after seven astronauts die in the *Challenger* explosion following takeoff at Cape Canaveral in Florida.
• *Brothers in Arms*, by UK group Dire Straits, is the first **MILLION-SELLING CD**.

1987 Terry Waite, the UK's Archbishop of Canterbury's envoy, travels to Beirut, Lebanon, to negotiate the release of hostages, and is himself **TAKEN HOSTAGE**.
• The US and the USSR agree to destroy one category of **NUCLEAR WEAPONS** when they sign the Intermediate Nuclear Forces (INF) Treaty.
• The **DIGITAL AUDIO TAPE** (DAT) player is introduced to rival the high-quality sound achieved by the CD.

1988 Northern Armenia in the USSR is hit by the region's **WORST EARTHQUAKE**; 100,000 people die, 500,000 are made homeless.
• The US announces the Lockheed F-117A "Stealth" fighter-bomber, which is claimed to be **INVISIBLE TO RADAR**.

1989 An international ban on the **IVORY TRADE** is declared at the Convention on International Trade in Endangered Species (CITES).
• The Berlin Wall comes down, marking the **END OF THE COLD WAR**.
• The **GLASS PYRAMID** sculpture by I. M. Pei at the Louvre in Paris, France, is unveiled by President Mitterrand.
• At the Liverpool v. Nottingham Forest FA Cup semifinal at Hillsborough, UK, 96 fans are **CRUSHED TO DEATH**.
• Christopher John Bollig is born, making Augusta Bunge of Wisconsin the world's first known **GREAT-GREAT-GREAT-GREAT-GRANDMOTHER**.
• An agreement to stop producing CFCs by the year 2000 is signed by 80 nations, with the aim of preventing further damage to the world's **OZONE LAYER**.

Imagine Ancient Egypt in the heart of Paris

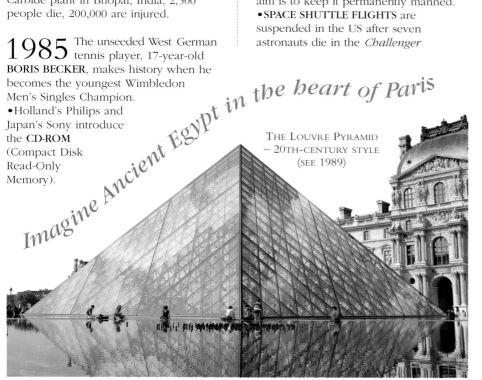

THE LOUVRE PYRAMID – 20TH-CENTURY STYLE (SEE 1989)

EXTRA EXTRA! In 1988, NASA scientist Edgar Whisenaut publishes a book foretelling the end of the world.

1990
The **KINGCYCLE BEAN BICYCLE** is invented; it is designed to reduce drag for extra speed.
- NASA's **HUBBLE SPACE TELESCOPE**, costing $1.5 billion to develop, is taken into orbit by the *Discovery* space shuttle.
- Six women are suspended from their teaching posts at King Saud University, **SAUDI ARABIA**, following their arrest for driving cars in public.
- The most expensive painting ever, van Gogh's *Portrait of Dr. Gachet*, is sold at auction for $75,000,000 at Christie's in New York City.
- The world's **LARGEST CHURCH**, the Basilica of Our Lady of Peace in Yamoussoukro, Ivory Coast, is finished.
- Imprisoned for 26 years, **NELSON MANDELA** is released from jail in South Africa; negotiations get underway for dismantling the apartheid system.

1991
The USSR is **OFFICIALLY DISSOLVED** and the former Soviet republics establish the new CIS (Commonwealth of Independent States).
- A **HEART ATTACK** warning device is invented by Kenneth Matsumura; worn on the wrist, it keeps constant track of the electrical signals that should be regularly emitted by the heart.
- Japanese company Matsushita introduces a **VOICE-ACTIVATED VIDEO**, programmed to be spoken to in the Japanese language only.
- In the Gulf War, Western Allied Forces mount their 100-hour **DESERT STORM** offensive to successfully liberate Kuwait from Saddam Hussein of Iraq.

1992
The Mall of America, the **LARGEST SHOPPING MALL** in the world, opens at Bloomington, Minnesota; it houses over 400 stores and a full-size Ferris wheel.
- The first of the world's largest telescopes, the Keck I, a **MULTIMIRROR TELESCOPE** with an aperture of 32.9 ft (10 m), is set up at Mauna Kea Observatory in Hawaii.
- **BROCCOLI** is found to contain a compound that helps fight cancer.
- The **SYNCRUDE TAILINGS DAM** is completed in Alberta, Canada; it is the largest-volume dam in the world, having taken 1,907,000,000 ft³ (540,000,000 m³) of materials to construct.
- The **EURO DISNEY** amusement park opens near Paris, France.
- France's **BAN ON SMOKING** in public is ignored by the nation's smokers.

1993
Norman G. Sharber from Arizona patents the **ELECTROFISHING POLE**. It creates an electrical field in the water that causes fish to fall unconscious; this becomes a great boon for fishermen.

- The **VU QUANG OX** is discovered in Vietnam; this is the first new mammal to be discovered in over 50 years.
- The **PENTIUM CHIP**, containing 3.1 million transistors, is introduced by Intel; the chip has a capacity of 100 MIPS, which means that it can process 100 million instructions per second.

1994
A new US regulation stipulates that air-conditioning systems in new cars must not contain chemicals that **DEPLETE OZONE**.
- UK schoolboy Richard Pryce is arrested after successfully **HACKING** his way into the US military computer system.
- The **CODEX HAMMER**, one of Leonardo da Vinci's notebooks containing his scientific drawings, is acquired by Microsoft billionaire Bill Gates for $30,800,000 at Christie's in New York City.
- The **CHANNEL TUNNEL**, first proposed some 200 years ago, is completed between France and England at a length of 30 mi (50 km). It is the second-longest undersea rail tunnel in the world; the longest, at 35 mi (55 km), was built six years earlier at Seikan, Japan.
- Nelson Mandela, leader of the African National Congress (ANC), becomes South Africa's **FIRST BLACK PRESIDENT** three years after the end of apartheid.
- Comet Shoemaker-Levy is observed crashing into Jupiter; the spectacular breakup of the comet is recorded by the *Galileo* probe.
- The **WORLD SERIES** is canceled for the first time due to a strike by North America's major-league baseball players.

The speedy Kingcycle Bean bicycle races to meet the new millennium

KINGCYCLE **BEAN**

A WHOLE NEW STYLE OF BICYCLE (SEE 1990)

1999! A total eclipse of the sun is visible, in varying degrees, in Europe, the Middle East, and western Asia.

EURO CURRENCY
IS INTRODUCED
(SEE 1999)

•**TONYA HARDING** wins the US Figure Skating Association championships after former champion Nancy Kerrigan is forced to withdraw following an assault; Harding's ex-husband is found to have been responsible for the assault and Harding subsequently loses her title and is banned for life from skating events.

1995 Over 500 people are killed in one of the century's **WORST FIRES** when flames engulf a school tent at Mandi Dabwali, India.
•The trial of the celebrated ex-football star **O.J. SIMPSON** begins; he is accused of murdering his ex-wife Nicole Brown Simpson and her friend Ronald L. Goldman the previous year; the televised proceedings attract a worldwide audience of hundreds of millions.

1996 The UK cattle industry faces ruin when scientific research indicates that the rare but deadly human brain disease, CJD (Creutzfeldt-Jakob Disease), may be caused by eating beef infected with bovine spongiform encephalopathy (BSE), known as "**MAD COW DISEASE.**"
•Canadian Donovan Bailey sprints 100 m in 9.84 seconds to become the world's **FASTEST MAN.**

1997 The world mourns the death of the UK's **PRINCESS DIANA**, killed in a car accident in Paris, France; the largest television audience ever, estimated at some two billion viewers, watches the funeral, which is broadcast worldwide.
•The UK's Gareth Griffiths survives a 13,125-ft (4,000-m) fall after his **PARACHUTE FAILS**; Michael Costello, the American skydiving instructor to whom he is strapped, twists over just before they hit the ground, sacrificing his own life to cushion the fall of his student.

•The arrival in the night sky of the brightly burning **HALE-BOPP COMET** precipitates the bizarre mass suicide of 39 Heaven's Gate cult members in California.
•"**DEEP BLUE,**" IBM's supercomputer, beats champion player Gary Kasparov in a chess tournament.
•*Titanic* is the first film since *Ben Hur* (in 1959) to be awarded 11 **OSCARS**, and is the highest-grossing film of all time.
•A new **LAND SPEED RECORD** is set by the UK's RAF fighter pilot Andy Green when he becomes the first man to break the sound barrier on the ground; he travels across the Black Rock Desert in Nevada, at 763.04 mph (1,227.99 km/h) in the Thrust SSC jet car.
•The *Pathfinder* probe lands on **MARS**, and sends out the *Sojourner*, a six-wheeled vehicle that is remote-controlled from Earth.
•A once-in-a-century party is held in Times Square on April 6 to celebrate **1,000 DAYS** before the year 2000.

1998 The AkasHi-Kaiko bridge at Kobe-Naruto in Japan is completed; it is the world's **LONGEST SUSPENSION BRIDGE**, with a main span of 6,529 ft (1,990 m).
•Florence "**FLO-JO**" Griffith, the American sprinter who became the fastest woman in the world in 1988 when she set the 100-m world record, dies of a heart attack at age 38.
•Images of one of Jupiter's moons, Europa, received from the probe *Galileo*, indicate the possibility of a warm life-sustaining ocean lying beneath its icy crust.
•The *Voyager of the Seas* is built in Finland; it is the world's **LARGEST CRUISE SHIP**, weighing 142,000 tons, and is able to carry 3,840 passengers.
•A dinosaur with feathers, *Protarchaeopteryx robusta*,

from which today's **BIRDS** are likely to have descended, is discovered in China.

1999 A single European currency, the **EURO**, is introduced into 11 countries of the European Union.
•Following NATO's intense air campaign to force the cessation of Serbian ethnic cleansing of Albanians in Kosovo, a UN peace-keeping force is sent in to attempt to stablilze the region.
•Two masked teenagers in black trenchcoats, armed with bombs and guns, launch a merciless attack on **COLUMBINE HIGH SCHOOL** in Littleton, Colorado, killing 12 fellow students and a teacher before shooting themselves.
•Twenty million **SIKHS** throughout the world celebrate the official founding of their religion 300 years earlier.
•George Lucas's long-awaited and heavily hyped *Star Wars: Episode One – The Phantom Menace* hits the world's **MOVIE** screens.
•A **TOTAL ECLIPSE** of the sun occurs on August 11 and is visible, to varying degrees, from parts of Europe, North Africa, Arabia, and western Asia. The Moon passes between Earth and Sun at roughly 1,054 mph (1,700 km/h).
•The Millennium Mars **MICROPROBE** is due to penetrate the surface of Mars.

THEN AND NOW

1993 Flav'r Saver tomatoes, whose genes have been artificially changed, are the first genetically modified foods to be sold to the public in the US.

1997 As fears grow about the safety of genetically modified organisms (GMOs), the UK government announces the establishment of a new committee to conduct a thorough investigation into the products of the world's most controversial new science.

EXTRA EXTRA! Sixteenth-century astrologer Nostradamus predicts that a great terror will come from the skies in 1999.

123

CELEBRATION

THE THIRD MILLENNIUM arrives on December 31, 1999, for most countries, and on December 31, 2000, for others. Whichever date you celebrate the new year, the new century, and the new millennium, it is a night to remember!

ASIA AND THE PACIFIC

TRADITIONAL GREETING SOUTH-PACIFIC STYLE

Welcome to the 21st century

2000 Viti Levu, the largest island in Fiji, lights a chain of **BONFIRES** stretching from the International Date Line to the center of the millennium festivities. As a chorus of drums accompanies the sun setting over the Pacific Ocean, children from different cultures voice their hopes for the future. The countdown to midnight is followed by a five-hour party.

• The highest point on Pitt Island in the Chathmas was to have been the first place on land to see the sunrise on the morning of January 1, but the Republic of Kiribati moved the Date Line so that the uninhabited Caroline Island achieves **FIRST DAWN STATUS**, followed by Pitt Island, which can claim the title of the first populated place to see the 21st century. One hundred young people from around the world are flown to Pitt Island to witness the arrival of the 21st century, and their names are recorded by history as the first of their generation to witness the event.

• The length of the Date Line across the islands of Tavenuni, Rabi, and Vanua Levu is illuminated by a series of lights that can be seen from space. The time threshold is marked by a wall of blocks, each containing a sealed glass **TIME CAPSULE** with a message to those who will open the capsules in 3000.

• Tall ships from all over the world take part in the **PACIFIC TALL SHIPS FESTIVAL**. The voyage starts in Sydney, reaches Wellington, New Zealand, for Christmas and then moves to Gisborne, North Island, for New Year's Eve, where passengers celebrate being in the world's first city to see the dawn of 2000.

• The first **MARATHON** of the millennium, covering a 26-mile (42-km) course, starts at 6 AM on New Year's Day in Hamilton, New Zealand.

• Sydney is the host of the **OLYMPIC AND PARALYMPIC GAMES** in 2000, which have been christened the Athletes' Games. More than 5,000 athletes, both male and female, are taking part, and the event is housed in a 110,000-seat Olympic stadium, the largest of its kind in the world.

NORTH AMERICA

2000 Times Square in New York City sees the New Year 24 times in one evening by means of huge TV screens showing the **COUNTDOWN TO MIDNIGHT** as it takes place in 23 other time zones worldwide.

• On December 31, **GRAND CENTRAL STATION** in New York, one of the world's busiest railroad terminals, is transformed into a vast ballroom where people dance their way into the 21st century.

• Vancouver, Canada, has invited nominations for people who have made a valuable contribution to its city over the last 200 years; their reward is one of the 2,000 **MILLENNIUM MEDALS OF MERIT** being created for the event.

• Los Angeles is the proud owner of the **FIRST CATHEDRAL OF THE THIRD MILLENNIUM**, built to replace the Cathedral of St. Vibiana, destroyed by an earthquake in 1994.

• More than 300 people have signed up to take part in **ODYSSEY 2000**, a bicycle ride around the world that will cover 20,000 miles (32,000 km) and pass through more than 50 countries. Starting and finishing in Los Angeles, the course takes a year to complete.

GRAND CENTRAL STATION, NEW YORK

FIREWORKS AT THE EIFFEL TOWER, PARIS

EUROPE

2000 The Roman Catholic Church has declared the year 2000 to be a **HOLY YEAR**, an award reserved for years with a special religious significance. At St. Peter's Church in Rome, Italy, the Pope attends a traditional High Mass on December 31, where thanks are sung for the year 1999, the 20th century, and the second millennium, which are ending.

•A huge **MILLENNIUM EGG** is hatched at the Eiffel Tower, Paris, just before midnight, to the sound of 2,000 drummers. The egg contains a bank of television screens that show the millennium celebrations taking place around the world. After midnight, revelers are able to send e-mails to anywhere in the world via the egg.

•The 12 avenues that converge at the Place Charles de Gaulle is used to form a large-scale **COUNTDOWN CLOCK** on New Year's Eve. One of the avenues is illuminated to form the hour hand, while a laser light shining from the top of the Arc de Triomphe serves as a second hand, counting down to midnight.

• The focus of the celebrations in the UK takes place in Greenwich, London, where the Millennium Dome opens with a night of partying. Designed by the Richard Rogers Partnership, the Dome, the largest of its kind in the world, covers 20 acres (49 hectares) and contains a 10,000-seat theater and 13 zones of attractions. Also in Greenwich a millennium countdown clock above the meridian line marks the start of 2000 at **MIDNIGHT GMT**, or zero hours at zero degrees longitude.

MIDDLE EAST AND AFRICA

2000 According to the Bible, **ARMAGEDDON** is the final battleground between good and evil. To see whether this ultimate battle really takes place, many people spend December 31 in Megiddo, Israel, which has been identified as the real Armageddon.

•For Christianity, the year 2000 marks the 2,000th anniversary of the **NATIVITY**, the birth of Christ. Two celebrations to mark this event are a reenactment of the Journey of the Magi and a five-month pilgrimage to Bethlehem.

MILLENNIUM DOME BUILT AT GREENWICH, LONDON

INDEX

ACKNOWLEDGMENTS

PAGE*One* and the Author would like to thank the following people: Aylla Macphail for research, compiling, and checking facts; John Farndon for writing the special features; Rick Eyre for additional information.

DK Publishing would like to thank the following for their kind permission to reproduce their photographs:

t=top, b=below, l=left, r=right, c=center

AKG London: 50cl, 108-109; Geneva, Barbier-Mueller Collection 98; Paris, Bibliotheque Nationale 51cl; Victoria and Albert Museum 61tc.
Ancient Art & Architecture Collection: G. Tortoli/Henry Moore Foundation 114tl.
Arcaid: Natalie Tepper,1980 16–17.
Archivo Iconografico, S.A.: 39tr.
Bridgeman Art Library, London / New York: *David* by Michelangelo Buonarroti Galleria dell'Accademia, Florence, Italy 32; *Map of Europe* by Mercator (1512–1594), c.1554 British Library, London, UK 48–49; The Copernican system, *Planisphaerium Copernicanum*, c.1543, devised by Nicolaus Copernicus (1473–1543) from *The Celestial Atlas, or the Harmony of the Universe* Amsterdam, c.1660 by Andreas Cellarius (17th Century); British Library, London, UK 35cr; Cupola of the cathedral designed by Filippo Brunelleschi (1377–1446), Duomo, Florence, Italy 29b; Christie's Images, London, UK 106l; Little Dancer, Aged 14 by Edgar Degas (1834-1917), Private Collection/Christie's Images 72; *The Gare St. Lazare*, 1877 by Claude Monet (1840–1926), Musée D'Orsay, Paris, France/Bulloz/ © ADAGP, Paris and DACS, London 1999 86–87; Trompe l'oeil oculus in the center of the vaulted ceiling of the Camera Picta or Camera degli Sposi, 1465–1474 by Andrea Mantegna (1431–1506) Palazzo Ducale, Mantua, Italy 37c; The *Lamentation of Christ*, c.1305 by Giotto di Bondone (c.1266–1337), Scrovegni (Arena) Chapel, Padua, Italy/Giraudon 22bl; George Stephenson by John Seymour Lucas (1849–1923) Institute of Mechanical Engineers, London, UK 89br; Cave painting of horses, c.15000 BC, Cave of Lascaux, Dordogne, France 112–113; Equestrian statuette of Emperor Charlemagne (742–814) 9th century (bronze) Louvre, Paris, France/Peter Willi 8tr; Vesuvius erupting, plate III from Sir William Hamilton's *Campi Phlegraei* 1779 (w/c) by English School (18th Century) Private Collection 52–53; *The Death of Robespierre (1758–1794) 18 July 1794* engraved by James Idnarpila, published 1799 by J. Geys (fl.1799), Musée de la Revolution Francaise, Vizille, France 71bl; Isambard Kingdom Brunel (1806–1859), standing in front of the launching chains of the *Great Eastern*, 1857, photograph by Robert Howlett (1831–1858), Stapleton Collection, UK 88br; *Feathered Star* and *Garden Maze* Quilt by Rachel Burr Corwin, New York, mid-19th century, Smithsonian Institution, Washington DC 64-65; *The Birth of Venus*, c.1485 by Sandro Botticelli, Galleria degli Uffizi, Florence, Italy 31c; Sistine Chapel Ceiling: *Creation of Adam*, 1510 (post restoration) by Michelangelo Buonarroti (1475–1564), Vatican Museums and Galleries, Vatican City, Italy 36–37; Louis XIV (1638–1715) of France in the costume of The Sun King in the ballet *La Nuit* c.1665 French School (19th century) Private Collection, Roger-Viollet 51br.
British Museum, London: 3bl, 4cr, 20l, 20tc, 59br, 71tr.
Bruce Coleman Ltd: Alantide 60b; Pacific Stock 124bl.
Corbis UK Ltd: The Academy of Natural Sciences of Philadelphia 79tr; Arte & Immagini srl 39b; Dean Conger 111cl; Michael Freeman 9bl.
Curtis Brown: Line drawing by E.H. Shepard copyright under the Berne Convention, coloring copyright © 1970, 1973 by E.H. Shepard and Methuen Children's Books, reproduced by permission of Curtis Brown, London/Cecilie Dressler Verlag 104–105.
Michael Dent 18b.
E.T. Archive: 8bl; Biliotheque de l'Arsenal Paris 15bc; Bibliothèque Nationale Paris 13br; Denis Cochrane Collection 102bl.
Mary Evans Picture Library: 30tl, 32, 44bl, 67tl, 75tr, 83bl, Tom Morgan 96–97.
Exeter Maritime Museum: 65tr, 116c.
Werner Forman Archive: Phillip Golman Collection, London 56.
Glasgow Museums Museum of Transport: 66br.
© Greenpeace International: 121tr.
Sonia Halliday and Laura Lushington Photographs: 18tl.
Robert Harding Picture Library: 12tl, 26–27, 98–99, 104b; Phillip Craven 21l; Gavin Hellier 42–43; IPC Magazines Ltd/Philip Craven 40l; Rainbird 52tc, 128; Roy Rainford 56–57, 121bl; J. E. Stevenson 72–73; R. Richardson 32–33.
Michael Holford: Collection of Senor Mujica Gatto, Lima 49br.
Image Bank: 112bl; Travel Photo Int. © Fotoworld 94tl.
Images Colour Library: 111br.
Image Select Ann Ronan 44–45.
Imperial War Museum: 108tr, 108bl, 109tc.
Lebrecht Collection: 97br.
Museum of London: 14–15, 22–23.
N.A.S.A.: 47tr; JPL 103tr.
National Gallery, London: Gerard ter Borch, *Portrait of a Young Man* 45bl.
National Maritime Museum: 48tr, 67br.
© Trustees of the National Museums of Scotland: 38tr.
Collection of the National Palace Museum, Taiwan, Republic of China: 14t.
National Railway Museum, York: 86bl.
The Natural History Museum, London: 85br.
NMEC licensed illustrations: QA Photos Ltd front cover br, 125b.
Polytechnic Museum Moscow: 93l.
Popperfoto: 110tr.
Roskilde: 12–13.
The Royal Collection © Her Majesty Queen Elizabeth II: 38l.
Rye Town Council: 58c.
Science Museum: 36br, 77br, 80l, 93tr, 100tl.
Tony Stone Images: Bruno De Hougues 125tl.
Tracks: 117br.
Trip: Liesti Associates 124br.
Courtesy of the Trustees of the Victoria & Albert Museum: 82tr.
Wilberforce House, Hull City Museums and Art Galleries, UK: 5tl, 34–35.
Woolwich Artillery: 90–91.